MW00610510

To Murissa

love, Mon + Dad

Your favorite teacher!

LIGHT IN THE QUEEN'S GARDEN

LIGHT IN THE QUEEN'S GARDEN

Ida May Pope, Pioneer for Hawai'i's
Daughters, 1862–1914

Sandra E. Bonura

University of Hawai'i Press
Honolulu

22 21 20 19 18   6 5 4 3 2

Library of Congress Cataloging-in-Publication Data

Names: Bonura, Sandra, author.
Title: Light in the queen's garden : Ida May Pope, pioneer for Hawai'i's daughters,
    1862–1914 / Sandra E. Bonura.
Description: Honolulu : University of Hawai'i Press, [2017] | Includes bibliographical
    references and index.
Identifiers: LCCN 2017009363 | ISBN 9780824866440 (hardcover ; alk. paper)
Subjects: LCSH: Pope, Ida May, 1862–1914. | Teachers—Hawaii—Biography. |
    Kamehameha Schools—History. | Hawaii—History—Overthrow of the Monarchy, 1893.
Classification: LCC LA2317.P66 B66 2017 | DDC 371.10092 [B]—dc23
    LC record available at https://lccn.loc.gov/2017009363

University of Hawai'i Press books are printed on
acid-free paper and meet the guidelines for permanence
and durability of the Council on Library Resources.

Contents

FOREWORD

Ida Pope's story began in a restless era—industrialization, government schools, and labor unions were expanding; women agitated for the right to vote; European and Asian immigration was at an all-time high; and teaching was the only respectable occupation for a middle-class, college-educated woman. Oberlin College, Ida May Pope's progressive, coeducational alma mater, encouraged service, and she chose to teach and serve in a foreign country called the Kingdom of Hawai'i. In Honolulu, few American teachers fared well. The Western expatriate community was insular, and male compatriots proved as challenging as they were supportive.

And she arrived just as a political storm was brewing. Western expatriates in powerful positions influenced by American constitutional, egalitarian ideals; cultural elitism; and technical supremacy clashed with recalcitrant Hawaiian monarchs and royals. On January 17, 1893, thirteen American sympathizers backed by an American naval force led a revolution seizing the government from Queen Lili'uokalani. The queen's personal lobbying efforts in the U.S. Congress and with high officials armed with the written petition of all her people proved impotent against a nation intent on global expansion.

Steadfast through the storm, Ida May Pope was the clear choice by the trustees to be the founding principal of the Kamehameha School for Girls, established in 1894 by the will of Ke Ali'i Pauahi written ten years earlier. Back in 1884, and up to the time Ida Pope arrived, Hawai'i was a sovereign nation recognized by European and Asian empires and a monarchy under the reign of King Kalākaua. Indigenous people were the majority of the population. 'Olelo Hawai'i (the Hawaiian language) was the common language.

Kamehameha Schools flourishes today because of the wisdom of its founders. Documentation of this history is the *kuleana* (responsibility) of a museum archive at Kamehameha Schools. Dr. Sandra "Sandee" Bonura was a frequent visitor conducting research on her first book, and the archivists were privileged facilitators of parts of the journey. The relationship continued with this story, which should have been told long ago but perhaps waited for Sandee's heartfelt affinity.

In publications and lectures, Sandee added to *'ike Hawai'i* (Hawaiian knowledge) with the *mo'olelo* (stories) of other individuals affiliated with Ida May Pope, like Lydia Aholo, Queen Lili'uokalani's *keiki hānai* (adopted child). Sandee's inquiries led far and wide to other people and institutions whose valuable connections she graciously shared. A meticulous and respected scholar, Sandee upholds high academic standards, including accurate citation and documentation of primary sources, respect for copyrighted material, and integrity in the use of historical resources.

The journey of writing any worthwhile history is arduous, but the result has broad implications. Sandee understands that while Ida May Pope was an exemplary leader, she represents a continuum of countless brilliant, morally upright, and accomplished women whose records are archived in their communities. She was as talented and as complex but as flawed as any of us, and because she possessed all those qualities, her story withstands the test of time. To miss the stories of accomplished, good people unheralded by celebrity or popular media or to not care at all is to have an incomplete understanding of the broad swath of human achievement and to miss truths that emerge from a long view of history.

E 'olu'olu, e kipa mai: Come, let us meet Ida May Pope!
Candace W. Lee, M.Ed., M.LISc
Kamehameha Schools Assistant Archivist

Acknowledgments

First and foremost, my biggest appreciation goes to my husband, Carl Bonura, who traipsed all over the country with me providing needed emotional and practical support while I conducted research. His thoughtful and critical evaluation throughout the process was essential to getting Ida May Pope's story into print.

This book would have not been as rich or intimate if it had not been for Ida's family members who embraced me like a long-lost relative. In particular, her great-grandnieces Joanne Calendar, Mary Lois, Kathy Losten, and Lois Taylor and great-grandnephew William Pope freely shared their personal archival treasures to bring "Aunt Ida" alive. I will always think of myself as their "Pope cousin."

There is no place in Hawai'i I would rather be than with my buddies in the museum archive of Kamehameha Schools, where Miss Pope's spirit lives. Archivist Stacy Naipo, the guardian of the school's history, has created a warm and vibrant atmosphere for researchers like myself. Her patience for my repeated requests has earned her a special place in my heart. I am indebted to Candace Lee, former assistant archivist, who went above the call of duty on my behalf through several of my publications and presentations across the islands to provide helpful guidance and the foreword for this book.

My research proceeded smoothly and provided consistent excitement and pleasure due to the help of some very capable people from other research institutions. Barbara Dunn, Jennifer Higa, and Ipo Santos-Bear made research enjoyable at the Hawaiian Historical Society. John Barker at the Hawaiian Mission Children's Society and the ever-welcoming Diane Ching of the gift shop rounded out my positive experiences. Many thanks to Paula Rath and Dee Okahara of the Pālama Settlement, Brooke Black of the Huntington Library, Barbara Austen of the Connecticut Historical Society, Ken Grossi at Oberlin College Archives, Barbara Moir at the Lyman House Memorial, Crystal Miles at the Bancroft Library, John Kurtz of the Bucyrus Historical Society, Claire Gabriel of the Russell Sage Foundation, and Peter Brueggeman, the final director of Scripps Institution of Oceanography Library and Archives. I thank them all for aiding and inspiring me with their knowledge of history.

Outside the archives, the living descendants of nineteenth-century missionary teachers reminded me that their ancestors were not "all cut from the same cloth." Particularly, I want to thank the families of Lilla Estelle Appleton, Amos and Juliette Cooke, Helen Norton, Iretta Hight Retan, and Carrie Winter Kofoid. Their offerings of old letters, diaries, photographs, and other documents supplemented and/or corrected Ida's perspective in rich ways.

During the research process, I encountered several Hawaiian descendants of Ida Pope's pupils. Family enthusiasts like Jeffrey Aholo Apaka, Puanani Mundon Gonsalves, Noa Horner, Sheila Johnson, R. Kawika Makanani, Pilialoha Lee Loy, and Nancy Spaulding continually reminded me that Ida's history was entwined with that of their Hawaiian ancestors, thus making this book personal. The collective enthusiasm from all of the above and more added legitimacy to the writing of this book, and I am humbly grateful for their input.

Finally, there is nowhere that transcends time and place for me more than when I am sitting beneath rainbow shadows in the beautiful Kawaiahaʻo Church, where I imagine the Hawaiian girls from the queen's era once sat, along with Ida Pope, reciting my favorite scripture, The Lord Is My Shepherd (O Iehova koʻu Kahuhipa):

ʻO IĒHOVA koʻu Kahu hipa; ʻAʻole oʻu mea e nele ai Nāna nō wau i hoʻomoe iho ma nā ʻāina uliuli: Ua alakaʻi ʻo ia iaʻu ma kapa wailana mālie. Ke hoʻāla mai nei ʻo ia i koʻu ʻuhane: Ke alakaʻi nei nō ʻo ia iaʻu ma nā ala maikaʻi no kona inoaʻOiaʻiʻo, inā e hele au ma ke awāwa malu o ka make, ʻAʻole au e weliweli i ka pōʻino: no ka mea, ʻo ʻoe pū kekahi me aʻu; ʻO kou mana, a me kou koʻokoʻo, ʻo koʻu mau mea ia e ʻoluʻolu ai. Ke hoʻomākaukau mai nei ʻoe i ka papa ʻaina naʻu ma ke alo o koʻu mau ʻenemi: Ua kāhinu mai ʻoe i kuʻu poʻo me ka ʻaila; Ua piha a hū koʻu kīʻaha ʻOiaʻiʻo, e hahai mau ana iaʻu ka pono a me ke aloha i nā lā a pau o koʻu ola ʻana; A ma loko o ka hale o Iēhova ʻo wau e noho mau loa aku ai.

Psalm (Na Halelu) 23

LIGHT IN THE QUEEN'S GARDEN

Introduction

Great historical events often accompany great forces of nature: a hurricane, a tsunami, an avalanche. Traced back to their origins, such natural cataclysms start as a gentle breeze, a single drop of rain, a small pebble falling. They appear harmless, but trigger life-changing events. Similarly, a swath of Hawaiian history can be traced directly to an unassuming woman from Ohio who set into motion a series of events that would ultimately effect social change for Hawaiian women.

When Ida May Pope died unexpectedly in the summer of 1914, it was front-page news in virtually every publication in Hawaiʻi. Remembered as Mother Pope, this gentle-but-tough Midwesterner was deeply mourned. It has been said that more people are affected by teachers than by any other occupation. Ida Pope lived her life with the passion of someone who sincerely believed this. With strength and perseverance, she led by example, and paved a way for Hawaiʻi's daughters to seek their own fulfillment. Her eulogist told the assembled mourners, "Someone should write the biography of Miss Ida Pope. It would make interesting reading."[1] A century later, here it is. May it tell her story honestly and lead us to press forward with the same passion and zeal.

I first discovered the indomitable Ida May Pope while reading antique love letters that had been retrieved from a steamer trunk found in a forgotten California attic. The trunk was crammed with century-old photographs, rare artifacts, and letters about life, love, politics, and education in nineteenth-century Hawaiʻi. The letters were from Carrie Winter, a Connecticut teacher who journeyed to Honolulu with Ida Pope. Each letter chronicling her three years with Ida has been preserved in its original postmarked envelope. They were systematically transcribed, edited, researched, and published in *An American Girl in the Hawaiian Islands: Letters of Carrie Prudence Winter, 1890–1893.*[2] As my research continued, the name "Miss Pope" kept appearing in multiple collections of the era. I soon found myself intrigued by this woman, who inspired and motivated a multitude but had been historically ignored.

Light in the Queen's Garden chronicles the life of Ida Pope, a transformational type of leader in any era, who was handpicked to establish the Kamehameha

School for Girls. This institution was established in 1894 by the estate of Princess Pauahi, the last of the royal Kamehameha line, and dedicated to the education of girls of Hawaiian ancestry. When twenty-eight-year-old Ida left Ohio, to accept a "temporary" teaching assignment in Honolulu, she couldn't have imagined it would become a lifelong career of service to Hawaiian women. Nor could she have envisioned she would become closely involved in the greatest political turmoil the Hawaiians had ever experienced.

Ida's personal impressions of King Kalākaua and Queen Liliʻuokalani, her interactions with members of the group who overthrew the monarchy, and her account of the days leading up to the revolution and long after give an insider's perspective on crucial events in Hawaiian history. Ida was present during the life celebrations of the last king of Hawaiʻi, and then his sad death rituals. She then had the extraordinary opportunity to travel with the last queen of Hawaiʻi on her controversial visit to the "leper colony" on the Island of Molokaʻi. Liliʻuokalani's adopted daughter, Lydia Kaʻonohiponiponiokalani Aholo, was placed in her care, and Ida played a significant role in mothering Lydia and shaping her future, especially during the years the queen was involved in the fight to restore her kingdom.

Ida Pope's firsthand account of the years that brought her pupils into womanhood during the annexation of their kingdom tells an important story about the Hawaiians and a rapidly changing world. Ida often portrayed her pupils as struggling under the weight of conflicting expectations imposed on them by the swiftly changing economy. To that end, she worked relentlessly to maintain relationships with important islanders, both Hawaiians and non-Hawaiians, who could help young women advance in their society. Nowhere is this more evident than in her cordial but sometimes tense working relationships with two of the most influential and complex figures in Hawaiʻi, the affluent Charles Reed Bishop and Queen Liliʻuokalani. As she worked with forces like the queen and Charles Bishop, Ida in turn became a force shaping society for future generations of Hawaiian women.

By the time the twentieth century rolled around, few places on earth had changed so completely as the Hawaiian Islands. In the midst of educating her pupils for the radical pace of modernization that was rushing Honolulu forward, Ida had a startling revelation. As time-honored Hawaiian traditions were subjugated under the transformations, she realized her pupils had been deprived of their culture and that she had, unwittingly, been a participant in this. Almost as an apology, Ida went into the new century at full steam, making sure those Hawaiian girls knew they had a distinct cultural identity, one that must be acknowledged, respected, and enabled to flourish in the midst of the Americanization of the islands.

Ida's personal life in the Hawaiian Islands was far from easy or even comfortable. She suffered isolation, loneliness, a shortage of necessities, and illness. She learned news from home only through slow-traveling correspondence and was helpless when loved ones at home became ill or died. Travel from island to island meant days of seasickness in rough waters, and travel overland was sidesaddle on treacherous paths through rugged mountains.

Her professional life was not much easier. Experiencing sexism throughout her tenure, Ida had to face the hurdle of "staying in her place" straight on and upset many of the nineteenth-century expectations for women. Regarding gender inequality, she privately stated, "To say that I am cross is 'putting it mild' I think it outrageous. It is one of the indignities that womankind suffers in the business world, in competition with mankind."[3] In addition to her educational duties, she moved into roles that maximized the natural-born leader she was, and because of this, her influence is visible today in several social institutions, including the Pālama Settlement, Honolulu's first social service agency; the Kaʻiulani Home; the Lanakila Home; and the Francis R. Day Cottage for Women at Lēʻahi Hospital, all developed to serve her alumnae as well as the community. Countless Hawaiian women today, current and former beneficiaries of the Ida May Pope Memorial Scholarship created in 1919, have no idea of the personal sacrifices she made for their collective futures.

Throughout her tenure at Kamehameha Schools, Ida continued her graduate work at the University of Chicago. The trustees agreed to sabbaticals for three separate semesters so that she could learn the latest educational methods from the most progressive leaders of her time. She also traveled throughout the United States to consult with the brightest minds in the budding vocational education and social change movement. In turn, the movement's leaders visited her. She was able to use her experiences to facilitate the first social survey of Honolulu, which contributed to the overhaul of labor laws, vastly improving working conditions for Hawaiian women.

This book pulls together many new primary source documents uncovered along the way, including Queen Liliʻuokalani's adopted daughter's long-lost oral history recording, diaries, scrapbooks, photos, and correspondence from descendants of many teachers who worked side by side with Ida. Contrasting viewpoints show why some missionary teachers from this era have been characterized as racists in some circles and saints in others. Though this book is about how the spirit of Ida Pope was forged, I hope that the voices of her Hawaiian pupils can be heard in some small way.

In the darkest era of Hawaiian history, the queen gave her people a garden as a sanctuary, a safe gathering place when it was illegal for them to gather in public.[4] This event coincided with Ida's opening of the Kamehameha School for Girls in 1894. The garden's name, Uluhaimalama, allegorically translates as "as the plants grow out of the dark into the light so shall light come to the nation."[5] For many Hawaiian girls, the school was their "Uluhaimalama," and Ida Pope was the bright shining light in that garden. Her legacy as a guiding light for Hawai'i's daughters may be seen in this poem, penned by the renowned Mary Dillingham Frear:

IDA M. POPE

How many darkened ways her presence lightened
In days of yore!
What cheerless hearts her courage brightened!
Still ring the echoes of her children's laughter.
God help the helpless ones and frightened
To whom she held a torch-lit door
And guide them feebly, feebly, groping after Her—
Gone before[6]

CHAPTER ONE

Ida's Heritage, 1862–1914

The Legacy of Thomas Pope

Ida May Pope grew up in a home where stories of early American settlers were told and retold in the family so children would remember the faith and courage of their ancestors, and the hardships they faced in order to bring them the comforts they now enjoyed two generations later. Magazines in the nineteenth century encouraged parents to tell their children their forefathers' stories in order to create "an interest, then reverence, and finally a desire to be like them, to be no less than they."[1] An added benefit, parents were told, was that when their children complained about their life, the adversities their ancestors faced in an "unknown wilderness"[2] would serve the purpose of humbling them. Ida's friend Lilla Appleton said it best: "We can fight our own battles better for knowing better the lives and ideals of those from whom we are descended. It links us to great accomplishments of the past, and makes us feel as if we also should do great deeds."[3]

The comprehensive family history book titled *A Bridge to the Past of Prosser and Pope Families,* compiled and created long ago by Ida's niece, Ruth Prosser McLain, still exists today. Its pages reveal that Ida herself traced both her maternal and paternal lines directly to early settlers of New England, several of whom commanded the attention of Plymouth Colony historians. Ida, along with her mother and sister, researched and created an "ancestral record"[4] that included notables such as Louisa Alcott, Colonel Benjamin Church, Richard Warren, George Washington, and Governor John Webster. But chief among their interests in the book, and particularly idolized by Ida's family, was the nonconformist Thomas Pope. Ida clearly embraced her past and liked to think that she inherited her strong spirit from her first feisty colonial ancestor in America.

Thomas Pope, Ida's first New England paternal ancestor, was twenty-two when he arrived at Plymouth Colony in 1630,[5] one of 140 immigrants who sailed from England to Massachusetts on the *Mary & John.* Many of these early colonists were fierce defenders of their rights, and Thomas stands out as a clear example of this propensity. There are several recorded eruptions of Thomas's temper, and "his promptness in resenting a real or fancied injury, and his independent expressions of personal opinion, more than once caused him to be arraigned before the magistrates of New Plymouth."[6] With a great deal of public fanfare, Thomas packed up his wife and four children and headed for Dartmouth, Massachusetts, to "seek a section of the country where man should be freer from restraint."[7]

The Popes settled on the Acushnet River near the developing village of Dartmouth. Historical records acknowledge that the "earliest record of any white inhabitant in the area was Thomas Pope, who built a grist mill on Sconticut Neck."[8] After moving to Dartmouth, Thomas knew that the security of his family would depend on establishing a strong relationship with other English settlers. He soon became reacquainted with the pilgrim John Cooke, who had arrived at Plymouth with his father, Francis Cooke, in 1620 on the *Mayflower*. John, "on account of religious differences,"[9] had moved to Fairhaven, a few miles from Dartmouth, and he and Thomas became close friends and later allies against the Indians.

After fifty-five years of shaky yet mostly peaceful coexistence with their native neighbors, the colonists engaged in a bloody war beginning in 1675. King Philip's War, as it is known today, between the tribes and the colonists lasted fourteen months. Chief Metacomet of the Wampanoag Indians, known as King Philip, led the uprising against the colonists in New England. During the battle, Dartmouth was virtually burned to the ground and Thomas Pope's twenty-two-year-old son, John, and his daughter Susannah and her husband were killed as they fled for safety to John Cooke's home, which he had transformed out of necessity into a garrison.[10] The protection of the rest of his family during the war deepened the Pope-Cooke bond, and Thomas assigned John to coadminister his will and look after his family after his death. Two centuries later, Ida Pope, her two sisters, and many Cooke descendants would again be fellow adventurers in a new land—Hawai'i—Ida, through family stories, very aware of the early bond between their first ancestors in America.

The Early Years, 1862–1883

Physician William Pope and Cornelia Rochester Waring began family life in Crestline, Ohio—a flat, unappealing, dusty town where 1,458[11] citizens resided on eight square miles and where[12] Ida, third of their seven children, was born July 30, 1862. Her siblings, in order of birth,[13] were William Jr., Lois, Katherine, Henry, Anne, and Frank. Although it was widely known that Dr. Pope and his family were not "members of any religious denomination," others nevertheless acknowledged his "temperate, moral and consistent life."[14] He was, however, a man of conviction and a devout democrat "earnest in the support of party principles and ever ready to exercise his right by ballot to maintain its precepts."[15]

Dr. William and Cornelia Pope. *Author's private collection.*

As a vital railroad junction, Crestline saw its fair share of serious railroad accidents, providing Dr. Pope with a small but steady income. However, because every train changed locomotives in Crestline and crews liked to drink and get rowdy, "it was an unlovely place in which to raise a family."[16] Too many "rough, unattached men and too many saloons" meant the parents had to keep a sharp watch on the girls, so "all significant life went on in the house."[17] Within the home retreat, Ida's reading of great literary works stirred her intellect, refined her taste, and intensified her desire for knowledge. Later, this would work to her advantage, as she devised ways to keep young Hawaiian girls entertained and occupied while boarding with them near numerous saloons in Honolulu.

Ida enjoyed assisting her mother with the younger children and her father with his medical patients. Family memoirs describe Ida as a curious, frank, spirited, and lovable child who easily won the affection of others. When she was nine, her mother gave birth to "little" Anne Elizabeth, who weighed only three pounds at birth. All the Pope children were short in stature, but Anne never grew to more than 4½ feet. When she was seven, she fell from the barn's hayloft and severely injured her hip. Anne's "sunny personality" despite her painful disability made her the "pet of the family," but no one was closer to her than Ida. They were "similar in temperament and natural bent,"[18] and Ida was fiercely protective of her little sister.

Despite his work as a physician, entrepreneurial Dr. Pope was never one to pass up a venture, and his first—to the astonishment of the community—was

Ida, showing her determination at two years
of age. *Author's private collection.*

All seven Pope children were born in this Crestline, Ohio, house. *Illustrated Atlas of Crawford
Co. Ohio* (Bucyrus, OH: Gould & Starr, 1873).

almost a success. Hearing that fortunes were being made by other Ohioans like John D. Rockefeller, through the discovery of oil, Dr. Pope jumped into action, and actually did discover oil in Crawford County, Ohio. Unfortunately, the project ultimately was unprofitable, forcing him to fall back on the meager income earned by practicing medicine. His fortunes took a more positive turn with his introduction to German-born William Franz—the first step toward a partnership that would eventually establish the Franz & Pope Knitting Machine Company.

True to the spirit of the Industrial Revolution, Dr. Pope and Mr. Franz set out to create an instrument that would simplify everyday life. Building on an existing design of Franz's, the two perfected a machine in 1868 to knit socks, one of the most tedious duties of the time. They obtained their first patent for the device in 1869,[19] and Ida's father gave up medicine for good to become the president and general manager of the Franz & Pope Knitting Machine Company, "the first enterprise of the kind in the United States."[20] In 1870, when Ida was eight years old, her father began selling the first of the machines that would knit "a stocking, heel, and toe complete, without taking it off the hooks, in seven minutes."[21] Only six years later, the family was elated to learn that the company won a medal at the Philadelphia Centennial, its invention lauded as the "most advanced knitting machines in the United States."[22] A newspaper of the day drew a fanciful and prophetic picture of the machine's future:

> Readers will have no difficulty in recalling a familiar picture—a room made pleasant by a genial fire on the hearth. At hand is a corner sacred to "Grandma," and here she sits, hour after hour, knitting, weaving stockings—this is her favorite employment. Gaze upon it while you may, reader, for soon grandma's occupation will be gone. In place of the loved old lady, whose eye is fast growing dim, and whose hands tremble with age, will be seen a younger generation—in place of the bright needles that "click" and glisten as the stocking is slowly fashioned, will be a little machine labeled "Franz & Pope's Patent"—the good wife or daughter seats herself, hastily turns a crank for a few minutes, and, presto! Here is a complete stocking.[23]

With the success of the company, the Popes were finally able to start a new life. In the early 1870s, they relocated to Bucyrus, Ohio; their new home, thanks to their surname, was dubbed "The Vatican." They held Shakespeare, Dickens, and Browning Clubs, where Ida, always in charge, would organize her younger siblings to "read from the appropriate author and later put on a costumed play based on their reading."[24] Most magazines of the time published "parlor theatricals,"[25] and

The Pope home, Bucyrus, Ohio, dubbed "The Vatican." *Author's private collection.*

the family subscribed to the most prestigious periodicals of the day: *Harper's, Century, Scribner's,* and the *Atlantic.* Dramatic readings by neighborhood clubs were encouraged by parents in the nineteenth century to formulate cultivation. Under the direction of Ida, "The Vatican" hosted many clubs and dramatic productions for the youth in the Bucyrus community.

Since Lois and Ida were the two oldest and hardiest of the four girls, they assisted their mother with the labor-intensive laundry work, using a large, round, galvanized tub and corrugated washboard. Once the clothes and bedding for nine family members were wrung through a hand wringer and hung out to dry even in the freezing winters, there were the sewing and darning each night. Their home was peaceful because their parents were "especially congenial" with each other.[26] Their father found "great comfort in his domestic family relations, where the same kindness and affection which ruled his own spirit was communicated to and shared by every member of the household."[27]

Every evening after supper, the family gathered together around the table to listen to Dr. Pope read aloud—Cornelia and Lois sewing and mending, and teenage Ida and her younger siblings picking out nutmeats from black walnut and hickory shells or crunching on apples from the bowl on the table. The only time they ever remembered their father being irritated with them was when they crunched their apples too loudly while he was reading. Life had become comfortable and lovely at last for the large Pope family.

Oberlin College and Teaching Years, 1883–1890

Ida discovered her passion for teaching at Bucyrus High School, where she excelled in all subjects. In 1879, as Ida graduated from high school, illness forced her father's business partner, William Franz, to retire. This required Ida to help with the bookkeeping of the booming business. While the Popes worked long hours, other manufacturers began infringing on Dr. Pope's patents. When he discovered this, Dr. Pope went on the offensive, publishing a notice in *Scientific American:* "I hereby caution and warn all persons" that it is our "intention to prosecute."[28] Dr. Pope did prosecute the Lamb Knitting Machine Manufacturing Company, an action that provided Ida a valuable lesson in standing up for one's rights, no matter the cost. The judgment awarded in 1881 included recovering "the profits and gains"[29] his competitors had earned using his technology, and paid for Ida's dream of going to college.

In the fall of 1883, brimming with enthusiasm and energy, twenty-one-year-old Ida traveled sixty miles from home and entered Oberlin College, fully aware of how rare the educational opportunity was. Not only was she a woman, she was also the only one of her siblings whom her father sent to college. Her oldest sister, Lois, was needed at home as "mother's helper"; her eldest brother, William Jr., temporarily left the family due to repeated drunkenness; and her fifteen-year-old brother Henry went door-to-door selling the family's knitting machines. But Dr. Pope had Ida pack her bags for Oberlin, knowing that his bright and strong-willed daughter would need a college education to fulfill her dreams of being a teacher and to ensure her independence.

Oberlin College, founded by Congregationalists in 1836 and named for a minister and social reformer passionately committed to free public education, claims to be the first educational institution that opened its doors to all Christians, "irrespective of color or previous condition of servitude."[30] Long before she left for Honolulu, Ida confronted the explosive issues of interracial socializing, coeducation, and women's rights.

Ida was enrolled in the "Literary Course" that replaced the "Ladies Course" in 1875.[31] Her coeducational program was a two- to three-year series of courses that did not culminate in a degree. This fact disturbed Ida, as she would note on her alumnae forms, along with any typographical errors discovered on their forms. After 1894, graduates of the Literary Course who completed additional correspondence

Ida May Pope, ca. 1880s. *Author's private collection.*

work could receive the degree of Bachelor of Letters (LB).[32] Ida took full advantage of this opportunity while in Hawai'i.

Immediately following her graduation in 1886, Ida moved back home and was hired to teach high school in Bucyrus. Soon, her sense of efficacy, organization, and leadership was noted and she was recruited to be on the executive committee for her state's teachers' association. The next summer, when the Crawford County Teachers' Institute was held, she was asked to present on "The Object of Education"[33]—a concept that she would continue to develop in her next assignment. After three years of teaching in Bucyrus, she was offered another opportunity and relocated to Columbus. The position to teach special needs children at the largest institution in her state, in a position vacated by her Oberlin classmate Helen Hoppin, must have seemed like a good opportunity at the time. Helen was leaving Ohio to join another one of their classmates, Lilla Appleton, to teach at a girls' boarding school in Honolulu.

The Ohio Asylum for Feeble-Minded Youth provided simple vocational training for "idiotic" or "peculiar" children between the ages of six and sixteen.[34] Built upon the mission of making "the deviant un-deviant," the institution touted the opportunities it gave to children with special needs who struggled in public schools.[35] Dr. Gustavus A. Doran, its director, claimed that children with disabilities excelled once they were enrolled in a more supervised and stringent setting. This was an undertaking for which Ida had particular empathy, based on the struggles of her own public school students, her interactions with her father's medical patients, and the experiences of her own disabled sister, Anne. Ida hoped for the chance to combine her two enduring passions of nursing and teaching to improve the lives and opportunities of the deaf children who were to be her students.

However, when Ida arrived in fall of 1889, it was not to a school that would allow her to realize her hopes and ambitions as a special educator, but to an overcrowded and disorganized asylum. The school had limited space due to a catastrophic fire, and Dr. Doran, occupied with the rebuilding efforts, had no time to train new teachers like Ida Pope. In addition, despite his written reports, requests for relief, and pleas on behalf of the teachers, overenrollment was a serious issue.[36] Ida, one of twenty-two teachers, was soon lost among the institution's 150 staff members and 869 students.[37] Without separate quarters, she slept alongside her pupils in the "deaf and dumb" unit. Not having learned any sign language herself, she waited in vain for training and struggled to communicate with her pupils. An internal report criticized the superintendent for hiring teachers like Ida, "who had to learn how to teach the deaf, after they had begun to teach"[38] and publicly accused the institution of negligence in regard to the deaf community.[39]

Despite the overcrowded conditions and her own regret, Ida persevered. When she began to search for a new position at the end of the year, it was with a changed perspective and a strong faith in the importance of manual training.[40] She was undoubtedly proud to learn that the American Association of Instructors of the Blind had publically endorsed the Franz-Pope knitting machines in 1877 to train sightless children for wage earning.[41] Ida was convinced that without training in some handicraft, those disabled children in the Ohio asylum would never gain employment or independence from the institution.

The asylum had other serious problems, as seen in the frantic petitions from Dr. Doran to the Ohio's governor regarding the housing of young women as they came of age. Many had no place to go and no way to generate income out on their own. The only humane and safe solution he saw was to house them in a separate building on school property. Ida would remember his futile campaign later when she confronted a similar issue in Hawai'i.

The Job Offer

Soon, her destiny appeared in a letter from Lilla Appleton, who urged Ida to take the place she was vacating at the Kawaiaha'o Seminary in Honolulu. Sure that she could do no more for the students at the Ohio asylum, Ida gathered multiple endorsements and formally applied for the teaching position with the American Board of Commissioners for Foreign Missions (ABCFM). A job offer soon followed, which she accepted. After she picked up her last paycheck from the asylum on May 23, 1890, she began to excitedly pack her newly purchased steamer trunk.

As excited as she was, the decision to accept the position was not an entirely easy one. Her father was ailing and the family business was struggling in a downturned economy. But practical-minded Ida knew that the American Board contract would allow her to terminate her employment at the asylum, pay her traveling expenses, give her three years of free room and board, and provide a salary that could help her family. Most importantly, since Ida had never been out of Ohio, she saw this as the adventure of a lifetime.

She broke the news to her close-knit family in the spring of 1890, and though they were apprehensive, the Popes knew their headstrong daughter would not be dissuaded. Had they known about the subversive revolutionary movement brewing in Hawai'i, they might have insisted she stay at home. As it turned out, their daughter would be in the right place at the right time. With the same independent spirit possessed by her pilgrim ancestor Thomas Pope, Ida would soon be fighting for the rights and liberties of Hawaiian women.

CHAPTER TWO

The Extraordinary Nineteenth Century

Books, songs, movies, and poems are plentiful about the extraordinary nineteenth century in which Ida May Pope lived. Themes include immigration, westward expansion, the rise of industrial America, the growth of political democracy, women's rights, temperance, public education, slavery, the Civil War, and more.

While all of this historical movement was taking place, the life of an average woman began to transform drastically while the life of an average man went unchanged. Men still dominated the nineteenth century. Only they could vote, execute a will, enter into a contract, own a home, or sue in court. Even a woman's child officially belonged to her husband. Rich women lived relatively idle lives and poor ones worked without ceasing. Poised between these two extremes, middle-class women like Ida Pope were bound by proprieties even more restrictive than their formidable undergarments. But growing social movements throughout the century began to change the balance between men and women. New cultural and social changes were overtaking America, overlapping and overwhelming old values and traditions.

Ida's alma mater, Oberlin, was at the forefront of social change in the United States, and the movement migrated to Hawai'i through her alumnae. They carried the torch lit by the legendary feminist Lucy Stone, Oberlin class of 1847, and the first female to graduate from their college. Lucy was a woman of "firsts." She was the first woman in America to keep her own name after marriage. She was also the first one to convene a national Women's Rights Convention in Massachusetts. Even in death, she achieved a "first" by being the first person cremated in New England. It was said that her dying words to her daughter, three years older than Ida, were, "Make the world better."[1] And the world did begin to look better for nineteenth-century women. What a woman could and couldn't do looked dramatically different at the end of the century compared to its onset.

Romantic Ida May Pope in the late 1870s. *Author's private collection.*

Early Nineteenth Century

In the first three decades of the 1800s, America was swept by religious revivalism. It was this revival wave, dubbed the Second Great Awakening, which led the first group of missionaries to Hawai'i. This migration was traced directly to a young Hawaiian runaway boy who unknowingly set into motion a series of events that launched this first American mission to Hawai'i.

In 1809, this boy's main goal in life was to escape the wars of King Kamehameha the Great. Sixteen years old and orphaned, 'Ōpūkaha'ia got away by working as a cabin boy for passage on an American ship. Soon, a series of events led to his Christian conversion and a burning desire to return home and spread the Gospel. He entered a rigorous program of academic study, prepared intensely for missionary work, traveled, spoke, and became the poster child for foreign missions among Congregationalists, raising funds throughout New England. It was as if God Himself had sent 'Ōpūkaha'ia to light the missionary fire. And then he inexplicably was gone, a victim of the typhus he contracted in the first week of January in 1818. His death on February 17 was the heartbreak of many, his unfulfilled life the subject of many sermons.

While his tragic and untimely death at twenty-six saddened a multitude, his life captured the imagination of New England evangelicals, particularly the newly formed American Board of Commissioners for Foreign Missions. The American Board swiftly called both men and women to take 'Ōpūkaha'ia's message to the Hawaiian people in proxy. In 1819, Reverend Hiram Bingham, like other volunteers, quickly found the required wife, and left Boston for the grueling thirteen-thousand-mile, six-month sailing passage around Cape Horn.

The first missionary wives were eager to participate because like the Great Awakening that preceded it in the eighteenth century, this second revival had a democratizing effect on their gender.[2] Women were stimulated and encouraged from the church pulpits in their communities to participate in the outpouring of religious enthusiasm and become partners in ministry with men. Women's involvement in teaching Sunday school and notably in missionary societies increased exponentially in the beginning of the nineteenth century. These meetings gave them an acceptable and proper way to gather, collaborate, and engage with the public outside their homes.

And as they formed fund-raising committees to support ministry efforts, a topic such as obtaining a higher education would have been cautiously discussed. Women in ministry were warned not to let their literary or intellectual pursuits get in the way of God's work. Up to the beginning of the century, being able to read, especially the Bible, would suffice as "book learning" for women. One writer proclaimed, "All a girl needs to know is enough to buy a peck of potatoes in case she becomes a widow."[3]

This attitude prevailed until Oberlin did a daring thing in 1833 and became coeducational. Others seized the opportunity to attend "women only" institutions, such as Mount Holyoke Female Seminary in Massachusetts. In an 1835 pamphlet outlining her plans, founder Mary Lyon stated that one of the goals of Mount Holyoke would be "to cultivate the missionary spirit among its pupils."[4] The use of "seminary" rather than "college" in the school's name was strategic because it was less threatening to those potential donors who did not think women should attend college. Until 1888, only men running colleges could hold the title of president; thus her title was "principal" and not "president." When Mount Holyoke opened in the fall of 1837, Mary Lyon proclaimed, "Young ladies, live for the good of others."[5] Thus inspired, droves of "Holyoke Ladies" were hired by the American Board and took off to the Hawaiian Islands, decades before Oberlin. Nineteen of Mary Lyon's graduates carried her ideals and teaching methods into schools throughout Hawai'i including four who were founding teachers of Kawaiaha'o Seminary, one of whom was Reverend Hiram Bingham's daughter.

Mid-Nineteenth Century

As the Second Great Awakening wound down in the mid-1800s, there was great debate all over the United States surrounding the topic of female education. But in Hawai'i, there was no such debate. Ironically, the American missionary influence on Hawaiians not only increased access to education for native women but also created a more egalitarian relationship between the sexes due to the abandonment of the religious practices that formerly subjugated women.

As a result of the investment in education for both sexes, Hawai'i became one of the most literate nations in the world during the mid-1800s, with an estimated 91–95 percent of the general population able to read and write. Not only did this surpass the literacy rate in the United States, which was barely 78 percent; this achievement was unparalleled anywhere in the world.[6]

Well pleased with the results of education in his kingdom, King Kamehameha III wrote a declaration to the General Meeting of Missionaries stating his desire to establish an exclusive boarding school for the kingdom's royal heirs, both males and females.[7] Hiram Bingham, the acknowledged leader of the missionaries, instantly recognized a good opportunity "to win and educate their juvenile heirs."[8] While all the missionaries agreed that the young souls should be "won" for Christ, many disagreed with the king's request of sequestering the royal children. Some advocated for a common school experience, believing "that chiefs and people

The close-knit, blue-eyed, and petite Pope sisters in order of their birth: Lois, Ida, Katherine, and Anne, ca. 1885. *Author's private collection.*

should be educated on the same footings."[9] The debate ended in favor of sequestration.[10] Royal children began to be isolated from their future subjects in 1840 and groomed for leadership by married American teachers Amos Starr and Juliette Montague Cooke in the "Chiefs' Children's School."

At the same time girls were being groomed for leadership in Hawai'i, many in the United States asserted that a "finished" education would take women away from their domesticity and the home life would suffer. For the most part, scholars decided that women should receive some education, but many disagreed about the subjects to be included. In 1844, Oberlin ladies were not even allowed to read their own graduating essays because faculty thought it "would be undignified and immodest for the ladies to deliver their productions from the rostrum."[11] Even though the Oberlin ladies were college educated, the popular culture of the mid-century still considered a woman's place to be in the home, with marriage and children as the ultimate goal, not up on a public podium.

But spinsterhood became less of a choice and more of a necessity as the numbers of marriageable bachelors declined. Of the American women born between 1860 and 1880, more than 10 percent remained single. One clear reason for the decline was the Civil War that began in 1861.[12] The four-year war cost an estimated 620,000 men their lives, creating more "spinsters" in Ida's generation than any other in American history.[13] Another reason was the large number of men who had taken off to seek their fortunes in the West. The reformer Mary Livermore gave a popular speech around the country urging parents to "train their daughters for self-support because their chances of getting a good husband were dwindling."[14] By midcentury, single women began to be celebrated for getting an education and serving the community. In a perfect illustration, of the four Pope sisters, only Lois married, leaving Ida, Katherine, and Anne to independently provide their own support.

When that first cohort of women left Mount Holyoke for Hawai'i in the middle of the century, the strict Victorian rules of conduct they were bound by at home still dictated their every waking moment—even more so because they were still attached to a New England puritanical missionary board. In fact, in the first decades of the missionary work in Hawai'i, few wives dared to challenge outright the boundaries that kept them silent in church. And when one did, it was noted. Mount Holyoke graduate and missionary daughter Martha Chamberlain recorded an auspicious event in her diary on July 16, 1870: "The *first* time a *woman* had ever spoken extemporaneously from a foreign pulpit in Honolulu."[15] The daring Lydia Vose Snow, recently returned from laboring for thirty years in Micronesia with her missionary husband, had a public statement to make to her Christian sisters. She brazenly headed toward the church platform, but stopped short "on the pulpit steps."[16] This event was gossiped about the town, with many weighing in on the appropriateness of her conduct. Martha privately applauded her missionary sister. "She was quiet, composed and self-possessed, her voice rang clear, her words were a testimony."[17] Lydia Snow, while not daring to climb past the church steps in 1870, paved the way for women like Ida Pope who, near the end of the century, could step right up to any church platform for the right occasion. In Hawai'i, Ida had other hurdles to face regarding "staying in her place," because she was still expected to adhere to the rigidly defined roles and restrictions of the era. But as the twentieth century dawned, Ida resisted.

Late Nineteenth Century

American women at the end of the nineteenth century represented a historical shift in education and work. Now that they were overeducated for the rural farming communities they came from, their diplomas would not provide the same career opportunities as they did for men. Ida was fortunate in that she was well known in the village of Bucyrus and was quickly hired. Other "educated spinsters" in her graduating class found themselves in a quagmire. What would they do with their education? While factories, mills, and shops had plenty of low-paying jobs for women, it was unrewarding work after the stimulation of college. And it was hard to take up factory work, which required "standing all the time, lifting heavy goods; no holidays."[18] Salaries for factory work were four to six dollars a week, and because women needed lodging, most of their pay went to boarding houses, and the rest to food. After they saw to their personal "washing, sewing, clothes, medicine, all extras," the "legitimate end was a coffin or hospital."[19]

Due to these harsh circumstances, the late nineteenth century witnessed the rise of a new group of young women who were willing to take risks and go against the old guard. In 1871, when Ida was eleven, Susan B. Anthony was arrested for trying to vote for Ulysses S. Grant in the presidential election. When Ida was twenty-four, Miss Anthony was finally granted an audience before the U.S. House Judiciary Committee to argue for an amendment to the U.S. Constitution granting women the right to vote. Neither Susan Anthony nor Ida Pope would live to see the suffrage amendment passed, because popular thinkers, authors, and orators, both men and women, still had restrictive views of appropriate roles for women. In 1873, a popular resort published this "Routine for a Lady" as an enticement to young ladies of Ida's generation. It underscores the lack of stimulating or engaging things to do in an educated middle class woman's day.

> Rise and dress; go down to the spring; drink to the music of the band; walk around the park—bow to gentlemen; chat a little; drink again; breakfast; see who comes in on the train; take a siesta; walk in the parlor; bow to gentlemen; have a little small talk with gentlemen; have some gossip with ladies; dress for dinner; take dinner an hour and a half; sit in the grounds and hear the music of the band; ride to the lake; see who comes by the evening train; dress for tea; get tea; dress for the hop; attend the hop; chat awhile in the parlors, go to bed.[20]

Despite the educational advances made, an educated woman still generated anxiety among many who were threatened by a possible abandonment of traditional roles. Some of the loudest voices still arguing at the end of the century against women's higher education came from prominent clergy. In 1882, when Ida Pope was in her last year of high school, the influential archbishop Reverend Dr. Roger William Vaughan, who laid the curricular foundation for colleges and Catholic schools, reminded Americans that "modern thinking" of educating women was going against God's plan.

> The modern idea that woman should become lawyers, doctors, and stump orators, is a painful and saddening blunder. Women are meant to be women, and not to be twisted and metamorphosed into female men—it is to be hoped that "modern thought" will turn its energies in another direction,

instead of that which would destroy the sweetness, rest, and purity of man's home, which is or ought to be his safest and securest castle.[21]

Despite views like those of Archbishop Vaughan, the culture had shifted enough so that women like Ida could become educated, independent spinsters—as long as they dedicated their lives to an acceptable noble pursuit, like teaching.

A Call to Teach

In 1841, educational reformist Catherine Beecher bemoaned the fact that a single woman like herself was forced to live with her parents and waste her mind in frivolity. She believed a single woman should be able to teach outside the home so she could share her feminine virtues with all society. Her counterpart Horace Mann may have inadvertently encouraged teaching not as a career but as an idealistic or charitable vocation with his own publicized sentiments. He reasoned that teaching was a woman's true calling, one that would take advantage of her God-given talent as nurturer.[22]

The reality was that most of Ida's classmates sought teaching positions only because it was one of the most, if not the most, socially acceptable position for single women. But teaching would not support a single lifestyle because women received only 40 to 60 percent of male teachers' salaries.[23] Ironically, because even male teachers were poorly paid, they avoided the profession, creating opportunities for women that otherwise would not exist. Even more ironic, when education itself became a feminine profession, women who previously had been considered intellectually inferior to men became the primary force educating boys to be strong male leaders.

Ida's friend Lilla Appleton recommended that women focus on primary school teaching, because even after completing a PhD she was repeatedly rejected. "The more advanced in age and scholarship the classes you elect to teach, the more you come into competition with men and the more you are likely to be rejected as a candidate. Even though your scholarship may be superior to his, the man is more likely to get the position."[24]

With numerous applicants for a single opening, public schools made extravagant demands that most middle-class young college educated women could not meet.[25] For example, those who had skill and passion for teaching but were not accomplished vocalists, or did not speak French or Latin, were often unsuccessful in obtaining a position. Advice to the unsuccessful applicant was to "know what you pretend to know."[26] Normal schools had evolved throughout the nineteenth century into teacher's colleges and then into colleges of education within larger institutions to provide focused teacher training. But it was financially impractical for most unemployed graduates to return to college for further training. The economic picture of the late nineteenth century in the United States was not cheerful. Ida's father ultimately lost his business to bankruptcy like many others in the 1890 economic depression. There were more workers seeking employment than there were jobs in Ohio, and the future looked grim for the Popes.

Hawai'i as a Vocational Opportunity

There was hope for jobless women when popular literature in the late nineteenth century proclaimed, "Mission enterprises are now opening a wide field to intelligent and religious young women."[27] Readers were informed that newly formed boarding schools in "distant outposts" offered a "wide field of good work and self-support to the right kind of women."[28] The role of a "missionary teacher" now provided an entry point for a woman to become a missionary, of sorts. Using the authority of a missionary vocation to enter the classroom was strong enticement for an adventurous, unemployed single woman.

But even at the end of the nineteenth century, the Hawaiian Islands still seemed impossibly wild and rough. Many parents were reluctant to send their unmarried daughters traipsing off to those "distant outposts." The Popes, too, were fearful that their daughter might be risking her life in the legendary dangerous conditions of the "Sandwich Islands." After all, they were a family of readers, and they had read sensational stories about Captain Cook's violent murder in 1778 at the hands of Hawaiians, and of cannibals living in neighboring Pacific islands.

Sending women to these dangerous lands had been controversial in some circles for decades. Even when the first American Board detachment was sent from Boston to Hawai'i, many in their own community criticized the fact that the company included wives and children.

> The idea of letting American women and children join this pioneer band was extremely repulsive to many who were heartily in sympathy with the evangelistic movement. To these it seemed unwise and unnecessary to subject delicate and refined ladies, as well as ingenuous girls and boys, to the hardships of life in a strange land, amidst uncongenial surroundings, and amongst cruel savages.[29]

And if sending married women to Hawai'i was controversial enough, sending unmarried women was a scandalous idea never entertained by the American

A warm and balmy 1890 Thanksgiving Day in Kapiʻolani Park, where the freezing weather back home would have been a topic of much discussion. *Left to right:* Carrie Gilman, Ida Pope, May Atherton, May Waterhouse, Helen Hoppin, Ruth Hoppin, Iretta Hight, Carrie Winter, and Carrie Castle. *UCSD Libraries.*

Board in the first part of the nineteenth century. There were concerns that living among a vast number of the unsavory seafarers from whaling ships and merchant vessels that defined Honolulu in those days might undermine a single woman's reputation.

But the advent of the female boarding school in Hawaiʻi represented a viable and respectable option for unmarried women. And the Hawaiian Islands offered opportunities these women would be hard-pressed to find elsewhere—a paid adventure of a lifetime and an occupation that coincided with their altruistic beliefs and college training.

From another angle, the advent of single women to Hawaiʻi also provided relief to the exhausted and often uneducated wives and daughters of missionaries, women who had previously been saddled with overwhelming teaching, school-administration, and other conflicting duties, including raising their own offspring. Missionary families could now turn over their mission schools to the new spirited breed of educated women like Ida Pope.

Oberlin "sisters." *Left to right:* Nellie Waterhouse (*looking over shoulder*), Iretta Hight, May Waterhouse, Ruth Hoppin, Helen Hoppin, Myra Davis, and Carrie Winter. *UCSD Libraries.*

One woman relieved to see educated teachers take over the mission schools was Juliette Cooke, still living in Hawai'i after the school for royal children closed at the midcentury mark. Even though Hawai'i had grown more American in character by the end of the century, the schism between the Americans and the Hawaiian leadership had grown wider. The Chiefs' Children's School was certainly the most significant cooperative effort between the American Board missionaries and the Hawaiian royalty.

Juliette's husband, Amos, left behind twelve leather-bound volumes of intensely private diaries full of self-admonition, frustration, and confessions that spanned his decade in the school. The diaries chronicle numerous occurrences of whippings of the royal children among other harsh punishments. In Juliette's own words, she and Amos were the wrong couple selected to raise and educate the sixteen royal children, five of whom became the last rulers of the Hawaiian kingdom, namely, Alexander Liholiho, Lot Kamehameha, William Lunalilo, David Kalākaua, and Lydia Kamaka'eha Pākī (Lili'uokalani).[30] Amos' method of breaking the will of the royal children may not have yielded what either side anticipated when the Chiefs' School was founded, but it certainly changed the course of history and left its own legacy.

By the time Alexander Liholiho, as Kamehameha IV, ascended to the throne in 1855, the Hawaiian government had already begun its separation from the American missionary influence that had up to that point defined Hawaiian education. The king's disdain for the unpleasant treatment he received during his childhood under the Cookes may have contributed to his choice of an educational leader. In 1865, Abraham Fornander, a Swede, who had always been very critical of the educational work of the American missionaries, was named inspector general of schools for the entire kingdom. And as educational historian Helen Gay Pratt put it, "The Americans who had created the public school system, created the written language, translated books into Hawaiian, printed the books, travelled the Islands and personally examined the children in the schools, trained the Hawaiian teachers—were thus cut off."[31]

Even though Hawaiian public schools were secularly restructured, there were still private mission schools that were receiving benevolent financial support and that could remain independent from the public school system. The rationale to create boarding schools like Kawaiahaʻo was to provide an education for select children who would be under the continuous influence of missionary educators.[32] In 1884, Oberlin president James Fairchild, also a corporate member of the American Board, visited Hawaiʻi and knew just who should be the ones to fill vacancies at mission schools. Once he returned to Ohio, several of his graduates were trading the comforts of home for rudimentary and often perilous conditions in the Hawaiian Islands. Once there, they began recruiting each other.

Being college educated gave Ida and her classmates not only a broader intellectual perspective but also a lifetime membership in a sorority of unusually talented and dedicated women. Those who were recruited as missionary teachers for Hawaiʻi formed a tightly knit family unit. On Sundays, they often met to share teaching experiences, news and gossip from home, politics, and most importantly, a shoulder to cry on, if need be. This sisterhood would be an important factor in Ida Pope's long tenure in Hawaiʻi. Their alumni magazine, *The Oberlin Review*, reported on the ladies' alumnae picnic and told its readers that despite the many male alumnae in Honolulu, the ladies made it clear: "No gentlemen invited."[33]

CHAPTER THREE

Kawaiahaʻo Seminary

Acorn to Oak, 1865–1890

Gulick Family School

Ida Pope was headed to a school with a storied history among missionaries, Hawaiians, and their royalty. It had its humble beginning as a "small family school"[1] in a house vacated in 1863 by Reverend Ephraim Wesson Clark. Reverend Clark had pastored many royal family members during his fifteen years of service to Kawaiahaʻo Church. Now, after experiencing much personal sadness and death in the house that sat directly across the road from his church, he was going back to America. At about the same time, missionary doctor Luther Gulick and his wife, Louisa, arrived in January 1864 and needed a home. They had been forced to leave the Micronesia mission field and return to Honolulu due to Louisa's sickness. Upon their return, Dr. Gulick was named secretary for the newly formed Hawaiian Evangelical Association Board. The Gulicks were very grateful to enjoy the stability of their own home after thirteen years of missionary work moving around the many islands in the western Pacific Ocean.

Early in 1864, Louisa Gulick took advantage of her newfound stability to earnestly train and educate her children. She soon learned a Hawaiian missionary couple being sent to the Marquesas Islands desired that their daughters remain in the safe confines of Honolulu.[2] Louisa, knowing the harsh conditions, was more than anxious to support her Hawaiian missionary sister by providing a loving and safe haven for her daughters. She viewed the opportunity to teach and house girls-in-need as "service to the people among whom they had come so far to live."[3] Thus, her two little boarders, along with her own five children, became the fledgling Kawaiahaʻo Seminary.

The community was impressed by the patience, love, and attention Louisa showered on the children. "Month to month the numbers increased, new girls were received and aid in teaching was rendered by kind neighbors."[4] Louisa's diary documents the increasing popularity of her school, with fluctuating numbers always above capacity for one teacher without any formal training. Louisa may not have had formal teacher training—"normal training," as it was referred to in

Kawaiahaʻo Seminary in 1892 on the present site of the Mission Memorial Building, King Street, Honolulu, ca. 1892. *Lilla Estelle Appleton private collection, Betsy Lang.*

her day—designed to train high school graduates to be teachers of children, but she seemed to have good instincts. Lack of formal training didn't matter much to her, since her main purpose was to create a warm Christian home environment with an informal curriculum that went beyond the activities of a structured course of study.

By 1867, Louisa's health and energy began to wane, and she couldn't keep up with the influx of Hawaiian girls and the requisite duties. At the same time, the Hawaiian Mission Children's Society (HMCS) was looking for a cause to support. Louisa's need to give up the school presented the HMCS with the opportunity they sought. There were many girls throughout the islands in desperate need of housing and an education. Converting the centrally located Clark space into a proper boarding school would solve a great problem. It was now apparent that an educated woman was needed to take the school to the next level. "After ten months spent in vain efforts to obtain a teacher among all the eligible young ladies on the Islands," excitement abounded when the news that Reverend Bingham's daughter Lydia had been persuaded to return to the land of her birth to assume control of the new school.[5] Her education, experience, and understanding of mission life would be invaluable.

Acorn to Oak

Lydia Bingham, who had been six years old when she returned to New England with her parents in 1840, arrived in Honolulu in March of 1867 in a ship under the command of her brother Hiram Bingham Jr., who was also moving back to Hawaiʻi.[6] Lydia was thirty-three years old, was unmarried, and, most importantly, had practical experience both as a teacher and as principal. Lydia knew how much her father had wanted to return to Hawaiʻi, and almost as his proxy, she stepped into the fully paid position of principal.

Once she arrived, it didn't take her long to discover that beneath the friendly smiles, there would be no practical support to help her set up the operational framework for the school, just downright apathy. On June 12, 1867, "with no little sorrow and discomposure," she assertively expressed her disappointment and reminded her missionary employers of her sacrifice. "I decided to resign my lucrative and desirable position as Principal of the Ohio Fem. College."[7] And while she would "deeply regret abandoning the enterprise," she might be forced to move elsewhere if she was not fully supported.[8]

It is unknown what or who changed her mind, but Lydia went full steam ahead laying out the purpose and plans for the "Honolulu Female Academy." Soon, the name changed to Kawaiahaʻo Seminary, after the district in which it was situated.[9] Diagonally across the road from the school was the greatest legacy of Lydia's father, Kawaiahaʻo Church, constructed in 1836 and dedicated in 1842, both designed and pastored by him. It was a constant reminder of her parents' twenty-one years of missionary work in Honolulu. The churchyard is also the last resting place of hundreds of missionaries and their descendants, including two of Lydia's brothers who died in infancy. Today the "Westminster Abbey of Hawaiʻi" is listed on the state and national Register of Historic Places. This impressive coral block church was once the center of religious life for the monarchy as well as for the school, as Ida Pope would discover. This church represents a link between the missionaries and the monarchy like no other institution in Hawaiʻi.

With a veteran educator in control, the school's reputation and enrollment grew exponentially, requiring expansion. In 1868, a building campaign began among the local missionary families, leading to the purchase of the Clark House where Louisa Gulick had begun her family school. The Clark House was then deeded to the American Board.[10] Adjacent to the school was the abandoned

Mission Press and Bindery, where the first completed edition of the Bible in the Hawaiian language had been created. This too was acquired for the rapidly growing school, which then began in earnest to develop as a respected and established institution.

Lydia Bingham began to supplement the basic curriculum with lessons on nutrition, hygiene, childcare, housekeeping, and needlework, viewed as a necessity for future wives and mothers.[11] The practical training became such an enticement that parents transferred their daughters from the Catholic schools, with their intellectual and theological curriculum, to the seminary—among them, Princess Miriam Likelike, youngest sister of King Kalākaua and Queen Lili'uokalani, and mother of the future Princess Ka'iulani.[12] Thus the school began to expand from a school for destitute Hawaiian children to one that served a diverse population.

Lydia recalled that the little "acorn" of Kawaiaha'o Seminary "planted in missionary soil, watered by some trials and tears, nourished by the prayers and gifts of many" soon grew into a "vigorous Oak."[13] By early 1869, the school had swollen to forty-six pupils, and Lydia, without assistance, "taught sixteen months on the stretch without vacation."[14] Lydia's unwed older sister Elizabeth "Lizzie" Bingham, aged thirty-nine, was then recruited from Illinois to lend a hand. Lizzie, a Mount Holyoke graduate with teaching experience at Rockford Female Seminary, worked tirelessly side-by-side with her sister for four years until Lydia left for Hilo in 1873 as the new wife of missionary widower Titus Coan. When he whisked Lydia away, Lizzie Bingham continued on at the helm of Kawaiaha'o for six more arduous years. Later, Ida would hear colorful accounts of the school's early history firsthand from Lydia Coan.

While the school continued to gain stature under the second Bingham sister, financial constraints meant that it remained physically cramped. Studying in a "dreary" basement that was filled with the "tiniest fleas" tormented these pioneering pupils.[15] After Ida arrived, she asked seventeen-year-old Maggie Powers, later the legendary teacher "Mother Waldron," to describe the earlier decade under the Bingham sisters.

> When I first came to school at the age of five years, the principal houses were adobe and stone. They were several feet apart, and in rainy weather, it was very inconvenient to go from our dormitories to our schoolrooms. We had old desks and chairs. Our dining room, which was the basement, was used for the recitation-room of the second class. The other three classes recited their lessons on the verandas. We ate with spoons from tin-plates and the tables, which were scrubbed snowy white, had no table-cloths. In the morning, milk and bread served for breakfast. For dinner

we had poi and meat or salmon. At 5 o'clock, a bell was rung, and all the girls would run, as fast as their legs could carry them to the kitchen steps and there, in a pan, was our supper consisting of a cracker and a half or bread with molasses. Our food, though plain, was the best to be had as our school was very poor; and sometimes when we were sick and needed better food, a teacher would go without and let us have her share.[16]

Clearly, the conditions at Kawaiahaʻo before Ida Pope arrived were austere at best. And yet, as Maggie Powers was virtually an orphan after her father was lost at sea and her mother and sister quarantined as "lepers" on Molokaʻi, it's hard to predict what would have happened to a girl like her without the boarding school. Even though times were lean and food scarce, resourceful teachers found ways to keep growing girls nourished.

Second Generation in Charge: Teachers' Loss of Autonomy

In 1870, fifty years after Henry ʻŌpūkahaʻia had inspired the exodus of twelve different companies of missionaries to Hawaiʻi, the American Board withdrew its support after deciding that the islands were successfully evangelized. Due to costs associated with the Civil War, the board had forewarned the missionaries a decade earlier that the day was coming when they would need to be self-supporting.[17] Despite the warning, many were unprepared when the time came and were apprehensive about returning to their changed country.

America was undergoing sweeping economic and political transformations after the Civil War and the 1865 assassination of Abraham Lincoln. At this point in time, the Franz & Pope Knitting Machine Company was prospering but others were not. Those missionaries who wanted to stay in Hawaiʻi realized that some central organization would be needed to carry on the benevolent work while providing financial support for their families. Thus was born the Hawaiian Board of Missions.[18]

Many other missionaries had no choice. They realized that without financial support, they would have to return to America.[19] Now, their grown children had to make a choice. Would they return to the unstable land of their parents' birth or stay in the land of their own birth? This group of men, native-born in Hawaiʻi yet not of native Hawaiian ancestry, would ultimately instigate the plantation economy that radically altered the cultural framework of the islands forever. Their economic power later translated into massive political power that would ultimately overthrow the Hawaiian government. But years before that happened, these men leapt into action and took firm control, not only of the finances of Kawaiahaʻo Seminary but of the total operation of the school, including the curriculum and instruction.

The earlier generation of missionaries had supported a relatively autonomous role for the teaching wives when they established schools throughout the islands in the first part of the nineteenth century. They relied largely on the wisdom of the women to get the job done in whatever way they could, as long as the children's physiological and spiritual needs were being met. To a large degree, it was a by-product of the early nineteenth-century attitudes following the religious revivalism in America that sent them to Hawaiʻi as "partners." But even though they were jointly called as couples to do God's work, they still had individual traditional roles: the husbands preached and the wives taught. But when children came along, the wives had even more responsibilities. These women left a lasting record of their experiences through journals, correspondence, reports, and records. Their records show their great capacity to endure hardship and danger. In fact, negative experiences seemed only to strengthen their resolve and underscore the spirit of sisterhood; hardship and resistance merely seemed to reinforce the rightness of their work. But when the second generation came along and formed the Hawaiian Board that ultimately took over the administration of Kawaiahaʻo Seminary, Hawaiʻi had changed and so had the goals of their descendants.

In 1876, due to the increasing enrollment of Hawaiian girls, the Hawaiian Board needed help in financing Kawaiahaʻo Seminary and approached the king for help. King Kalākaua had often shown his deep appreciation for American missionary teachers who often sacrificed their own lives for the kingdom's children. In order to recognize humanitarian services rendered to the kingdom, he had instituted the Royal Order of Kapiʻolani and had bestowed this medal on teachers.[20] Without hesitation, the king stepped in to partner with the missionaries and "liberally" subsidize Kawaiahaʻo Seminary.[21] This now required financial oversight by a board of trustees. The Reverend Dr. Charles M. Hyde's timely arrival in the summer of 1876 to train young Hawaiian pastors coincided with the Hawaiian Board's need of a governing president.[22]

When the trustees, mainly second-generation missionary sons, assumed leadership of Kawaiahaʻo, they wanted to ensure that indigent pupils like Maggie Powers would be self-supporting in the new changing economy and not a burden on the community. To engender self-sufficient adults, the children would need to be taught the practical skills that would provide them jobs during and after their school years.[23] This necessitated, in the trustees' opinion, the micromanagement

Kawaiahaʻo Seminary pupils before the days of uniforms. *Courtesy of Hawaiian Mission Children's Society.*

of the principals and their teachers, and the sanctioning of stern discipline techniques to make pupils fall in line. Mount Holyoke graduate Martha Chamberlain remembered one example of the discipline administered at the new board's direction: "The perforated door step will long live in the memory of the girls of old Kawaiahao Seminary, whose misfortune it was, as very naughty girls, to be locked in the dark cellar, and fed on bread and water for a while."[24] The free-spirited homeschool that Louisa Gulick began in 1864 looked very different governed under a board of trustees.

The first school board initially filled the second principal, Elizabeth "Lizzie" Bingham, with hopefulness. Lizzie, overwhelmed by duties, stated that she was "not so blind as not to see that it might be for the best interests of this institution to have a board of trustees who would assume the whole responsibility."[25] However, as she privately wrote to Reverend Sereno Bishop, her views soon changed, and she increasingly felt that board decisions were not "just"; that she was left "hurt," made to "feel in opposition," and "pushed."[26] For Lizzie, who had nurtured the school to its present stature—first with her sister and then completely on her own—it was hard

to work under board president Hyde. It wasn't long before Lizzie lost the autonomy she had enjoyed in former days because of Dr. Hyde's need for absolute control in everything. In 1882, in poor health and feeling defeated, Lizzie Bingham
resigned.

The next cohort of teachers, wary of being undermined, quarreled with the
trustees, who did not have their teaching experience. They also complained bitterly over needed repairs to the buildings. The school was in crisis, and Princess
Bernice Pauahi Bishop generously stepped up with $5,000 to update the struc-
ture.[27] Despite this, tensions increased between the board and the royal family,
especially with those who lived inside the palace. The first trustees, all but one of
them Christian ministers, disapproved of the monarchy; there was often friction
between them and the king due to differing values toward religion and society.
King Kalākaua, educated and Christianized by the Cookes in the Chiefs' Children's
School, had begun to revert, in their minds, to darkness. He began to incorpo-
rate the ancient shamanic priesthood (kahuna) into his religion and resurrect
the hula (Hawaiian traditional dance). To the trustees of Kawaiahaʻo Seminary,
this indicated the kingdom was moving backward, not forward, and board president Hyde believed the king to be "thoroughly vile and unworthy."[28]

Ida believed "King Kalakaua was a fine
looking man. He had a fine military
bearing, an intelligent expressive face
and affable courteous manners." *UCSD
Libraries.*

The King Snubbed on His Birthday

These tensions came to a head in 1886 when the missionary teachers accepted, on behalf of forty excited older pupils, a formal invitation to attend a glittering ball at the palace celebrating King Kalākaua's fiftieth birthday.[29] It was also a historical opportunity for both teachers and girls to see the ʻIolani Palace illuminated by electricity for the first time. David Kalākaua had entered the Chiefs' Children's School at age four, and knew firsthand how important outings were to boarding school children. He certainly remembered all too well his own childhood, devoid of merriment in the Cookes' strict boarding school. At the appropriate time, the excited children were assembled and dressed up in their best clothes, holding lei made expressly for their king. But just as they were to walk up the road, Reverend Hyde, president of the Board of Trustees, sent notice to the teachers that the children could not attend their king's gala, where there would be hula dancers among other degrading spectacles.[30] As a result, the disappointed children sat out the celebration in their dormitory.[31]

The fallout was swift. Community members, teachers, and parents were enraged that the trustees dared to prohibit Hawaiian children, innocent of politics, from the once-in-a-lifetime "royal" opportunity. The teachers, in particular, saw firsthand how personally involved the royal family was with Kawaiahaʻo, and they felt that Reverend Hyde had gone too far. For the first time, they publicly denounced a trustee's actions and insisted that either he would have to quit or they would.

In his view, though, Reverend Hyde had acted as a protector of the pupils' souls, driven by a firm belief that King Kalākaua was "seeking the overthrow of Christian institutions and the utter demoralization of society."[32] Teacher Lilla Appleton illustrated, in a letter to her mother, Fanny, how complicated the relationships were between the Hawaiian royalty, American missionary descendants, and the Kawaiahaʻo teaching staff.

> I think the Creator was just as well pleased to see the children wearing those birthday leis as He would have been to have them give them to the King, and perhaps a good deal more so. But the mean way in which the trustees overruled the teachers' decision half an hour before it was time to start for the Palace was quite as distasteful to Him as it would have been for the children to go to the Palace and make a bow to the King. It was not the thing done but the way in which it was done that gave offense. And the Christian community including those who support children in school stood with the teachers almost to a unit.[33]

And although Lilla seemed to hold the king in low esteem, believing that God didn't want to see the children bow to an immoral king, in her mind, keeping them from the event was a worse action. Unsettled by the tide of public sentiment against him, Hyde defended himself brazenly and sarcastically to the board. He seemed to wag his finger at his Christian brethren who dared to align themselves with the king merely based on his royal status.

> The lines must be drawn, and they all divide not on the color line, not on church lines, but on the lines of social purity and fundamental righteousness. White folk and good folks will be on the side in favor of heathenism and indecency, because forsooth! It is the King's side and we must honor the King. I expect to be blamed and misrepresented for the stand I have taken but no duty ever seemed to me clearer or more unpleasant.[34]

Prominent Charles Reed Bishop, even though married into Hawaiian royalty, often sided with the tight circle of white businessmen running the economy. But when it came to royal protocol, he differed. "So long as he is King he is entitled to respectful treatment, on account of his office if for no other reason."[35] Ultimately, the king's birthday gala was Hyde's undoing, and he wrote an unapologetic, emotionally charged five-page resignation letter on January 11, 1887, that signified victory for the women teachers. "I give up the Presidency of the Board of Trustees, or they [teachers] will resign."[36]

In full support of their president, fellow board members Sereno Bishop and Alfred F. Judd, whose grandfather had been trustee over the Chiefs' Children's School, immediately resigned. Board member Reverend M. Kuaea followed soon after, leaving William Castle, whose father had partnered with Amos Cooke in business, behind to mollify the staff and students. Later, it would be up to Ida Pope to forge a good relationship with the controversial Reverend Hyde in his future role of trustee for Kamehameha Schools.

The Hyde episode was an outrage not only to the teachers and their pupils but also, as one could imagine, to the royal family—and not merely because of Reverend Hyde's attack on the king's morals. The relationship between the monarchy and the school was deep and long, involving many layers. Many pupils in Kawaiahaʻo Seminary were orphaned or made destitute by circumstances and were fully supported by the Liliʻuokalani Education Society, organized in 1886 and named for its founder. Liliʻuokalani took an active leadership role in the education of all of Hawaiʻi's children, but preferred the "pure, good, beautiful faces"[37] of girls. Liliʻuokalani had declared that she created the society to help "in the proper training of young girls of their own race whose parents would be unable to give them advantages by which they would be prepared for the duties of life."[38] Liliʻuokalani sought out affluent donors among the "female membership of Kawaiahaʻo Church" and was successful in creating scholarships for "those of our sex who were just beginning life."[39] One can only imagine the royal family's fury and sadness at being publicly rebuffed by Reverend Hyde when he detained girls who were financially supported by the Hawaiian government, by the Liliʻuokalani Education Society, and from both the king and queen's personal accounts.

Two Lydias

Some of the girls who were kept from the king's celebration were even attached to the royal household. Liliʻuokalani's five-year-old *hānai* (adopted) daughter, Lydia Kaʻonohiponiponiokalani Aholo, was one of these. Her father, Luther Aholo, was a close friend and adviser to King Kalākaua. Her biological mother, Keahi Aholo, had died a few days after childbirth. The forty-year-old princess Lydia Dominis, later to become Queen Liliʻuokalani, adopted the newborn. She had been married to American John Owen Dominis for sixteen years, with no biological children of her own. The baby was soon given the princess's own birth name, Lydia. It is likely that King Kalākaua had made arrangements for his sister to *hānai,* or adopt, Luther's motherless daughter.

Later in her life, Lydia herself described *hānai* as meaning "to feed or bring up."[40] Under Hawaiʻi's *hānai* system, it was customary for children to be given to grandparents, or to dear friends, not as a severing, but as an extension of family ties.[41] Ida Pope once told her sister Lois that she had to be careful not to "over compliment" a parent, or she would find herself a "hanai mother" of a dozen children.[42] In its simplest form, to *hānai* a child was essentially "a paperless, non-legally binding adoption."[43] It was a widespread practice throughout the history of Hawaiʻi with no corresponding American word to describe this kind of arrangement. Indeed, as an adult, Lydia Aholo herself struggled to characterize her origins.

> She took me—It's the funniest thing. Everybody asks me, "Are you related to the Queen?" I tell them, "I don't know!" I have no way of knowing and I was never inquisitive. I never asked her why she reared me, or anything. All I know is, my mother died when I was eight days old, and—before I

was a year old, they brought me to Washington Place. Then, she put me in school, a boarding school, Kawaiahao.[44]

As if repeating history, both Lydias were adopted in similar fashion and then abruptly taken, as small children, from their adoptive mothers and placed in a strict Congregationalist-run boarding school. Both of them vividly recalled the emotional trauma suffered when placed in the school. In her published memoirs, the first Lydia, future queen Lili'uokalani, remembered her emotional arrival at the Chiefs' Children's School when she was four years old.

Crying bitterly, I turned to my faithful attendant, clasping her with my arms and clinging closely to her neck. She tenderly expostulated with me; and as the children, moved by curiosity to meet the new-comer, crowded about me, I was soon attracted by their friendly faces, and was induced to go into the old courtyard with them.[45]

Lydia Aholo, in an essay she penned at age fourteen, recalled her own emotional arrival at Kawaiaha'o Seminary when she was five years old.

The first night that I slept in school I cried. When I was sleeping that night I fell on the floor. I felt the floor it was so hard. I was under my bed, then I began to cry. And when one of my teachers heard me crying she asked the girls who was crying. I did not understand English at that time. Then my teacher came with a lantern in her hand and she found me under my bed. She took hold of me and put me on my bed again.[46]

That Lili'uokalani would send her *hānai* daughter to an American missionary–run boarding school after her own mixed experience is made only more poignant by the record of similar hardships they endured as very small children. Despite those early struggles, she still valued the rigorous education provided by the missionaries as preparation for her own leadership role in the kingdom.

Lili'uokalani's memoirs attest to her strong feelings about education. "I was a studious girl; and the acquisition of knowledge has been a passion with me during my whole life."[47] She viewed her "education in intimacy"[48] living alongside American missionaries as a distinct advantage when they attempted to politically blindside her. As queen, when asked to read documents that would do her nation harm, she stated, "It is easy for me to detect the purpose of each line and word—and even to distinguish the man originating each portion of it."[49]

"Work from Sunrise to Sunset"

In 1886, the principal of Kawaiaha'o Seminary, Nancy Malone, tendered her resignation. She began to think of any educated and resilient women she knew from her home state of Ohio who might consider a position in Hawai'i. She wrote to a couple of Oberlin classmates. Ida Pope was already contracted for a teaching position in Bucyrus, but Lilla Appleton was available. Principal Malone described the reality of the position to Lilla, whom she hoped to recruit for the school's ninety-three pupils, aged four to twenty. "The work of this school is to make true home-keepers of Hawaiian girls. These girls come to school with little idea of dress, no habits of industry. All the work of the school is done by the girls; cooking, washing, cleaning, etc. The oversight of this is what makes the teacher's work in Kawaiahao hard. Should the teachers be efficient, disciplined workers, able to carry their departments and assume the responsibilities of extras, the hard part of this work would be greatly lessened."[50]

To downplay the overwhelming responsibilities, she then appealed to Lilla with the intrinsic benefits of the job in a postscript. "Do I write discouragingly? You would love these girls, they are kind hearted, loveable. We are very happy in our work for them. There is a strong sympathizing Christian element in Honolulu to support us. Now Miss Appleton could you be our matron?"[51]

Lilla ultimately accepted the job offer but found the conditions at Kawaiaha'o more taxing than anticipated. When she left the post, she wrote to the new trustees that only a superhuman could survive in a school where 130 "girls work from sunrise to sunset" on a punishing schedule. In her "Sketch of the Work"[52] on a typical day, it is easy to see the roots of exhaustion for both pupil and teacher.

The rising bell rings at six o'clock. At half past six the girls come from the dormitories and the day's work begins—two or three girls excused to build fires, and make bread. By seven o'clock, breakfast for both teachers and pupils is prepared and choruses of voices unite:

God is great and God is good.
And we thank him for this food.
By his hand are all things fed,
Bless o Lord, our daily bread.

Breakfast over, the work has renewed. By nine o'clock everyone in school from the principal and her associates to our four-year old Bella has been at work. The back and front yards have been swept, bed trunks and

Missionary teachers. *Top:* Susan V. Hopper, Nancy J. Malone. *Middle:* Lilla E. Appleton, Mary E. Alexander, Fannie G. Morley. *Bottom:* Margaret Brewer (Fowler), ca. 1888. Fannie died soon after this photo was taken. *Midpac.*

closets put in order in three dormitories and every room in the house swept and dusted. One circle of about twenty-five girls have washed or ironed as the case may be, while fifteen others have washed or ironed table-cloths, napkins and towels. The seven o'clock breakfast has been prepared and eaten, vegetables, meat and dessert for the most part made ready for dinner, baking done, and floor and verandahs swept and scrubbed. At noon the children again assembled for prayer and lunch, followed by another two hours of kitchen and dining work.

After lunch, more than a hundred pairs of hands are as busy as two teachers can keep them. Sewing class is followed by two half-hour singing classes. It is now half past four, time for the girls to prepare the five o'clock supper. The hour following is the freest time of the day and teachers and neighbors are usually entertained by some very uproarious singing and game-playing in the back yard. At half past six the little children retire and the older ones gather in the school-room for an hour and a half of silent study at the end of which time they go to their dormitories accompanied by three teachers. The retire bell rings at eight o'clock and, except for the dormitory teachers, the busy day's work is done.[53]

Not surprisingly, as there were many mouths to feed at the school, the majority of the day's instruction involved preparing, serving, and cleaning up after meals. Lilla humorously recounted that "sometimes we meet with surprising results as when we find the coffee sent to the table in the dry state."[54] In addition, Lilla explained how the school needed to be vigilant about hygiene, particularly given the propensity toward head lice, and other minor conditions that could flare up into epidemics. "Every Friday afternoon the girls bring an investigation of each other's heads. Now and then some skin disease or other epidemic breaks out and the poor little victims file out from the dispensary, bandaged and plastered and anointed with various salves and ointments in a way which gives them a most remarkable appearance."[55]

Stepping into Her Predecessor's Shoes

Throughout the history of Kawaiahaʻo Seminary, ships continually took the fatigued teachers back to their homes long before their families expected them. One Kawaiahaʻo principal desperately wrote to the Board of Managers that the high attrition rate of her "faithful and hardworking faculty" supported the school's "established reputation as a woman-killer."[56] Music teacher Fanny Morley's eulogy speaks volumes: "Her labors have proved too much."[57]

Kawaiahaʻo wasn't the only "woman killer." Martha McLennan, who graduated the year before Ida and Lilla, lasted only four years as principal of Maunaʻolu Seminary. Her obituary in *The Oberlin Review* explicitly described her death in 1896 "as the result of breakdown from overwork in Hawaiian Islands."[58] It is unknown what Lilla wrote to Ida Pope in 1890 that persuaded her to contemplate a teaching position in the "Sandwich Islands," but the timing was perfect, and she accepted.

CHAPTER FOUR

Ida to the Kingdom, 1890–1892

Carrie Prudence Winter

"Look for a young lady in a dark red dress, carrying a canvass bag, looking as if she came from Connecticut and were going to the Sandwich Islands."[1] Armed with these instructions, Ida and her twenty-two-year-old brother, Henry, arrived at the Chicago train station on the morning of August 16, 1890. Henry, for whom Chicago had been the pinnacle of the adventure, would soon return home. Ida would make the remainder of her journey to Hawai'i with a fellow Kawaiaha'o Seminary teaching recruit: Carrie Prudence Winter, the young lady in the dark red dress. Ida most likely wore the blue gingham dress she favored. More practical than pretty, she nevertheless had received many comments on how it complemented her bright blue eyes.[2]

Carrie, the daughter of a Congregationalist minister, and new Oberlin graduate, left her fiancé, Charles Kofoid, behind so he could pursue a PhD at Harvard. Once in Hawai'i, every single steamship sailing toward the United States held a letter from Carrie to Charles that contained good insights on the doings of Ida Pope.

Sizing Up Miss Pope

In one of her first letters, Carrie struggled to describe Ida. "Miss Pope is short, but has the appearance of being tall, very fair, wears glasses, is older, I think, than I, is not pretty but has something, and I don't know what yet, which saves her from being common-place. She is a little talkative but not green."[3]

Although she couldn't put her finger on it, Ida's commanding presence may have overwhelmed Carrie. "Miss Pope has hardness and age, and experience mixed in."[4] Ida, twenty-seven, was only four years older than Carrie, but may have intimidated the sheltered daughter of a Congregationalist minister. Soon Carrie told her fiancé that Ida may not be as pious as she herself was. "Miss Pope—She and I run to each other I suppose because we feel better acquainted than with the others.

Carrie Prudence Winter, 1890
Oberlin senior picture. *Courtesy
of UCSD Libraries.*

We have many ideas in common but in some things I find her a little freer in thought than I care to be, i.e.—card playing, dancing and a few such things."[5]

After making each other's acquaintance, the trio used some spare time before the departure for San Francisco to see the magnificent new Chicago Auditorium Building that the whole country had been talking about. After its opening the year before, it was immediately acclaimed as one of the most beautiful and well-designed theatres in the world; the travelers couldn't miss the opportunity to see it in person. And see it they did—Ida, Carrie, and Henry climbed clear to the top of the auditorium's eighteen-story tower, and marveled at the "bird's-eye view of the city" afforded by such a skyscraper.

Soon enough, however, they were back on the ground. Ida sorrowfully waved goodbye to her brother in the waning hours of the day, and boarded the *Overland Flyer* for the eighty-four-hour journey to San Francisco. The trip from one side of the country to the other would be an unanticipated trial. By the second day, Ida and Carrie were yearning to reach their destination.

Ida Pope, 1886, Oberlin.
Courtesy of Oberlin Archives.

It was the beginning of the never to be forgotten day in Nevada. It was hot and every window and ventilator in the car had to be closed, while even then the sand seemed to sift in from every point. It was hazy from one end of the car to the other. It filled all the pores. You tried to wash it off your hands and they became rough and chapped. The lips, the nose, the eyes all smarted. We could only sit and gasp the long hours of the day away with such patience as we could command.[6]

Their stop at a train depot on the last evening of their long journey was a welcome relief. "How thankful we were when in the early evening we stopped at the foot of the Sierras. The air was cool and fresh. It was hard to go back into the stuffy sleeper but realized that we were nearing civilization again. The early morning found us in Sacramento. Hours later we rolled into Oakland. How glad we were to leave the car for good and be out on the bay."[7]

They arrived in San Francisco on Friday, August 21, 1890, and booked into the four-story, lavishly furnished Occidental Hotel. Neither had ever seen such opulence. In their rooms, the first thing they did was to lie down on beds "that did not bounce up and down and this way and that."[8] After thirty minutes, the bellboy knocked on their door and handed the two wide-eyed young ladies a beautiful basket of flowers "with the compliments of the manager."[9] They were off to a good start.

Ida and Carrie boarded the *Zealandia* the next morning at eleven o'clock and excitedly spent the next three hours before it sailed exploring the ship. Unfortunately, they were to learn that the arduous cross-country train trip paled in comparison to the debilitating seasickness they were about to experience. All the romance of the handkerchief-waving departure at the wharf disappeared along with the coastline as the ship left the harbor. Carrie recounted that "Miss Pope turned pale" and required assistance. "Oh the misery of what followed. We were on the storm side and every crack was stuffed tight. Not a bit of fresh air till Monday. The waves pounded, the boat rocked, the awful sounds, and smells!!! The sickness was bad enough but then there was that indescribable feeling of being poised in the midst of the air and sky and water and swaying there with nothing to grasp."[10]

But both young ladies recovered by the third day, and not long after that, they enjoyed the camaraderie of other passengers and the romance of moonlit nights on deck. On the morning of the seventh day, Ida finally caught her first glimpse of the Hawaiian Islands. She was told that the first island they were passing was Moloka'i, the home of exiled "lepers." Little did Ida know, as the *Zealandia* passed the forlorn brown island, that she would be traveling there in a year's time as a member of the royal entourage of the Hawaiian monarchy.

First Impressions

When they arrived in Hawai'i at 9 a.m. on August 30, 1890, everything on the islands was in the midst of change. Every social and political institution was straining at its seams, ready to break out into something new. Did they feel that energy from the deck of the *Zealandia*, before they ever set foot on Hawaiian soil? Certainly, what they saw, as Carrie recorded, mesmerized them.

> There before us lay the harbor, the city of Honolulu. I had never seen anything so beautiful. From the dull tint of the ocean we were suddenly transported into a world of color. Before us was a stretch of water of the deepest blue, broken only by long lines of white where the encircling coral reef broke the water into foam. Next came the tender green of the city's abundant foliage, and beyond rose the mountains, their summits lost in a mist of white, their sides varied with many a valley in which lurked vivid

purple shadows. We had read of such scenes, but they did not seem really possible till we saw this."[11]

They eagerly watched all the waterfront mayhem and the crowded wharf as the captain skillfully maneuvered the ship through the narrow reef to the dock. "Out in the harbor," Carrie wrote, "were brown-skinned natives, fishing in queer little boats. These boats were very narrow with huge outriders. We noticed that all had garlands of flowers about their hats. A thousand new impressions were crowding upon us!"[12]

The wharf where they arrived was a hub for commerce, and itself a symbol of the changes in Hawaiian society in the late nineteenth century. Carrie accurately described Honolulu as a place where "most of the business of the city has to do with plantation supplies."[13] At the wharf, thousands upon thousands of baskets of sugar were constantly being loaded and unloaded from the other islands onto sailing vessels.

Warships of many different nations were also evident in Honolulu Harbor, and although the young, naïve teachers did not then understand their political significance, they soon would. With all the harbor commotion, it is no wonder that Ida and Carrie, staying close together, walked down the gangplank and then "stood still and let ourselves be found."[14]

It was not long before Principal Helen Pepoon enthusiastically rushed toward the two fresh recruits for the Kawaiahaʻo Seminary. Carrie recorded in cheerful words, "At last—we were hearing greetings on all sides and here was the sweet-faced principal of our school greeting us and introducing us to trustees and making inquiries and hastening us to a two-wheeled brake and driving us through a maze of muddy streets and green foliage."[15]

The "maze of muddy streets" contained a hodgepodge of homes and buildings reflecting the mix of extreme wealth and poverty that defined Honolulu in the 1890s. Interspersed in the neighborhoods were varying denominational churches surrounded by beautiful foliage—but a trek beyond one of those fragrant church arbors could easily lead to dismal lanes of squalor.

As their horse-drawn carriage trotted down dusty King Street, they passed the ornate new palace, named ʻIolani, or "Bird of Heaven." The stately palace, with its neoclassical façade, verified the legitimacy of the Hawaiian monarchy for many. David Kalākaua, the king who lived inside ʻIolani, had been dubbed the "Merrie Monarch" due to the pomp and splendor of the events he hosted. By the time Ida arrived, the five reigns of the Kamehameha line had come to an end, and David Kalākaua had been ruling the kingdom for sixteen years. The palace had been commissioned at a great price just eight years earlier. Ida was awed by her

The ʻIolani "Bird of Heaven" Palace, the official residence of Hawaiʻi's monarchy, 1871–1893. *Lilla Estelle Appleton private collection, Betsy Lang.*

first glimpse of a royal palace, and didn't yet feel the strong political undercurrents of anxiety brewing within its inner sanctums. Unbeknownst to her, ʻIolani Palace would be occupied by royalty for only four more years and would ultimately represent tragedy and struggle for brother and sister, the last king and queen of Hawaiʻi.

Arrival at Kawaiahaʻo Seminary

Upon arrival, Ida and Carrie "were greeted by pleasant-faced teachers" and led to their rooms, which were "made fresh and beautiful for us by thoughtful hands, and adorned by beautiful roses."[16] Juliette Cooke, now a sprightly seventy-eight-year-old, walked across the road and embraced the two new teachers as both a kindly grandmother and a teaching adviser.[17] News of their arrival brought Oberlin alumnae May and Nellie Waterhouse in the early afternoon to pick them up and show them the most popular site on the island, Waikīkī Beach. Little did anyone know that their father, Henry Waterhouse, would play a key role in the overthrow of the Hawaiian monarchy just two years hence. In a "nice double carriage," the four girls, according to Carrie, "started right down our road toward

Waikiki a place 2½ miles out right on the water and the constant resort of all the city people."[18] Ida was informed that a public horse car went to the beach, where the Castles owned a cottage that was "always at our disposal for bathing purposes or to pass a quiet Sunday."[19]

On the way to Waikīkī, Ida realized that she was a long way from home when she saw women with long, swirling skirts riding astride horses. Back home, such a sight would have caused a scandal, but Honolulu was well filled with lady equestrians riding astride, as only the men would have done in Ohio. Apart from horseback riders, the dusty streets were crowded with every manner of commercial vehicle—familiar sights to Ida, fresh from Ohio at the height of her state's industrial development. Water wagons, trams pulled by mules, bicycles, and horse-and-buggy combinations of many varieties had found their way to Honolulu by the 1890s.

Outside the city, much of the arable land was covered with sugar plantations, which had become exceedingly profitable to the white businessmen who owned them. Hawai'i was defined by these sudden intersections of native and white culture, of modern and traditional society, of urban and rural. Any social gathering could bring together these different strains in Hawaiian society, creating a constant intermingling of Hawaiian and American cultures. Ida would frequently find herself in the middle of these shifting cultural sands.

For instance, a simple baseball game might bring together missionaries, Hawaiian royalty, natives, and teachers. Alexander Cartwright, the father of baseball and adviser to the royal family of Hawai'i, feverishly taught this new game throughout O'ahu. The Kamehameha School for Boys, with a staff of American teachers, had caught baseball fever. Shortly after her first fall term began, Ida decided these events should be an extracurricular activity for her pupils. Though she wasn't the least bit athletic herself, she had enjoyed watching her previous high school students and her three energetic brothers compete with each other in many sports and activities back in Ohio. It was very natural for her to take the Kawaiaha'o girls to cheerlead the boys to victory from the sidelines, as she herself had done.

Hobnobbing with Hawaiian Royalty

The first lū'au Ida and Carrie were invited to was in honor of one of the Kamehameha School for Boys' baseball victories. The event provided Ida her first up-close look at the royal family, including King Kalākaua and his wife, Queen Kapi'olani; and Princess Lydia Dominis (later Queen Lili'uokalani). Carrie asked her fiancé in a letter to try to imagine the event, which was to her a strange mixture of native traditions and familiar refinements.

Ida's first introduction to the monarchs in October of 1890: "Kamehameha gave a big luau on account of their base-ball victories and invited their parents and relatives, the King and his sister the princess Mrs. Dominis, a large number of White people and thirty of our girls." Note King Kalākaua is at the head of the third table from the bottom. To his left, the future queen Liliʻuokalani in white lei, head bowed in prayer. *Courtesy of UCSD Libraries.*

Contrary to the usual custom we sat in chairs instead of squatting on the ground. On the tables were white tablecloths covered with a large leaf called tea-leaf. On each plate was either a baked fish or a funny greasy meat done up in tea-leaf which proved to be pork. These delicacies had been cooked under the ground wrapped up in tea-leaves, then scattered all around were big dishes of raw fish of which the natives are very fond, bowls of poi, dishes of coarse salt, funny little crabs, a mixture of coconut and sweet potato, big sweet potatoes, baked fish, watermelons and bottles of soda water, no bread or butter and not a knife, fork or spoon for anyone, even the King. It was a little bit trying at first to see the natives eating their meal and fish till their hands were all smeared and then see two or three dip a couple of fingers into the same bowl of poi give a graceful twist and raise a big gob of the sticky stuff to their mouths.[20]

Though the king had made the concession of moving to chairs for this school-sponsored event, Carrie remained focused on the absence of silverware—a continued thorn in the teachers' sides in their efforts to teach their pupils "civilized" manners. Not even Her Royal Highness Liliʻuokalani could escape Ida's education in proper manners when she attended a school fund-raiser a year later. As Carrie wrote, "The Queen bought from all the tables and Miss Pope found her on a verandah devouring a large hunk of cake breaking out the mouthfuls with her fingers. Miss Pope found a napkin and plate for her and she ate in more civilized fashion."[21]

Though the royals practiced table manners that the teachers deplored, they were the hosts of lavish evening galas that Ida and the other schoolteachers eagerly attended at the gracious invitation of the monarchy. Royal balls at ʻIolani Palace were legendary under King Kalākaua, and an invitation was highly coveted by Hawaiian society. The king and his wife often extended invitations to the Kawaiahaʻo teachers for celebrations, honoring the sacrifices they made on a daily basis for the kingdom's youth.

The ladies were also invited to other social events in the city. For the young teachers, working in difficult conditions at the school, these evenings were rare opportunities for refined dress. At one such gathering, Carrie noted that the "Opera House was full and it was really quite an elegant affair, the ladies dressed in evening dress and without hats. Miss Pope wore her dainty blue and I my white silk."[22] When the last child was tucked in bed, the young teachers spent the quiet evenings recapping events with each other. The royal events would be dissected, with special attention given to the lavish costumes. They would speculate on whether a particular gown was made from silk or satin, and on its precise color: was it lilac or lavender?

King Kalākaua "Sleeping His Last Sleep"

Soon after the fall term began, the school received news that the king, in poor health, needed to leave for San Francisco on November 25, 1890, to seek medical treatment. He left his sister, Princess Lydia Dominis, now using the name Liliʻuokalani, in charge of the government, and in this role she filled all of his functions, including those at the school. In describing the princess's appearance at a school event, Carrie wrote, "You may judge how puffed up we feel," and made a special point of noting that the students all rose upon Liliʻuokalani's entrance and "remained standing till she was seated."[23] Staff and students realized that Kawaiahaʻo Seminary was in every way Liliʻuokalani's school, and their pride in her sponsorship was evident.

As for the king, after he spent a couple of weeks in frigid San Francisco, his old friend Claus Spreckles sent him south by rail to the warm port city of San Diego. Claus's son John D. Spreckles had invested heavily in that city and had purchased the entire island of Coronado along with the beachfront, red-roofed Hotel Del Coronado, an elegant destination where many went specifically to improve their health.

King Kalākaua arrived in Coronado on December 28 to find an "immense crowd" waiting to greet him. Even though it was after 10 p.m., a "company of troops snapped to attention, and the City Guard Band played" followed by the "State Militia and its Brass band" to signify the importance of his presence.[24] The *San Diego Union* reported the following day that Kalākaua was "one of the most enlightened and thoroughly able monarchs of modern times, a patron of art, science and literature, a friend of liberal government and a wise and sagacious ruler."[25]

The *Union* also reported the king was ill, but nonetheless he was given a whirlwind tour of San Diego that extended to Tijuana, Mexico. By all reports, King Kalākaua was smitten by all he saw and asked "informed questions" on industries that could benefit Hawai'i. He showed particular interest in San Diego's newly built, six-billion-gallon Sweetwater Dam and a thriving olive grove.[26]

On New Year's Eve, he was entertained lavishly in the Hotel Del Coronado's beautiful Crown Room. He returned to San Francisco the following day not realizing that he just had his last royal gala. Back in San Francisco, he died on January 20, 1891, in the Palace Hotel, from Bright's disease of the kidneys, turning his sister's temporary regency into a permanent seat on the throne.

The death came as a shock in Hawai'i, where the most recent news, from several weeks before, had been that the king's health was improving.[27] In a letter of February 2, 1891, Ida poetically described the reaction in Hawai'i to the death of the man who had been king for seventeen years.

My Dear Popes,

About nine o'clock we noticed an unusual stir. We inquired the cause there of and were informed that the U.S.S. Charleston had just been signaled off Coco Head with the U.S. and Hawaiian flags at half mast. Half an hour later she came into harbor draped in mourning and the news came that Kalakaua King of Hawaii was dead. The sad news was a terrible shock to the royal family. I went to a news stand to get a paper. Papers were selling like hot cakes. Invitations had been issued for a grand ball at Iolani Palace the evening of the King's return. Arches were being erected and most elaborate preparations were being made to welcome back the King. The Schools of the Kingdom were to be at the wharf and scatter rushes

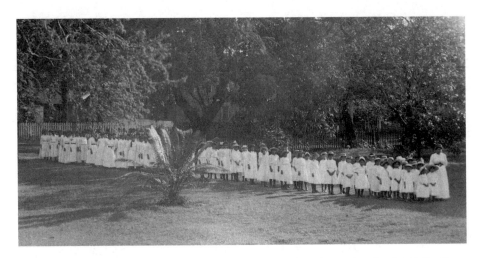

Kawaiaha'o pupils lined up by age in their best dresses, ready to depart the school. *Lilla Estelle Appleton private collection, Betsy Lang.*

along the line of march. Everyone was looking forward to a gala day—but alas the first and last of the Kings of the Kalakaua line was sleeping his last sleep—a sleep from which no sound of revelry will ere wake him.[28]

Ida described the procession, featuring the complete spectrum of social and political forces in Hawai'i at that moment.

At five o'clock in the evening the remains of the King were placed on a barge. The barge was towed to the wharf by a boat. Followed by sailors from the different war ships—Admiral Brown landed first. He was followed by marines bearing the coffin. The coffin was put in the hearse drawn by four black horses. The line of march was down Fort and to King and from there to the Palace. The Charleston Band led the procession. It was followed by marines with arms reversed—then by standard bearers with the American flag; then came one hundred and fifty sailors from the U.S. warships—following these was the hearse escorted by the Hawaiian police—then came the Hawaiian Ministers—officers of the war ships and clergymen. The streets were literally packed with people. The members of the Supreme Court and the Chamberlain met the procession at the door—and the coffin was carried into the throne room. Heralds were on the streets proclaiming—the King's Sister—Princess Liliuokalani Queen.[29]

School preparations for a grand welcome home for the king transformed into somber arrangements to pay their respects to the king who was lying in state at the ʻIolani Palace. Ida wrote, "At half past eleven our school paid their respects to their dead monarch. I wish you could have seen them. The girls were dressed in white with black ribbon belts and black ribbon in their hair. They marched two by two—one hundred and twenty of them—the little ones in front. They went with uncovered heads. The line was straight as an arrow—the royal Band played a march—and the Chamberlain ushered us into the throne room."[30]

The girls, with their display of unity and propriety, seemed to inject a proud note for Ida into proceedings that to her were otherwise surreal indeed, without precedent. The honoring of the dead king struck Ida as a strange and extraordinary event.

> It seems to me like a dream now. It was gruesome and awful. The wailing of the natives haunt me—the bier was in the centre of a hollow square covered with a pall of black velvet that hung in heavy folds and trailed on the carpet. Over this was thrown the King's feather cloak—a robe of yellow feathers—valued at a million of dollars—The coffin rested on this cloak—a feather cloak was thrown over the foot of the coffin and at the head was the King's crown and sword. Queen Kapiolani stood at the head of the coffin sobbing. She was enveloped in black and looked very mournful. The four corners of the square were marked by standards bearing kahilis—huge feather ornaments used at royal funerals. Queen Liliuokalani and the Prince consort Mr. Dominis formed one side of the square—and a lady in waiting—opposite them was the Queen Dowager's Maid of Honor—The Household Guards made up the other two sides of the square. They were in black with yellow feather capes on their shoulders—Their kahilis will be waved over his coffin day and night until he is buried.[31]

Mourning on such a scale made a deep impression on Ida. From the moment of her arrival, as a necessary part of her stewardship of the school, Ida was in close relationship with the ruling monarchy due to their keen interest in the school. And unlike Carrie, Lilla, and other teachers who thought King Kalākaua immoral and wrote disparagingly about him, Ida clearly broke with their ranks and thought otherwise. "King Kalakaua was a fine looking man. He had a fine figure—a military bearing—an intelligent expressive face—and affable courteous manners— His reign was marked by great material prosperity to Hawaii—ever since his accession to the throne in 1874 has the Kingdom made great advancement— intellectually and materially."[32]

King Kalākaua lying in state, 'Iolani Palace. Queen Kapi'olani and the future queen Lili'uokalani in mourning. Photo by Gonsalves, 1891. *UCSD Libraries.*

With its long history in relationship to the monarchy, the school was fully represented at the funeral; indeed, the king's death seemed to bring about a degree of unity that had been absent under the trustees while he lived. Reverend Hyde—the man who kept a school full of girls away from the king's birthday party three years earlier—walked in the funeral procession at the head of the Protestant clergy.[33] The entire seminary of grief-stricken girls, who no doubt remembered their missed opportunity to honor the king for his birthday, walked behind Miss Pope, the newly promoted principal of Kawaiaha'o Seminary, on that somber day in February.

Comforting the New Queen

After the saddened girls had returned to their school routine, Lili'uokalani, needing personal comfort, sent word to Miss Pope that she wanted the girls to return to the palace and sing directly to her, placing the school from the very beginning at the center of her reign, as Ida recorded.

Ida proclaimed, "Long live Hawaii's Queen, Fair may her reign be—for she has a land flowing with milk and honey—a people amiable and lovable to a fault." *Kamehameha Schools.*

At three in the afternoon the Queen sent for our girls to come and sing for her—The girls sang "Nearer My God to Thee" in native—and sang in English "Abide with Me" "Lead Kindly Light"—"Rock of Ages" and "Safe in the Arms of Jesus"—They sang like seraphs. It was indeed an impressive sight. The natives stopped their wailing and listened with the most rapt attention. I think it must have been quite a relief to the Queen—the wailing is kept up almost incessantly.[34]

As the girls lined up for departure, Koni Puuohau, one of the school's known troublemakers but Miss Pope's favorite pupil, broke away and ran to the grieving princess, dropped on her knees, and kissed the royal hand. Koni received no reprimand because Lili'uokalani was more than responsive and receptive to the young girl's actions.[35]

Soon shy Lydia Aholo, whose social rank was elevated in the school and the community as the *hānai* daughter of Hawai'i's reigning monarch, would be excessively proud. For the new queen, Ida was equally delighted and had nothing but good wishes. "Hawaii is for the first time in her history to have a Queen—Liliuokalani has borne her honors gracefully and has been so long associated with the late King that she is conversant with public affairs. Long live Hawaii's Queen—Fair may her reign be—for she has a land flowing with milk and honey—a people amiable and lovable to a fault."[36]

The Death of Ida's Father

Mail delivery in the early nineteenth century was accomplished by slow sailing vessels, improving in efficiency during the latter part of the century with the advent of steam-powered ships. Even so, steamers arrived only once or twice a month and tended not to keep to their posted schedules. As a result, mail was frequently weeks or months behind. Ida, now isolated from her close-knit family, was frantic for letters from home and the opportunity to send updates on her well-being. Transoceanic telegraph cable hadn't yet reached Hawai'i, so the devastating news that her beloved father had died soon after she departed Ohio came too late for her to make any plans to return home.

Carrie Winter wrote that Ida "was quite broken hearted" and that she went "to Waikiki for a quiet Sunday where she could be alone with her sorrow."[37] Ida's personal sympathy for the new queen's loss may have increased since they were both caught off guard by unexpected deaths. Lili'uokalani, too, learned of her brother's death only as the steamer made its way to Honolulu with the flag at half-mast. In another coincidence, the death of Ida's father, coming within weeks of the king's, was also from Bright's disease.

Ida had always had a unique relationship with her father and was "Daddy's Girl" because she was the "one most like him."[38] Knowing how deeply Ida would feel the loss of her father, the Popes sent a steady stream of letters. Unfortunately, the letters only intensified Ida's grief by the sense of distance. Carrie noted, "She tries to be brave but it is very hard for her to keep up."[39] More bad news soon followed. Ida's family reported that the Franz & Pope Knitting Machine Company went bankrupt in the nationwide economic downturn.

Since Ida was under contract at Kawaiahaʻo, she could send money home, but it would now be up to her twenty-two-year-old younger brother, Henry, to provide for the family. Like Ida, he may have been small, but he was strong willed and action minded. His first move was to sell the inventory of unsold knitting machines for capital. Then he packed up his mother; his two younger sisters, Anne and Katherine; and the baby, Frank, and headed to Illinois. Ida's oldest sister, Lois, and her new husband, Joseph George Prosser, would join the family at a later date. Henry informed Ida that he was going to create a new family business making hosiery by utilizing every family member available.

Henry Pope (1868–1947) to the right of Franklin Delano Roosevelt. *William Pope private collection.*

No one at the time knew, of course, but in a few decades, "Little Father," as his sisters called him, would run one of the largest enterprises in Illinois, the Paramount Knitting Company, reorganized as Bear Brand Hosiery in 1922. Like his sister Ida, Henry Pope sought solutions for problems. The annals of history have recorded his dramatic impact on rehabilitation methods for polio victims. He also personally funded his good friend Franklin Delano Roosevelt's fight against polio. Meanwhile, Ida had her own work to do in Hawai'i.

CHAPTER FIVE

Miss Pope in Charge

Revamping the Curriculum

Principal Pope appeared to bury her grief over the loss of her father in school-work and in the school itself. Now in charge, she frenetically began devising ways to improve anything that in her mind was outdated. The first of these to fall under her scrutiny was the curriculum, or the lack of it.

When she assumed leadership, Kawaiahaʻo Seminary at that moment stood poised between educational imperatives. After the Bingham sisters departed, its focus had shifted away from the initial purpose of preparing pupils to be Christian housewives toward supplementing Bible training with a manual training program.

This educational change was justified on the grounds not only that it would help the girls find employment but also that the school might be able to fund itself through the proceeds from selling the goods that were made as part of the manual training. This would go some way toward reimbursing expenses for the charity cases—those girls on scholarship. For the girls, this meant learning all aspects of the textile arts such as weaving, sewing, knitting, and garment making.

Miss Pope, however, was not completely satisfied with this narrow focus on handcraft training and sought to reorient the curriculum yet again. She wasn't opposed to a manual training component; her own life had been shaped by the industrial shift. The value of this training, both for its own sake and as a necessary basis for knowledge, was indisputable. Her father, as a practicing physician, couldn't make enough money to support their large family until he invented a knitting machine for socks, a product whose success meant that, unlike her older siblings, Ida was able to attend college. So it was natural for her to embrace the concept of manual training with its practicability and application. Plus, as a woman from rural Ohio, she believed in the value and dignity of hand labor, *to a point.*

The educational landscape of the United States had already shifted from a classical to a progressive model, but Ida's key insight—from which generations

Kawaiahaʻo Seminary produced accomplished dressmakers. *Lilla Estelle Appleton private collection, Betsy Lang.*

of her graduates would benefit—was that the hands-on practical arts need not replace the classical subjects that spoke to the heart. Ida preferred those subjects that fall under humanities such as drama, history, literature, music, and poetry. Much of her correspondence quotes her century's greatest writers, artists, and poets. Her parents cultivated the arts in all their children, and their home had been a well-known gathering place for those who sought cultural refinement. As a result, her overhaul of the curriculum switched the order of importance. Where manual training including intensive housekeeping of both the school and grounds used to occur after breakfast, Miss Pope devoted mornings, assuring more alertness, to general education instruction.

Ida had another key insight related to the curriculum's reform. For it to succeed, she saw that academic subjects would require a progressive focus of an experience-based learning. Ida was both idealistic and aware of the distance between progressive teaching methods and the traditional practices previously practiced at Kawaiahaʻo, and she would need to develop a standardized curriculum.

But with money short, gathering the new materials for such a curriculum required ingenuity and initiative. Ida sent urgent requests home to family mem-

Queen Liliʻuokalani loved the baked goods the school produced. *Lilla Estelle Appleton private collection, Betsy Lang.*

bers seeking literature, schoolbooks, sheet music, and anything else that would help provide the girls with an education well beyond the traditional manual instruction. Up to that point, books weren't a part of any comprehensive course of study—with the exception of the Bible, the lone textbook. All of the new books—on subjects like arithmetic, physical education, and English—trickled in bit by bit from family members and friends back home. Ida's competitive nature is revealed in this plea home for a published group recitation that would beat out that of any school rival. Concert recitations were in vogue back home, where groups of pupils actively recited and displayed their knowledge dramatically "in concert."

February 2, 1891

My Dear Popes,

I want to ask Katherine if she knows of any concert recitations that would be suitable for girls in my room—something striking and pretty—any song suitable for twenty girls for an exhibition. The natives are fond of anything fancy and I am at a loss to find anything. Now please don't forget—because I must begin to plan for closing exercises. It takes a long time to drill these girls and there is much rivalry in the schools here. Something dramatic and would require fancy dressing. If you find anything don't fail to send it by the next steamer—it is almost impossible to get anything here and I want my first exhibition to be a howling success.[1]

Though her methods for implementing her ideas involved scraping and scrabbling, the ideas themselves lay at the forefront of contemporary notions of a modernized educational program. William Bramwell Powell, educated at Oberlin, radically reshaped the nineteenth-century world of teacher training. He fervently called on the teachers of Ida's generation to lecture less and experiment more. He predated Ida's contemporary, the progressive John Dewey, in telling teachers that children "learn by doing." Powell believed that learning to read should be more than just recognizing words and pronouncing sentences. He encouraged teachers to tap into a child's interest and context. He also encouraged teachers to introduce students to great masterpieces of literature.[2]

Because Powell taught in some impoverished neighborhoods, he told teachers to prepare students for their future experiences, not merely from the standpoint of employment, but in order to elevate them above their impoverished circumstances.[3] This philosophy would guide Ida's choices in the following years but cause conflict with those who thought boarding school girls did not need to be elevated, just trained to earn income or be wives.

Powell, who cofounded the National Geographic Society, loved the beauty of nature. His Powell Language Series, unique for its time, contained hundreds of beautiful pictures to captivate the imagination of children. His books *How to See, How to Talk,* and *How to Write* had attained great success in the late 1800s.[4] Ida Pope was probably the first educator in Hawai'i to pioneer Powell's methods of object teaching, of training her girls not just by listening to a lecture, but by seeing and doing.[5]

Carrie Winter was at first enthusiastic about Powell's books. "[They aid] me very much in teaching English," she bragged, "the girls are a little worked up mentally."[6] But privately she worried that "Miss Pope has had to work too hard."[7] Maybe there was ground for worry, because the curriculum still had to address the school's constant need for revenue. Just as selling the handmade products of manual instruction had funded the school for years, the new curriculum also would need to generate income—and on this point, Ida hit on an innovation: what better way than to train her older girls to work in schools?

Miss Appleton Returns as Teacher Trainer

In 1891, Ida convinced the trustees that adding teacher training for the older girls would actually bring money back to the perpetually cash-strapped school. Pupils trained as teacher assistants could be hired out to other schools to provide help as needed in the afternoons, thereby earning a bit of money to defray expenses for their room and board. Since many of the girls were on scholarships, this money directly benefited the seminary's account books. This experience would also give the girls an opportunity to use their newly acquired knowledge professionally. But the teacher assistants themselves needed someone to train them—ideally an educator with firsthand knowledge of life in Kawaiahaʻo. For this, Ida turned to a familiar figure—Miss Appleton.

Ida readily persuaded Lilla Appleton to return to Kawaiahaʻo Seminary in the role of teacher trainer. Lilla was especially desirable because she had just learned the latest teaching techniques, and would be an ally in implementing the

Lilla Estelle Appleton. *Lilla Estelle Appleton private collection, Betsy Lang.*

Girls in their handmade blue and white "sailor-style" uniforms. *Lilla Estelle Appleton private collection, Betsy Lang.*

new curriculum. She was soon steaming her way back to Honolulu and arrived on the dock in March of 1891, several weeks after the king's death. Lilla, having taught during the king's reign in previous years, loved Hawai'i but had never been as enchanted with David Kalākaua as Ida had been. As Lilla passed the palace on the way to her old school, she couldn't understand why the community was still in public mourning after several weeks. She wryly noted to her mother in her first letter home that his "funeral drapings were still hanging on the streets and buildings" with a large arch spanning the street proclaiming, "We mourn our loss."[8]

At the school, however, Lilla was joyous over the "pleasant" and "great many changes" the efficient Ida had implemented in such a short time.[9] An immediately visible change was that all the girls now wore crisp, navy blue uniforms, which they had made themselves on their new sewing machines. Miss Pope's organization was everywhere, from "little racks on the back verandah for the girls' hats," to "expanded classrooms," to "new shelves," fresh paint in the "kitchen and poi room," and "remodeled bathrooms and more bath tubs."[10]

Other changes included new protocols, including the morning ritual of the girls marching to music as they took their seats in their first class. The changes Lilla observed may seem minor given the breadth of Ida's ambitions, but they served a crucial function in the school in terms of giving the girls a standard set of expectations, a fair and neutral environment, and a new sense of pride in their education. This was a marker of the larger changes that had occurred since Miss Appleton's first experience as a teacher at the school.

Ida's predecessor, Helen Pepoon, rarely visited the classrooms and gave the teachers more or less free rein. That all changed under Principal Pope, and for accountability purposes she instituted a weekly public recitation. At eleven o'clock on Friday, each grade performed its recitation, requiring the teachers to demonstrate what their pupils had learned during the week. Ida designed it to be a very celebratory event. However, she did not anticipate that the arrival of three new teachers would soon thwart her plans and dampen her enthusiasm.

Unfit Teachers

Having the qualified Lilla Appleton was looked at with great relief, but more teacher replacements were urgently needed to help manage the 140 pupils. Ida and Carrie had virtually worked alone after Helen Pepoon and her staff left, so they anxiously awaited the September arrival of three newly recruited teachers with great expectation. But on their arrival, Carrie reported for herself and Ida, "We are very much disappointed in our teachers and we fear what lies before us through them."[11] Carrie believed that Miss Anna Hadley, aged thirty-seven from New York, and her friend, Miss Anna Armstrong, aged thirty-five from New Jersey, were too old for the job and would be useless since they were "small bundles of bones."[12] Carrie liked "pretty little" twenty-three-year-old Miss Eva Harris from Ohio much better, but Carrie worried, as did Ida, over her youth and her lack of "spunk and assertiveness."[13]

Immediately upon the new teachers' disembarkation, the gossip mill began to churn with stories about the two older recruits from those who took the voyage with them from San Francisco to Honolulu. The tongue-clicking was that they chose to spend the seven days at sea with "gamblers and vulgar people" over other missionary teachers who were also on board. Among the latter was Principal Oleson from the Kamehameha School for Boys, who reported to Ida and Carrie that "Miss Hadley would have been in better health if she had played cards less and drunk less wine. She drank wine freely, took in the late evening with the dissolute ships officers, invited them into her state-room at ten o'clock at night and allowed the chief gambler to bet publicly in her name."[14]

Carrie was even less impressed with Anna Armstrong, whom she described as having "come here for her health with 4 trunks, traveling expenses of $20 where it should be $180 and a nose way up in the air."[15] Neither Carrie nor Ida had brought more than one trunk of clothes, and here was Anna with four trunks, expecting to change clothes for imagined parties and galas around the city that she expected to attend at someone else's expense. Worst of all, as Carrie wrote to her fiancé, was Miss Armstrong's demeanor. "She complained all the time and has tried to order me around like a kitchen girl, without success mind you for somehow I don't hear her. She is surprised that we don't keep servants."[16]

In the days to follow, according to Carrie, the situation went from bad to worse, to the point where communications between the women nearly broke down entirely. "They are women that I wouldn't have anything to do with anywhere else and I shall pursue the same course as far as possible here."[17] Ida assigned Anna the afternoon duty of teaching instrumental music, but Carrie reported, "She can't play herself the songs the girls have to sing."[18] And when Ida confronted Anna with her inabilities, the new teacher put all on notice that it wouldn't take much to make her take the next steamer home. Carrie reported, "Miss Pope is almost sick over the prospect and I suppose that if the school ever needed sympathy it is now."[19] Four weeks after their arrival, the trustees set up a meeting to discuss the disturbing rumors about Anna Hadley and Anna Armstrong. As Carrie reported, "They questioned Miss Pope so closely that she had to tell just how unsatisfactory they were and they really considered the question of sending them right away but it was decided that we could not afford to do so and they are simply to be informed of the dissatisfaction with them."[20]

Resigned to keeping the unfit teachers at least for the time being, Ida tried to keep a close eye on their erratic behavior. But Carrie reported that "Miss Hadley had to whip 6 or 8 girls after her study hour last night. She has very little control over the girls."[21] It seems the students showed no respect for their new mistresses, either. Soon, Anna Cooke, Juliette's daughter-in-law, perhaps not getting sufficient information from Ida, sent privately for Carrie, who wrote, "She wanted to draw me out on the subject of Miss Hadley and Miss Armstrong. I did not allow my personal feelings to get into my remarks but I held to the opinion I have always held that they are not the right women for the place. How horrid it is."[22]

It seems as if Anna Cooke had influence, because two weeks later Carrie reported to Charles: "The trustees decided to dismiss Miss Hadley and Miss Armstrong. They'll get their little notes tomorrow and I haven't any idea what will happen then. I am something of a coward and would like to be somewhere else. However they might as well make me suffer in a good cause as in a bad one. They are as serene and high and mighty as ever."[23]

The fact that Miss Hadley and Miss Armstrong needed an inordinate amount of supervision allowed Eva Harris' uneven behavior to go unnoticed in the first few weeks. But young twenty-three-year-old Eva was slowly unraveling mentally. She began to take to her bed for long periods of time complaining of an undefined "sickness." But it was her erratic behavior within three months of her arrival that confounded Ida and Carrie. "Miss Harris is all the time doing such horrid little things, getting heated over trifles and being rude, without sufficient excuse. She sometimes is very miserable over it herself."[24]

When the 1892 school year was over, Ida asked Eva to "give up her position," but Carrie snidely reported that the "willful little thing"[25] refused. While all the rest of the teachers went off on a summer expedition to observe a volcano, Ida sacrificed her vacation to oversee Eva. Carrie wrote sadly, "I wanted our Miss Pope on this trip very much but she could not go on account of Miss Harris who seems to get weaker all the time."[26]

By October, Eva was hospitalized with "hysteria," and the doctor told Miss Pope that the young woman "is not accountable for much that she does and says."[27] With unpaid hospital bills mounting, Ida convinced Eva to return to the school, hoping she could then be persuaded to go home. By December, Eva was back at the school monopolizing the guest cottage reserved for sick children. But in January her hysterical outbursts were startling the staff and children to the point where, as Carrie wrote, things were "rapidly coming to a crisis."[28]

> The community is nearly in despair over that girl. She's out of her head most of the time and is very trying. Her true pride seems all to have left her and she does not seem to realize in the least how much she is receiving from the community at large. While threatening to kill any one who shall write to her parents of the true state of the case. There is an insane asylum here but it is not at all the proper place for her to go, not having the right treatment. Everyone says she must go, but the difficulty has been to get *anyone* who would look after her, and to get her *willing to go.*[29]

Ida surreptitiously sent several letters to Eva's parents pleading for help that never came. Ultimately, the fact that her parents never responded would be a blessing in disguise for Ida in a few months' time when politics became tumultuous.

Finding Delight with the Girls

In the midst of school mayhem, Ida learned to find pleasure in simple and carefree fun with her girls, as revealed in this letter home.

My Dear Popes,

I will tell you of my picnic I had last Saturday—It was a Zoological picnic. My girls and I went a hunting for Radialarias and Mollusks—Our investigations did not add much to the enlightenment of the nineteenth century—but such a lark as my brown fairies had—and such blessings as were called down upon my head, did us all good. I wish you could have seen us start. The girls all had on pretty light frocks and sun hats—"every man" carried his own dinner and we stopped along the way and bought some bananas. It was a perfect morning and we trudged along with merry hearts—Our way lay through a large coconut grove across the fields—where we had a fine view of mountains and sea. In about three quarters of an hour we reached the beach. The girls donned their bathing dresses—short Mother Hubbard wrappers. One girl—in a belted blue gown—and hat tied with a broad ribbon—and with a basket over her arm—I longed to put her on a canvas—or have a Kodak and just press the button. I did not bring a bathing dress but the girls tempted me to take off my shoes and stockings and paddle in the water. The girls swim like fishes—you should see them in the water. We caught crabs—fish—snails—gathered shells and pelted each other with sand. We dined under the Algarroba trees—the girls ate poi with their fingers—salt salmon—sea weed and bananas—I had a U.S. lunch all to myself—we came home in a pelting rain—but we did not mind for we had had such a delightful time.[30]

Queen Liliʻuokalani was also finding delight in Kawaiahaʻo's girls. Despite her heartbreaking losses and increasing political difficulties, she took a keen interest in all school activities. Indeed, the queen may well have found the innocence of girls to be a respite from her growing political difficulties. The frequent participation at school fund-raising exhibitions during this time by the queen and her retinue is well documented. Between 1891 and 1893, the newly crowned queen, according to Charles Bishop, was involved in many schools across the islands, but none more than Kawaiahaʻo.[31] This preference was often reflected in planned visits, reported by the *Hawaiian Gazette:* "The Queen visited Kawaiahao Seminary Tuesday morning being present at the opening exercises. She made an address to the young ladies which was duly appreciated."[32]

But there were unplanned visits as well. The queen undoubtedly heard the distressing news about the upheaval among the teaching staff, because all of a sudden, one never knew when she would drop in. As Carrie noted, "The Queen visited us one morning this week. It was an entirely unexpected visit but we understand she was pleased with all she saw. She was present at devotions in the chapel and spoke to the girls and afterward spent some time in the school-rooms."[33]

And, of course, one pupil she was most interested in seeing was her adopted daughter. The queen, a gifted musician and composer, made sure Lydia had preferential treatment by the music teacher. Lydia joyfully recalled making the queen laugh at one school recital.

> When I was eight years old she paid for piano lessons. And when I could play something real nice, we had a recital and we invited the Queen, and she came. And every so often she used to look at me and she used to laugh, because I was so small and my feet never touched the floor.[34]

The school may have been the only place the queen was laughing, because she had suffered one more devastating loss. Just seven months after becoming queen, her husband, John Owen Dominis, died. And the political pressure was boiling. Three years before Ida arrived, in 1887, the king had been coerced to sign a new constitution that lessened the power of Hawaiians and increased the power of non-Hawaiians. As queen, one of her first actions was to look for a way to restore power to the monarchy. Growing political turmoil and the devastating loss of her brother and then of her husband—amid such conflicts, the school was a bright point for Lili'uokalani. At Kawaiaha'o Seminary, the innocent and eager schoolgirls—excited to see their queen and to sing her compositions—would have been a refreshing contrast.

Partnering with the Queen

The trustees were well aware of Miss Pope's increasing reputation with the queen and the community, but to Ida's frustration, they still managed the money too tightly, limiting her options. She complained to her staff that she wasn't happy that the trustees weren't allowing her "insight into the money matters of the school."[35] So she took matters into her own hands and went around them.

The problem of books was ever present at Kawaiaha'o—how to get enough of them and how to make them accessible to the girls. After obtaining textbooks from various places, Ida was then intent on broadening the girls' minds by including a wide genre of books, poems, and literature for general reading. Having unsuccessfully beseeched the trustees for a school library, and determined to expose the girls to great literature, Ida decided to host a concert fund-raiser in April of 1891. She banked the success of this end-run around the trustees upon support from a different, more powerful quarter—the queen.

SECOND CONCERT

.. GIVEN BY THE ..

Pupils of Kawaiahao Seminary,

ASSISTED BY THE

ROYAL HAWAIIAN ORCHESTRA,

— AT —

Kawaiahao Church, Saturday Evening, April 18, '91,

AT 7:30 O'CLOCK.

PROGRAMME—Part I.

1—Overture,	"The Knight of Breton,"		*Herman*
	ROYAL HAWAIIAN ORCHESTRA.		
2—Chorus,	"How Bright and Fair,"		*Rossini*
	KAWAIAHAO SEMINARY.		

3—Songs, with Motions by the Little Folks.

     a—"The Breadmakers,"
     b—"Rock-a-Bye Baby,"

4—Chorus,	"Maikai Waipio,"	*Her Majesty Queen Liliuokalani*
	KAWAIAHAO SEMINARY.	
5—Trio,	"The Reapers,"	*Clapisson*
	PUPILS OF THE FIRST CHORAL CLASS.	
6—Chorus,	"The Waking of the Birds,"	*Concone*
	KAWAIAHAO SEMINARY.	

PART II.

7—Solos and Chorus,	"The Fishermen,"	*Gabussi*
	KAWAIAHAO SEMINARY.	
8—Quartette,	"The Rustic Dance,"	*Resch*
	PUPILS OF THE FIRST CHORAL CLASS.	
9—Duett,	"Quis est Homo,"	*From Rossini's Stabat Mater*
	MISS SUSANNE PATCH AND MRS. J. F. BROWN.	
	With Organ Accompaniment by Mr. F. M. English, B. A.	
10—Chorus,	"Liko Pua Lehua,"	*H. R. H. the late Princess Likelike*
11—Quintette,	"Sleep, the Bird is in its Nest,"	*Barnby*
	PUPILS OF THE FIRST CHORAL CLASS.	
12—Chorus,	"Friends, Good Night?"	*Flotow*
	KAWAIAHAO SEMINARY.	

HAWAII PONOI.

The Audience is respectfully requested to remain until the Conclusion of the Concert. E oluolu ke anaina e noho a hiki i ka pau pono ana o na hana.

Benefit concert planned by Ida Pope, attended by Queen Lili'uokalani. *UCSD Libraries.*

Strange allies that they were, Ida and the queen created a successful, if hybrid, event. It was held in the Kawaiahaʻo Church, which had been decorated with beautiful yellow vines, ferns, and sugar cane.[36] More importantly, it was the queen's first public appearance since the death of her brother,[37] and she seemed eager to collaborate with Miss Pope for the big musical event. The queen, who

Beautiful Princess Kaʻiulani, 1893, adored by all. *Library Congress 3b19305u.*

loved flowers as much as Ida did, was up early on the day of the event, and oversaw the selection of a big "load of flowers" from her private garden for decoration.[38] She also sent her royal chamberlain to prepare for her grand entrance in the evening by replacing some pews with a rug and her royal chair.[39]

That evening, the church was packed, and all stood as the queen walked down the aisle to her place of honor as the band played "Hawai'i Pono'ī," the national anthem for the Hawaiian kingdom. As the queen sat upon her throne, she would have seen on one side of the stage an easel displaying a portrait of "little princess" Victoria "Ka'iulani" Cleghorn that had been presented to the school by the princess' father.[40] Miss Pope felt it appropriate protocol, that as the next in succession, Ka'iulani should be honored in her absence. Besides, the elegant and beautiful crowned princess near their age bedazzled all the girls.[41]

The girls, in their freshly laundered white dresses, included two songs at the concert composed by the queen and sung in Hawaiian. The concert was a huge success, as were all of the evening galas that mixed the royals and high society

Music was an important part of the life of the seminary. *Lilla Estelle Appleton private collection, Betsy Lang.*

with the school. Still, the trustees must have been surprised when Ida's fund-raising event yielded between $400 and $500, which was more than they expected and more than enough for her library.[42]

Despite her remarkable progress, the relationship between Ida and the queen was beginning to get complicated. Just as Ida didn't appreciate being micromanaged by the trustees, she didn't want to become the servant of the queen. Though the school depended on its royal ally and most ardent supporter, Miss Pope also wanted to run the school independently. In some cases this meant disappointing her patron. As Carrie noted, "Miss Pope heard the Queen wished to put 20 new girls in here. We couldn't possibly find room for them. Miss Pope has sent word that 6 more can come in."[43] Even though Ida stood her ground against the queen's edict, there began a cementing of the relationship between them, a respectful bond that would have its ups and downs but would endure in the end for the sake of female education, both their passions.

Proving Her Worth

At the end of 1892, the school duties began to take their toll on Ida. Money was tight, the infrastructure insufficient, staff unfit, and curriculum sparce. Her family noted that she was exhausted and homesick. Before she thought about how and when to go home, Principal Pope would have to get through the public examinations at the end of the 1892 school year that proved her worth to the community and to the school's benefactors.

Those community events also sold student handiwork such as clothing and baked goods, which brought in necessary revenue. The fund-raiser was imperative because Ida confidentially reported to Carrie that the trustees had informed her that the school was not "in a very good condition financially."[44] It's doubtful, however, that Kawaiaha'o's near-insolvency was public information at this point. To the outside world, Miss Pope enjoyed both the queen's support and the appearance of a successful, prosperous school, as described in a newspaper article of June 8, 1892.

> The annual public examination of Kawaiahao took place this morning at 9 o'clock. Her Majesty the Queen attended and a large number of visitors and parents of the scholars. The exercises opened with a chorus sung by the whole school. Bible recitations were then had, after which Mr. W. R. Castle conducted the school through scriptural quotations. Miss Pope, principal, occupied a position on the platform near the Queen and superintended the different examinations. Miss Pope then escorted Her Majesty

Annual Examination of Kawaiahao Seminary.

Shortly after 9 o'clock yesterday morning Her Majesty the Queen arrived at the Seminary, and within a few minutes the large school was filing into the main school, or Rice hall, in her presence, and to the evident admiration of the large concourse of spectators. Among the visitors, besides Her Majesty and her attendants, were Mother Cooke Mother Rice, Mesdames Judge Judd, Dole, Severence, Hartwell, Haalelea, S. C. Allen, Lyons, W. H. Rice, W. R. Castle, Andrews, and others, besides a few gentlemen and a large number of the parents, guardians and other friends of pupils.

After opening with prayer, by Rev. Dr. Beckwith, and the announcement, by W. R. Castle for the Board of Trustees, of the date of opening in the fall, with a few words of encouragement and cheer for both teachers and scholars, the examination opened with an excellent instrumental duet by Misses Lima and Aholo. Besides this there was other music, both piano and vocal. In the latter the girls of the school excel, and always give great pleasure to the hearers, and this occasion was no disappointment.

In reading, the girls showed excellent training, and by their clear enunciation and intelligent rendering indicated that they have been appreciative pupils. The exercises in arithmetic also showed fine training with like appreciation. In short, all of the work showed thorough drilling and conscientious training. The work in English speaking and like exercises was most praiseworthy. The kindergarten class of little ones made an interesting exhibit, as did the class of Liliuokalani Educational Society girls, who were decorated with pretty shields bearing a crown and suspended with blue ribbons.

Far from being a dull and prosy affair, there was much to interest every one who is watching the advancement of the Hawaiian race.

One exercise especially, would add a desirable feature to any school. It was an illustrated lesson in anatomy. A large class of girls stood erect and graceful while they indicated the different bones of the body by gesture.

Another notable example was in language, the subject being given by an object presented. One girl described the object, another told a story about it.

Everyone must have observed the ease and skill shown by the pupils in writing letters and figures. It does seem that a people so gifted in mathematics and in drawing, must have the foundation upon which to build a well-balanced education.

Later in the morning, we saw elevated maps of Oahu most pleasingly and accurately arranged showing

of Trustees, of the date of opening in the fall, with a few words of encouragement and cheer for both teachers and scholars, the examination opened with an excellent instrumental duet by Misses Lima and Aholo. Besides this there was other music, both piano and vocal. In the latter the girls of the school excel, and always give great pleasure to the hearers, and this occasion was no disappointment.

In reading, the girls showed excellent training, and by their clear enunciation and intelligent rendering indicated that they have been appreciative pupils. The exercises in arithmetic also showed fine training with like appreciation. In short, all of the work showed thorough drilling and conscientious training. The work in English speaking and like exercises was most praiseworthy. The kindergarten class of little ones made an interesting exhibit, as did the class of Liliuokalani Educational Society girls, who were decorated with pretty shields bearing a crown and suspended with blue ribbons.

Far from being a dull and prosy affair, there was much to interest every one who is watching the advancement of the Hawaiian race.

One exercise especially, would add a desirable feature to any school. It was an illustrated lesson in anatomy. A large class of girls stood erect and graceful while they indicated the different bones of the body by gesture.

Another notable example was in language, the subject being given by an object presented. One girl described the object, another told a story about it.

Everyone must have observed the ease and skill shown by the pupils in writing letters and figures. It does seem that a people so gifted in mathematics and in drawing, must have the foundation upon which to build a well-balanced education.

Later in the morning, we saw elevated maps of Oahu most pleasingly and accurately arranged showing
the native conception of proportion, which also appeared later again in the music to which we listened.

Shortly after eleven, the company adjourned to the dining room where specimens of the handiwork of the pupils were on sale. The progress in the sewing department has been very great and the plain and fancy work would have been a credit to the finest millinery establishment. The guests thought so for in less time than it takes to write this all was sold. In cookery a variety of cakes, candy and the whitest and lightest of bread spoke for themselves of attainments in the pantry. In short the whole exhibit must encourage the friends of Hawaii to hope for the future when her future mothers have done so well. All praise is due to the patient, untiring and able corps of teachers headed by Miss Pope.

"Her Majesty the Queen" presided as Ida Pope officiated the annual examination of the pupils, June 1892. *UCSD Libraries.*

the Queen and ladies to the dining room where were laid out all for sale on tables cookery of every description and fancy articles, pictures, ribbons, etc. The fancy lace work and underwear were very pretty and reflected credit on the efficient staff of Kawaiahao Seminary.[45]

At fund-raisers like this, Liliʻuokalani's presence, spending money to show her support, encouraged the close-knit Hawaiian community to follow her lead: "The Queen stayed through and bought over $20 worth at the fair." And she balanced her generosity with impartiality: "The Queen bought from all the tables."[46] And the queen herself set an example by ordering bread from the Kawaiahaʻo kitchen for the palace.[47] This publicized event demonstrated all the forces at play in the history of the school—the religious element, the manual instruction, the allegiance with the queen, and the desire to elevate Hawaiʻi's daughters.[48]

Charles Reed Bishop

At this event, for the first time, Ida got her first glimpse of the prominent Charles Reed Bishop, sitting alongside Queen Liliʻuokalani in the audience. Ida learned early that no other non-Hawaiian name outside royalty evoked more respect in the community than that of Charles Bishop. His name was associated with the Bishop Bank, Bishop Estate, Bishop Hall, Bishop Museum, Bishop Street, and Bishop Trust, but romantically, he was the tragic widower of Princess Bernice Pauahi Pākī Bishop.

The princess had been the beautiful great-granddaughter of King Kamehameha I, the establisher of the Kingdom of Hawaiʻi. The compliant Bernice Pākī, one of the first arrivals at the Chiefs' Children's School, appears regularly in Amos Cooke's diary and Juliette Cooke's correspondence, as the most obedient and talented golden scholar among the group. In 1848, having been in the school for nine years, Bernice caught the eye of New Yorker Charles Bishop, who fell hard for the talented beauty with exotic Hawaiian royal blood and the Western education and etiquette with which he was at ease. Charles, twenty-eight, began courting Bernice, seventeen, under the approving eyes of the Cookes, despite the princess having been pledged by her family to marry fellow royal classmate Prince Lot. In a love story full of twists and turns—and in an extraordinary act of independence—Bernice ended up marrying Charles despite great opposition.

Her parents accused the Cookes of turning their daughter away from her heritage and refused to attend the 1850 nuptials held in the school parlor. Throughout the following decades, Mrs. Bernice Bishop, reconciled with her family, inherited staggering amounts of royal wealth while her prosperous husband earned his

Princess Pauahi and
Charles Reed Bishop,
purportedly on their
wedding day. *Kamehameha
Schools.*

own fortune, in ventures from banking to agriculture, making them the most
influential couple of their time.

In 1872, Lot, the dying King Kamehameha V, who expressed his desire that
she succeed him to the throne, summoned Princess Bernice Bishop. When she
rejected his plea, wanting to maintain her existing lifestyle and her life of philanthropy, the Kamehameha dynasty was brought to an end.

Ida penned an article, dramatically and sentimentally, telling American readers that by "refusing a crown, she so lived that she was crowned. Refusing to rule
her people, she did what was better—she served by her example. She hated that
which was impure with intense hatred. Neither place, power, wealth, nor influence could win her favor if it was joined with degraded character."[49]

At age fifty-two, Bernice Pauahi Bishop discovered a lump in her breast and
underwent surgery in San Francisco. But once she returned to Honolulu, the tu-
mor returned with a vengeance and the cancer painfully spread throughout her
lymph nodes. In her last days, she told a friend that "happiness was not in money"
because "having so much" made her feel "responsible and accountable."[50] Before
she died in 1884, she told her husband where she had decided to bestow her great

wealth. Though childless, she left a will that revealed her great love for children. She bequeathed nearly all of her property in trust to establish two schools that would stress the practical arts, one for boys and one for girls, to be called Kamehameha Schools.

The school for boys had already been completed and Ida and Carrie, frequent visitors, were enthralled at what Mr. Bishop had already completed in his wife's name. In fact, in Carrie's account of the school ceremonies, Mr. Bishop even upstaged Queen Liliʻuokalani. "Something like a 100 people came in the evening. Everyone seemed pleased. The Queen was there with quite a large party of followers. More interesting to me was the Honorable C. R. Bishop of whom I have heard so much but had never seen before."[51]

A New School for Hawaiʻi's Daughters

By 1892, there were many reports going around that Charles Bishop was finally fulfilling his late wife's wish by creating the school for girls. Seeing an easy way out of financial trouble for the seminary, the Kawaiahaʻo trustees petitioned Charles Bishop to transition Kawaiahaʻo Seminary into the proposed Kamehameha School for Girls,[52] keeping Miss Pope at the helm. William Castle, board president, reasoned that an already existing structure, with an established history in the community, would make perfect sense. This would also relieve the members in the community who were benevolently funding the school alongside the queen.

However, Mr. Bishop had a different vision, and was not interested in adopting or adapting the Congregational-run Kawaiahaʻo Seminary to his wife's master plan. He never identified himself with the missionary party, having always made it known that he was a "liberal Protestant, and [that] the differences which divide Christians into denominations and sects seem to me to be nonessential, petty and weakening."[53] But he was in need of an extraordinary female to create the new school and had been convinced, probably by the queen, to attend the ceremonies to observe Ida May Pope in action.

Unbeknownst to Ida, the public examination of the schoolgirls was effectively her job interview. And Charles Bishop must have been mightily impressed with what he saw that evening, because Miss Pope, undoubtedly with Queen Liliʻuokalani's highest endorsement, was offered the esteemed position of founding principal for the soon-to-be-built new school for native Hawaiian girls.

CHAPTER SIX

Pilikia

Culture Clash

Viewing the black-and-white still photos of pupils sitting demurely at their school desks, it is easy to forget the color and energy these girls brought into the school. The girls were far from being blank slates; the mixture of their various backgrounds, family relationships, physical and emotional health, personalities, and attitudes created an animated environment that was a challenge for teachers to contain. In Hawaiian, *pilikia* means "trouble," and there was plenty of that in the school.

The transition from traditional Hawaiian to Western culture was a harsh and abrupt one for many boarders at Kawaiahaʻo Seminary. Rebellion, often resulting from the dramatic clash of cultures, began the moment girls crossed the school threshold—with roots that began long before the girls ever saw a classroom. This culture clash is clearly seen in the diaries and correspondence of many American teachers who registered their disapproval at the way Hawaiian children were allowed to run and play with few noticeable limits. The teachers' indifference to the cultural upbringing of the girls meant that the girls suffered the consequences.

Many American missionary teachers embraced the Victorian "seen but not heard" policy with regard to training children. But this was a belief foreign to Hawaiian indigenous cultures. Hawaiian society valued childlike behavior, and had no expectation that their children would act like little adults. Children were allowed to frolic and explore their ocean environment and in general had a great deal of physical freedom.[1] Conforming to a newly restricted, even regimented, physical environment was just the beginning of abrupt change. For some Hawaiian children, the experience of boarding school as a prison was magnified. Unfamiliar behavioral expectations imposed by Americans often contradicted their own cultural norms. Many teachers wrote home sourly about the perceived surly looks of pupils that required additional reprimands. But, as Hawaiian historian Mary Pukui noted, Hawaiian children were often misunderstood by the American teachers who required them to look directly at their accusers, when they had been raised to avert their eyes out of respect.[2]

78

Carrie Winter at the back of her classroom. "Do you see little Annie Wong (Chinese Dress), a little saint, deformed but bright and quick? Beside her is pretty Violet Lima (*holding book in front row*) and behind her Malia Kapali who can't keep still two minutes, has something to say on every subject and is amusing for all she is so trying." *UCSD Libraries.*

Carrie Winter was exasperated that Hawaiian children, used to sleeping on mats, did not value pillowcases, two proper sheets, and dedicated nightgowns that had been required of her in New England.

> The chief things to look out for here is the tendency of every girl to pick up and destroy everything that comes in their way. I have rescued a pillow-case and some handkerchiefs from the dust-pan so far. Then again they are fond of making up their beds with but one sheet on, or if they have two they put the blanket on before the top sheet. At night they like to sleep in anything but the proper garment and are fond of other beds than their own.[3]

One recorded incident highlighting the desecration of the Hawaiian language reveals that pupils were punished at Kawaiahaʻo for speaking their native language. As Carrie described, "I have a long list of girls to give extra work to. They have been talking native and that is against the rules."[4]

Pupils were also forced to forsake the hula, an important tradition that made up the core of their native culture. The hula had been a key transmitter of the cultural history of the Hawaiian people throughout the ages, with legends and traditions, all told via swaying gestures—gestures that the early missionaries to Hawai'i found lewd and immoral. They did their best to stop the hula, and it was forbidden at Kawaiaha'o Seminary. One of Carrie's letters prudishly revealed to her fiancé that she was worried about losing some of her "genteelness" by association. "I have to sit up half an hour with a couple of girls whom I caught dancing the 'hula.' I don't think you will ever know till you have worked among a people so few years removed from barbarism as these are. You will be anxious for the effect of this upon my own character and I sincerely hope that I have not lost genteelness."[5]

While dancing the hula was forbidden at school, Lydia, who went to Washington Place on most weekends, was encouraged by the queen to practice. "We danced the hula. Oh I tell you it was lots of fun. When she wants us to dance, she gets her guitar out."[6] Lydia, attached to the royal court, would have been caught more than others between the culture of the West and her Hawaiian culture. In late adulthood, she remembered her preference during her years at Kawaiaha'o Seminary. "And, we have to go back to boarding school. And we'd gather around her, tell her all kinds of hard luck stories so she wouldn't put us back to school. Nine o'clock [clap] back to school. That's how she used to do."[7]

The Queen's Support

Even though Kawaiaha'o Seminary did not point to the Hawaiian culture as a source of pride, the power of an education to uplift her nation superseded cultural transmissions at this point in time for Lili'uokalani. In her autobiography, she recorded an event that revealed her interest in the behavior of the schoolgirls.

> I could not think of leaving without saying farewell to some little girls, the charge of whose education I had assumed, and who were at Kawaiahao Seminary. So on the day of departure, I stopped at the schoolhouse. At my coming all the pupils were gathered together into the large room, where I made them an impromptu address, telling them to be faithful to their duty to their teachers, and warning them that it would distress me more than could be expressed should I ever hear that any of them had done other than right during my absence. After these few farewell words I left. I must confess with some fears in my heart, some misgivings as to the future of some of the girls whom I had addressed. But these doubts were set at rest

by their letters, and it made me very happy while I was abroad to hear accounts of their progress and continued good behavior.[8]

While Carrie struggled to take control of her students, Ida managed much more easily. As Carrie wrote, "Miss Pope seems to govern the girls with little trouble and it just cuts me to the quick to think I can't."[9] While classroom management seemed to come naturally to Ida, she also learned an effective means of addressing the severe behavior problems. Why resort to corporal punishment when she had Her Royal Highness to support the management of the school? As one of Carrie's letters revealed, all of the girls respected their queen, whether or not they felt warmly toward the school's rules and restrictions.

> The Queen told Miss Pope to tell all the girls that if any ran away from here she would have them arrested and put in the station house. I had Bible class last night and Miss Pope came in and gave the girls a talking to. And when she gave them the Queen's command you should have seen the change in those girls' faces. All through the school now you can feel the change and the readiness to obey. We are delighted to have the support of the Queen.[10]

A *Chicago Tribune* reporter, while doing an exposé in 1893 titled "Women in Hawaii," inspected Kawaiahaʻo Seminary. The front-page article gave high praise to the teaching and learning observed and substantiated the queen's disciplinary support. "Occasionally there is a refractory case for the teachers to attend to, and then it is said that Liliuokalani's influence has a good effect. She lectures stubborn pupils in a motherly fashion and generally manages to change ill-temper and insubordination to repentance and submission."[11]

Harsh Discipline

Not all cases were referred to Liliʻuokalani for one reason or another. To Ida's dismay, trustees encouraged the missionary teachers to whip pupils, and Carrie documented doing so on several occasions. Carrie, who had no prior teaching experience, recorded several instances when she administered corporal punishment. When she lost control of her emotions, the result was severe for seemingly petty student infractions. Girls identified as being overly noisy could be kept "all day long in a dark closet, with nothing to eat but bread and water."[12] Sometimes discipline was administered with a "bamboo rod" to the point of submission. "At noon I went up and applied a pretty good bamboo rod to her feet. She struck out at me and I applied it to her big, fat body. She subsided but would not promise to keep her feet still so I switched them some more. Then she gave in and since then has been quiet and peaceable."[13]

Carrie reveals that she didn't show preferential treatment to girls attached to the queen's household. The toll on her patience is revealed when she whipped Mary, the daughter of Milania Ahia, one of the queen's closest friends and royal retainer.

> I told her to go to my room and I got the strap and went to her. She seemed to be all right, stood out in the room, held up her skirts and I laid on two good strokes. Then she seemed to go wild and just flew at me with both of her hands into my hair. I used every bit of strength I had in that whipping. Mary was just crazy. When I stopped she just raged up and down the room screaming at the top of her voice and tearing at her clothes. It was really awful. When she was some calmed down I took her to the closet and she was locked in all day. When I went upstairs to repair damages I combed a good bunch of hair out of my head and found my watch chain broken.[14]

Pupils Retaliate

It is not surprising that many of the pupils, like Mary Ahia, rebelled against the American teachers. The weight of bridging this cultural distance lay on the pupils themselves, and in many cases it was more than they were willing or able to do. The girls expressed their frustration in a variety of forms of rebellion, ranging from stealing food to dancing the hula to intentionally provoking the anger of teachers. Carrie described how Ida did not use physical force but relied, as did the queen, on the authority of the police force to encourage obedience. "A lot of girls have been taking food and money from over the fence—some girls have been over the back-yard fence and off with boys—one of the biggest girls rebelled, refused to obey Miss Pope till a threat of the police was made."[15]

Some students fought back by trying to set fire to the school. One incident was posted in the *Hawaiian Gazette* about pupil Julia Jacobs, who was arrested for attempting to set the school on fire.[16] This was not an isolated incident—more than one fire was intentionally started at Kawaiahaʻo. Julia first said she was smoking but ultimately admitted arson to the police. The newspaper reported that she had been disciplined previously for bad conduct and "took the precaution to pack her own trunk previous" to setting the fire.[17] But Lydia Aholo seemed strangely naive to this, as her 1892 essay observed.

One day our house was set on fire because one of our girls had a box of matches in the pocket of her dress and I think the rat ate her pocket and it set our house on fire. We children did not know where to go to. So we just got out from our beds and ran. Some children got hurt because they were very excited. We had our night gowns on and mind you we were all standing in the hall. One of the older girls was so frightened that she cut her hand.[18]

Alice Goes to the Ball

When the queen illuminated 'Iolani Palace with her first state ball, it was worth the risk for Alice Lewis to defy Miss Pope and attend. It was, after all, as a March 18, 1892, newspaper stated, "the grandest entertainment on record."[19] "Thursday night a state ball was given, when Miss Pope found that Alice Lewis wanted to go she was told to stay home. The foolish girl went in spite of Miss Pope's request that she should not do so. She paraded around with one of the worst men in town till after one o'clock. She is in deep disgrace now and it may end in her leaving."[20]

Alice was not going to miss the event no matter the cost. It was simply too much to forgo for a young girl who experienced so much boarding school drudgery day in and day out. It's not known what action Miss Pope ultimately took, but Alice Kalahikiola Lewis Ordway never regretted her childish defiance. Later in life, it was a sweet memory and she repeatedly told this "Cinderella" story to her granddaughter, Sheila. Sheila remembered her aged grandmother's smile recollecting the beautiful French heeled shoes she wore to the queen's ball.[21] Still, an action like Alice's, in the eyes of her teachers, threatened both her future and the school's reputation.

Koni Puuohau

One girl caused the school more than her fair share of stress. Her name continually surfaces in letters from teachers as a troublemaker. Where many girls eventually embraced the structured life the boarding school offered, others, like Koni, financially supported by the queen, felt imprisoned at Kawaiaha'o Seminary.

There was just something about Koni that made Ida feel maternal toward her. She championed and cared for Koni as much as Carrie ostracized and punished her. Ida saw that beneath her disobedience, Koni was pining for love and security. Ida's approach to unruly children was to "kill with kindness." These divergent perspectives are mirrored in their different approaches to Koni. For Carrie, Koni is seen almost exclusively through the lens of disruptive behavior. "We have a certain girl here, one by name of Koni Puuohau, who is capable of giving any amount of trouble and has unsettled the whole school and made disobedience the fashion. She kept talking till late in the night and asserted several times that she should run away the next day. When she is in this fit she is like a great street rowdy and is capable of committing anything."[22]

Meanwhile, Ida saw beyond the acting out and realized that kindness would be the only way to unlock the child's potential.

> Koni Puuohau. She is so bright and mischievous—all the time up to some fun. She is not good, but she likes me just about as much as I do her. She is but fifteen and one of my most promising cherubs. She has not borne an angelic reputation, but she can be killed by kindness. I have been quite partial to her, but poor child! She has never been appreciated, and was just pining to have some one love her. She had a regular fight with one of the teachers last year and tried to run away.[23]

Yet despite Principal Pope's undoubted intervention on Koni's behalf with others, Koni ultimately ran away from the school in 1893 and nobody could convince her to come back. Lilla Appleton described the events, with her opinion seeming to fall somewhere in between that of Carrie and that of Ida. On the one hand, she evidently wanted the best for Koni, but in her letters, Lilla seemed resigned to losing the girl. "At half past ten, having borrowed Miss Winter's horse, I rode to Waikiki to visit Koni who ran away from school last Saturday with her sister's seducer. I felt that I could not rest satisfied without one last attempt. It was a fruitless attempt. Koni was insolent and thankless and I could not talk to her without crying, so finally gave it up and came away."[24]

Ida found Koni a year later and wrote to Carrie despondently, "I saw Koni for the first time last week. She looks ghastly and I do not believe will live long. She is hardly able to move about. She has lost all her dash. I feel very sorry for her."[25] Sadly, Koni died the following year from an undisclosed malady.

Predators

Trespassing by strange intruders, burglaries, and attempted break-ins frequently occurred on school grounds. Kawaiahaʻo Seminary was on the main thoroughfare of King Street in downtown Honolulu. The school was near saloons as well as the harbor and easily accessible to predators who could easily wander onto the property. Carrie described her disbelief at seeing the girls' panic spread like wildfire when a strange man was sighted one evening outside a window. She strangely noted her repugnance at their collective lack of nerve.

Miss Pope and I noticed a man in the yard evidently listening to the girls. As we stood looking at him, he stepped a little nearer into the light that came through the open doors. The girls saw him and instantly there was the most unearthly weird scream of absolute terror from the 100 girls and they began to rush into other parts of the house. We all rushed in at once and met the girls as they were tearing out of chapel. I put myself in the way of one of the biggest girls who was perfectly wild with terror and struck at me in her efforts to get away. I caught a glimpse of my pupil teacher rushing down the back plaza with her dress half torn off her. It was some time before we could get them into the chapel where the girls were all jumbled together, crying and trembling. Very few had seen the man but all had caught the fear. I never saw a panic before and I never want to see another but the incident shows considerable about the girls—their want of grit and backbone—just as though they had anything to fear from one man.[26]

Ida knew the girls' fear of intruders was justified. She, having grown up in two different Ohio railroad junctions, knew firsthand the dangers of living near saloons and the men who frequented them. Ida, as principal, needed to keep the same keen eye out for her pupils just as her mother had. But instead of the four girls her mother looked after, she had 144.

Despite the terror triggered by a single stranger on school grounds, many of the girls still did not understand the risks of bringing young men onto the school grounds, and the girls courted danger by secretly entertaining the young men on campus. Worse yet, curious girls would sneak away from the school grounds to meet up with them. Even though the teachers were vigilant, keeping them apart remained a challenging task, and incidents of boys and girls caught together were regularly documented. In the early days, when the girls wore long, wide, loose-fitting gowns, Ida wrote home that after searching the school buildings for a girl who was late for lunch, she found her giving birth in a bathtub. Lilla Appleton described a scene of either a planned attempt to escape or break-in: "The window blind is cut so that the hand could be slipped through to unfasten the window, [and] the marks of such effort are plainly visible on the window sill."[27] Deterring amorous liaisons required more than threats. It demanded good detective work, as Carrie described.

We have lately heard that there have been men hanging around our grounds at night. Robert Pahau, an ex-Kamehameha boy told us about it and yesterday I learned that he had again seen a man come in here and go into our wash house. We are assured that some girl must be going down there and last evening Miss Pope and myself, after the girls were abed, went down into one of the school-rooms and sat there in the dark in front of an open window to see if we could catch any girl going down. We sat there till toward 11 but saw nothing.[28]

However, it seems as if Robert Pahau might have been the culprit himself, because soon enough Mary Ellen Bridges was pregnant by him, left the school quickly, and lied about the reason to Miss Pope. Ida felt very much like a mother in an age-old story, furtively discovering the truth and hurt by the knowledge that she had been lied to and kept out of the loop.

Mary Bridges is living with Robert Pahau and has been for several months— but they are not married. She will be a mother in a few months. I tried so hard to get her back—never dreaming that she had gone wrong. Her excuses for not coming back were all so plausible that I believed her until I found out the state of affairs in a letter Eunice Kahuila wrote to Margaret Powers. The girls knew about it all along—but never enlightened me.[29]

The Toll on Teachers

As stressful as the school environment could be for the students, it was at least equally so for the young teachers, who, like their pupils, had to adapt to an environment for which nothing in their home or college experience had prepared them. Carrie, and perhaps Ida, felt "crushed" and demeaned by some of the wealthy citizens outside school as she tried to fit in.

There is something quite wrong with society here—they didn't prepare me for this in college when they told us of the responsibilities we would have to meet and how whole communities would look up to us as the educated people. Some of these rich, ignorant people give me a feeling as though they regarded me as of little higher social position than a mere girl. I really think teachers are looked upon here somewhat in that light. Miss Pope and I have determined however, to go wherever we are invited and do our best.[30]

Teachers quickly discovered that their role was just as much that of nurse, custodian, mediator, and guard. Besides alternating Sundays, they rarely had a break as long as school was open, sharing the responsibility of providing for the girls' every need around the clock. Exhausted teachers were often called to dormitory duty at night, despite their long workdays. And when they came on duty, they needed to be ready for anything, as described by teacher Lilla Appleton: "Every teacher is expected to know how to do everything, from giving the school an extemporaneous half-hour discourse upon the Sabbath school lesson to pulling teeth. We live, too, in a constant state of expectation not knowing just what may happen next, but fires and panics, robberies and run-a-ways as well as various other 'pilikias' of past years, have taught us to be on the alert for any emergency at any time."[31]

Rebellion, illness, tragedies, violence, and betrayal were all circumstances a young teacher had to learn to manage. The ongoing stress of corralling and shepherding lively girls led Carrie to question her worth in one letter to her fiancé, Charles.

> I have been "going on four months" and I seem to be almost a failure in the way of discipline. Perhaps that seems a little thing, but it means real suffering to me. I have about resolved that if things don't straighten out before the year is over I shall give up and go home. I think it grows out of an entirely weary system of governing these native girls—to have them in complete subjection and punish every slight deviation. I don't think you can realize Charlie, what work it is to punish a lot of girls.[32]

Carrie also revealed that perhaps some members of the community showed outward disdain for the school's discipline methods. "I think one of the hardest things we have to bear is the attitude strangers sometimes take toward us. They see the beautiful and poetic side of the girl's nature and it seems to them that we are hard and cruel and all their sympathy is for the girls when it really ought to be the other way."[33]

Indeed, any act of trust in the students might be repaid with betrayal, in some cases with costly results. As part of her efforts to train the girls in self-sufficiency, Ida looked for ways to help them gain a sense of worth. Carrie wrote about one of Ida's efforts that must have caused great disappointment. Ida purchased a small number of expensive chickens for the school and put a few older girls in charge of collecting the eggs for the purpose of teaching them responsibility. However, Ida discovered that instead of turning over the eggs to the school's kitchen, the girls were stealing them from the school for their own benefit. "The next thing was Miss Pope discovering some of the girls roasting eggs at the rubbish fire in the back yard. Four or five were involved and in one girl's pocket were found three eggs. They lied like everything over the matter but there is no telling how long they have been thieving. Eggs are 60 cents a dozen here so it is no slight matter."[34]

Illness

Rebellious or unruly girls were not the only heartbreaks teachers had to endure. Serious illness was a fact of life and caused teachers great distress. Staff had to nurse gravely ill students, and students often had to cope with the death of a family member or schoolmate. Teachers often wore the hat of a grief counselor to help their students through these difficult times. As Lilla Appleton wrote, such events could be sudden and traumatic.

> We received a telephone about midnight, asking if one of our girls could come out as the mother was dying. Miss Pope was afraid there was some foul play and asked me if I would go with her to accompany the girl. Miss Pope and I were driven to a native house. On the floor lay Annie's mother, unconscious. The doctor said there was no hope for her. Every little while she was seized with frightful convulsions, which were simply terrible to witness. Annie hid her face in her hands and Miss Pope and I went out of doors. We could not witness it. The Dr. added to the horror of it all by explaining that the woman could not breathe during these convulsions,

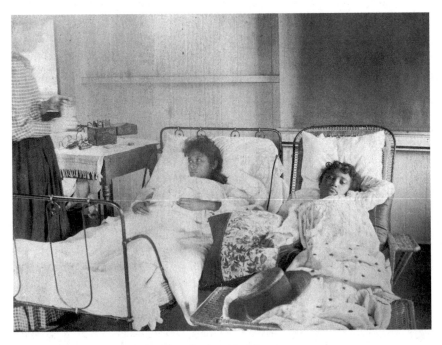

Serious illness was a fact of life in the school. *UCSD Libraries.*

that the spasms would grow longer and longer until finally the last one would last so long that the flickering breath could not be caught again. We staid until half past two. Annie staid and the next day her mother died.[35]

The medical treatment that the school could offer was superior to almost anything the parents could often acquire, but the girls often ran home instead of accessing it. It could be that the medical treatments of the time were themselves so traumatic to witness that this was another level of horror. One incident involved a mother who required her ill daughter to recuperate at home. By the time Miss Pope went to her home and found out how sick Mary Makaimoku was, it was too late. Influenza, or the grippe, could have been treated more successfully in the school's sick room, but at home, the condition advanced to a terrible conclusion. Ida fainted when the doctor drained the fluid from Mary's body.

We found her very sick, with no doctor for two weeks and in a little hot room with no ice or milk. Miss Pope sent Dr. McWayne down at once. He was very anxious to have her brought up to the seminary. It was Monday night before she at last got here and her condition was worse as dropsical symptoms had set in. She was very much bloated and he said were she his own child he should tap her at once. It took the 3 teachers who were here to help in the operation. Miss Pope turned faint. I should think the doctor drew off 3 quarts from her. It relieved her right away. The doctor feared a collapse any moment and kept his finger on her pulse all the time and every few minutes gave her brandy.[36]

This arcane treatment of "tapping" involved a dangerous maneuver that punctured the abdomen in several places. Ida would have witnessed the fluid shooting out from the body of her student, and this is probably why she fainted. It took a long time for the nineteenth-century medical community to realize that patients often died from the infection of the puncture wounds. Sadly, little Mary Makaimoku did not survive much longer, much to the distress of everybody in the school.

Equally distressing were hopeless situations when death was an absolute certainty. Consumption, or tuberculosis, claimed many boarding school lives, due to its highly contagious nature. Even as a daughter of a doctor, nothing in her background prepared Ida for dying girls. But even so, she quickly stepped in for parents who were unable or unwilling to care for their sick child. "She is a little girl of about 12 dying of consumption. Miss Pope took care of her all through the week. Wrote to their friends some time ago but the inter-island service has been very poor of late owing to bad storms. We were much disappointed this morning because the sick girl's father did not come. The doctor thinks the child is no better, even a little weaker. There is no knowing how long she will have to be nursed."[37]

Though medicine was still hampered by practices that a century later would be wildly out of date—bleeding, for instance—Ida was willing to seize hold of whatever nineteenth-century medical innovations she could get to protect her school. In January of 1892, a China steamer with plague-infected laborers arrived at the Honolulu dock just a week after a Japanese vessel had carried two cases of smallpox into Hawai'i. Fear of infection abounded in the community. As soon as she heard the news, Ida immediately requisitioned Dr. McWayne to vaccinate over one hundred girls in a single afternoon.[38] Ida's foresight is impressive in the light of history. Her quick thinking at the very least protected the school's population from what could have been unimaginable misery.

Kahuna

Kahuna is a Hawaiian word that has been defined by missionaries as a "priest, sorcerer, magician or wizard."[39] In ancient Hawaiian healing traditions, kahuna were the medical doctors. Kahuna were always a source of anxiety, not only for the medical doctors at the time but for the teachers. Because kahuna communicated with spirits other than their God, Ida and the other teachers deemed them pagan. They attempted to dissuade pupils from relying on the healing methods of kahuna, but parents were out of their reach.

Lilla Appleton wrote home about a German father who sought medical aid through a kahuna, which harmed little Louisa Esse enough to require hospitalization. Ultimately the father's custody was taken away in a court case that Ida was mandated to testify in.

> We have one very pitiful little German girl about six years old. She was taken to the hospital to be treated for injuries which she had received at the hands of some witches and then brought here to prevent repetition of the trouble. The case was taken into court and Miss Pope was called down to testify much to her horror. The end of it all was that it was decided the father should have no more authority over her. He torments us, however, by coming to try to see his "kleine kinder." On Christmas night he came apparently the worse for drink, stood in the door for ten or fifteen minutes and harangued us bitterly, that we should let him see the child on the day of the Krist Kind, finally ending with an appeal to Miss Pope "Have you ever been a Mother?" Miss Pope quietly slipped out and telephoned

for a policeman who soon arrived on the spot and nipped his sentiments in the bud.[40]

The desperation and reliance on the healing methods kahuna used frustrated Ida and other teachers. And despite their best efforts, the girls would not completely denounce their faith in them as long as their parents respected them as healers.

Domestic Violence

Ida was concerned for some of the girls who returned to their homes among the islands during summer vacation. Sometimes it was because when they returned to school from the carefree summer months, they needed to be retaught and retrained. Some amount of this was a contest between Hawaiian and Western culture, but most of the teachers were also genuinely concerned for their students' safety and welfare. The teachers recorded numerous incidents of domestic violence.

Carrie reported on one case of abuse that brought children back to school. "Perhaps most dreadful of all, two of the little children, gentle little things, have been half-killed by their cruel step-mother. I am thankful to say they are no longer with the beast."[41]

One of the most notorious cases of domestic abuse involved Kawaiaha'o Seminary alumna Lizzie Naone. After years of spousal abuse, her husband, Phillip Naone, ultimately killed her. The newspapers reported that "five shots from a revolver were fired into her body while she was attempting escape."[42] It would be up to Ida to manage her own grief as well as that of Lizzie's little sister, Keahiloa.

Lilla wrote home about one pupil who had witnessed a horrible case of domestic violence who more than likely suffered from post-traumatic stress disorder.

> Sunday night there was a great uproar in the dormitory. Dora was screaming and talking incoherently and struggling to get away while several girls were holding her into bed by force and doing the one thing they know how to do on all occasions, lomi-lomiing[43] for dear life. I showed the girls how to hold her without bearing down on her so hard, rubbed her head and called her by name.

Dora's problems continued, however, and at last Lilla discovered the root cause.

> Next night—The girls called me again—to say that Dora was trying to get away. I went in and she said "I hear the house is going to break down." "O, no" I said, "that is a mistake. You'd better come back to bed." "No!" she

insisted, I smoothed out her bed wondering what I should do, and in a moment she came back and lay down. Ice and a cloth wet in cold water comforted. We have since learned that Dora's father has just died in the insane asylum here and also that he killed Dora's mother by sticking scissors into her.[44]

While sickness and death were problems Ida might have faced in Ohio, the level of turbulence and upheaval in the school astonished and exhausted her. The harsh punishment as vividly described in several teachers' letters were methods used for most of its twenty-five-year history. Despite her efforts to treat students more reasonably and humanely, Ida fought an exhausting battle at Kawaiahaʻo Seminary. She spent her four years dealing with incompetent colleagues who stirred up trouble in and out of school, pupils who made bad decisions and courted disaster, nonstop pupil mischief, multiple deaths, battles with trustees, and never-ending politics. Ida could not wait to begin a new life as principal at the Kamehameha School for Girls, where she anticipated great autonomy. And her first administrative act would be to tell both trustees and parents that no child would be "corrected by force."[45]

CHAPTER SEVEN

Off to Moloka'i with the Queen, 1892

On May 3, 1891, Ida wrote to her sister Lois that she did "something a trifle out of the ordinary."

> In the past week I have had the experience of a life time, but when I tell you what I have done I fear the family will "rise up as a single man" and disown me. Few pale faced women have ever attempted such an exploit. I have been to Molokai and visited the leper settlements. I went with royalty—so do not be utterly cast down by my madness.[1]

In her letter she wrote, "You never did think I was brave, did you?" But in her day, visiting a quarantined leper's colony on the island of Moloka'i was an act of extreme courage, if not, as she mentions, madness. Known today as Hansen's disease, leprosy[2] was not a swift and deadly killer like measles, smallpox, or cholera. Those diseases had already killed prodigious numbers of Hawaiians in the early and middle parts of the century. But few actually died from leprosy and instead lingered a long time, anywhere from five to fifteen years, until they caught pneumonia or other ills.[3] Leprosy was viewed as the "worse-than-death disease" because victims were torn from their families with little expectation of seeing them again. In the early days of the colony, particularly before the Roman Catholic priest and reformer Father Damian arrived in 1873, the afflicted were simply shipped there to die.

Isolation had long been considered an appropriate response to leprosy. Leper asylums, or leprosariums, were a common feature in Europe and Asia since the thirteenth century. But Hawai'i was the first country to isolate the afflicted on an inaccessible and remote island.[4] By some reports, this horrible malady had begun to spread throughout the islands as early as 1830.[5] But it wasn't until 1863 that the rapid growth had begun to alarm the medical community in Hawai'i.[6] When some doctors from the Board of Health observed healthy people sharing poi out of a communal bowl "with a leper who had lost two or three fingers,"[7] their response was swift. They deemed enforced isolation critical for counteracting what they felt they could not stop. It appeared to the doctors that family members and friends exhibited little fear of the disease, even when their loved ones were in obvious advanced stages.

In 1865, after an urgent appeal from Kamehameha V, the Hawai'i legislature quickly passed the Act to Prevent the Spread of Leprosy that made isolation enforceable by law. Hundreds of acres on the remote cliff-bound Kalaupapa Peninsula of the island of Moloka'i were then secured for segregation. But getting victims of the disease to Moloka'i was not easy. Newspapers of the time are replete with stories of family members and friends hiding their afflicted loved ones all over the islands. When discovered, patients were immediately shuttled to the pier, where heart-rending permanent farewells were expressed poignantly in loud wailing.[8]

In 1890, Ida arrived at the very peak of the epidemic, with more than one thousand people, or 2 percent of the Hawaiian population, confined on Moloka'i.[9] The colony of those afflicted with the disease had improved since the early days when food, clothing, and hospital equipment were in very short supply, but the horrifying circumstances shocked and saddened Ida. Within only weeks of arriving in Honolulu, she was confronted with the magnitude of the situation by the public proclamation of a day of prayer and fasting for the sick and dying on Moloka'i.

School Sorrows

At Kawaiaha'o Seminary, Ida experienced the horrifying disease from every side—from the point of view of its victims and their grieving families, and as a school administrator who had to wrestle with handling students who contracted the malady. Often this meant traumatic removal of students to Moloka'i, and each new removal triggered memories of prior losses and other girls gone forever. Many Sunday sermons at Kawaiaha'o Church surrounded the healing of Naaman the leper in the Bible, and after such a sermon, many of the girls wept, especially those who had relatives on the island. It was up to the teachers to comfort and console them and to offer them hope of healing when in their hearts they were uncertain.

If Ida had been privy to the statistics reported by the Office of the Board of Health only six years earlier, she may have never accepted the position out of fear for her well-being. In the Official Report on Schools, Kawaiaha'o Seminary was singled out as a major health threat from leprosy.[10] Comparing it with other schools, the Board of Health found Kawaiaha'o as "the most unhealthy,"[11] with a startling loss of 13 percent of its student population to leprosy.[12]

Afflicted schoolgirls waiting to be transported to Moloka'i. *Courtesy of Hawaiian Historical Society.*

Therefore, Ida was constantly on the lookout for the first signs of leprosy in the girls. The first alarm would be the sight of "a firm, dry patch in which there is no sense of heat, cold or touch" particularly on the face, ears, nose, or cheeks.[13] Carrie described the peculiar version found in Hawai'i. "It shows itself in swollen, distorted features, missing finger tips, purple bunches, etc."[14] When teachers detected indicators, sometimes long before the girls themselves suspected the affliction, the school's legal responsibility was to call the doctor before the family could hide their daughter from the authorities. Knowing this, girls often lied about or hid their symptoms, even simple wounds, fearful that they would be sent away. As Carrie described, this led to a sense of both heightened vigilance and secrecy.

> Friday I was watching two of my girls at work. I went out of the room for a few moments and when I came back I noticed the fingers of a hand bent over the edge of the door. The queer appearance of the finger arrested my attention. The end seemed to be gone. I went in and found that it was Mary Ahia. When I asked her about it she was very much confused and said something about Nancy cutting it with an ax. I made inquiries of Miss

Pope and she knew nothing of it. In fact none of the teachers had ever seen that finger and when Mary was spoken to about it she burst out crying and refused to show it. The doctor looked at it today and said it was all right but I don't quite believe him.[15]

On the other hand, sometimes the girls themselves suspected the disease long before teachers or the doctor. At the start of one school year, Elizabeth Awai easily passed the "leprosy checkup" by the school's doctor.[16] One month later, the "quiet, retiring girl"[17] went secretly to Miss Pope with her trembling suspicions of actually having the dreaded disease. Ida at once had the girl examined by a different doctor. Once again, Elizabeth was declared healthy and the matter was dismissed. However, Elizabeth's fellow classmates did not dismiss the matter as easily as the doctors and avoided all contact with her. Three months after the doctor's appointment, Elizabeth requested to "be out for a day" with her family. When she did not return to school, Ida went looking for her.[18] To Ida's astonishment, Elizabeth had been diagnosed by a community doctor and was in quarantine while awaiting transfer to Moloka'i. With a heavy heart, because "the girl knew better than the doctor," Ida ordered the fumigation of the entire dormitory and the disinfection of every room Elizabeth frequented. Ida then had all her school possessions including her school desk burned.[19]

The teachers as well as the school's doctors faced a difficult decision in turning young afflicted girls over to the Board of Health. If they followed the letter of the law, a girl might never get a meaningful and private chance to say goodbye to her family. "One of the saddest experiences in the school, perhaps, the saddest—one of our little girls, of 11 or 12, is a leper and has had to leave. She is a very docile and sweet child and we feel badly over it. Sarah's face got very swollen and slimey and there were dark blotches on her neck and body. Neither the doctor nor Miss Pepoon wished to report her to the Board of Health. Perhaps it's only right to let her see her family once more."[20]

In Sarah's case, the rules were bent so her family could see her one final time. Despite their anguish, the parents let their daughter go—but the results of a report to the Board of Health were not always so peaceful. Reactions often spilled over into the criminal. Margaret Brewer, once a teacher at Kawaiaha'o Seminary and a good friend of Ida's, fell in love and was engaged to Dr. Jared Knapp Smith.[21] He diagnosed a young lady with leprosy one day and informed her he would be sending in a report, as was required, based on his findings. That very evening her twenty-year-old boyfriend showed up at his home and shot the doctor through the heart to prevent him from filing the report that would exile his loved one.[22]

Conflicting Faiths

As the Smith incident demonstrates, the threat of quarantine triggered desperation. During Ida's era, there was little hope to offer those who were sent to Moloka'i, and there were few who would go to minister to the afflicted, for fear of contracting the disease. The primary solution offered was faith, and is illustrated in the fact that the lighthearted King Kalākaua solemnly appointed a specific day of fasting and prayer. The Kawaiaha'o girls joined the king at one of those services, as described by Carrie.

> I was the only white person there and all was in Hawaiian but I could easily see what an earnest meeting it was. One old white-headed man made a very earnest talk and at one time all the people began to cry. Most of the girls wiped their eyes many times.
>
> When it was over I asked one of the girls what he said. It seems he was telling them of the earnest Christian life of the first converts of one Queen who became a Christian and that now he feared the people were Christians only in name and he thought if they would arouse themselves and pray earnestly like the old Christians, the good God would take the leprosy from the nation.[23]

Even though Hawaiian preachers called for repentance and faith, sometimes that faith took on a different form. Teachers attempted in vain to dissuade pupils from relying on the healing methods of a kahuna, but it was pointless. For the girls, the promise of a cure proved worth pursuing. There was a recorded act that took place behind the school: "A Kahuna in the rear of Kawaiahao Seminary spit down the throat of a little child, in order to expel the demon that made it sick."[24] While spitting down a child's throat by a Hawaiian faith healer was ineffectual, so was the carbolic acid that the missionary teachers favored, and carbolic acid was much more dangerous. Carbolic acid was often used as an antiseptic to treat leprosy during the nineteenth century, and teachers thought it wise to act preemptively by requiring children to bathe with it.[25] Anne Pope, Ida's sister, later a teacher at the Pālama Settlement in Honolulu, would gratefully acknowledge the bathtub where "we have used pints of carbolic acid and boxes of carbolic soap. It is not a pleasant thing, but you know leprosy is a veritable truth here."[26] The use of carbolic soap fell out of favor in the following century when it was found that concentrated carbolic acid behaved as a poison and created horrible side effects, including death.

"Royal Permission"

With no known cause of how leprosy was being spread or cure for the disease, it took everyone in the community to join forces to curb the widespread panic, including the new queen. As Ida wrote, "Her Majesty the Queen, is just coming out of mourning and like a wise sovereign as she is—she intends making a tour of the islands. She desired the favor of her subjects and what better way to impress them than to give them a glimpse of her most gracious self?"[27]

As princess, Lili'uokalani went to the leper colony in 1884 and responded to the heart-rending needs generously.[28] Eight years later, as queen, despite numerous criticisms and concerns over risking her personal health, she proclaimed that she would be going to Moloka'i to see "her people."[29] Ida also had "people" and was "consumed with desire" to see them.[30] Former pupils Ella Bridges and Emma Powers were quarantined there, and Ida was resolute in her desire to visit them.

Ida was disappointed but not intimidated when she and fellow teacher Helen Hoppin were summarily denied a permit for passage by the Board of Health. Ida wrote her sister Lois in Ohio that she did "not intend to be daunted" and boldly enlisted the help of the royal chamberlain to personally petition the queen on her behalf. Lili'uokalani immediately granted her "royal permission" and sent word she was to report to the Board of Health's office to pick up her permit. Ida smugly recounted how she circumvented government policy with the queen's aid.

> We went promptly at nine the next morning. The President of the Board looked upon us in as frigid a manner as possible for so warm a morning. He irritated me, but I smilingly produced my royal commission. He looked upon it as though it were but an ordinary bit of paper. The other members disapproved but we were as obdurate as they. Finally the Pres. said (after removing his coat) he would interview Her Majesty and inform us of the decision. You can imagine the state we were in the rest of the day. The conclusion of the whole matter was that the Pres. himself brought us the permits about half past five in the evening. We never doubted but that Her Royal Highness' sanction would but be an "Open Sesame" to all gates.[31]

The fact that the queen took healthy people with her, including Ida Pope, risking their health, was hotly criticized in the newspapers. Carrie, while envious of Ida's opportunity, privately thought it showed bad judgment on the part of the three-month newly crowned monarch: "Her Molokai expedition is exciting considerable comment. She is allowing a lot of natives who have friends there to go with her, which is a bad thing and not allowed under a careful administration."[32]

Surely the queen was motivated by the pleas of her subjects who craved to see their loved ones again. For Carrie it was a sign of an inept administration to allow its own laws to be overruled by the queen. For Ida, it was a rare opportunity. She left on the *Likelike* at ten in the evening on Sunday, April 26, and noted the "quiet orderly" boarding process followed by mayhem on the deck.

> Natives swarmed everywhere—each one had his own bed, a piece of matting—blankets and pillows. I was sick most of the night—there were natives talking and tobacco smoke thick enough to cut with a knife. There were three hundred and forty on the ship and it is a small inter island steamer. The Queen slept on the deck on a rug—She was accompanied by her nephew, Hon. Samuel Parker—Minister of Foreign Affairs, and by her maids—We paid our respects to the Queen twice—backed out of her presence and did not stumble.[33]

Emotional Arrival

The ship arrived at six the following morning, and Ida asked Lois to imagine her miserable disembarkation. "There is no wharf and we had to be landed in row boats. Imagine me clambering down the side of the Likelike clutching the rope with one hand and frantically holding on to my permit with the other. When we reached the landing we were pulled up over the rocks by two stalwart natives."

Ida recounted the queen's emotional landing:

> An arch was erected at the foot of the landing twined with ropes of fern— and branches of the leaves on the arch were these words, "Aloha Ika Moi Wahine" (Love to our Queen). She came in the last boat—It was a scene that baffles description—It seemed to me that I was walking in a charnel house.[34] When Her Majesty landed, the leper band played Hawaii Ponoi and greeted her with a wail—It sounded to me like the sloughing of the wind on a lonely night but it is a cry of welcome with the natives.

As delighted as the residents of Moloka'i were to see their queen, they were beside themselves to see her retinue, made up as it was of family members who had been parted for years in the expectation of never meeting again, as Ida expressed. "The meeting of the lepers with their friends was most pitiful. Husbands and wives—fathers—mothers—brothers and sisters that had not met for years. They scattered about in little groups embracing each other—sobbing and crying. I felt like an intruder—as though I had no right to witness such a scene."[35]

Ida began to see the queen, and indeed the Hawaiians themselves, in a newly humane light. "The Queen has been criticized for taking the friends of the lepers to Molokai. The natives have no fear of the disease and they kissed those diseased lips and cheeks without a shudder. But had we father, mother, sister or brother there, would we not do the same? If there is aught to cure the hurt of this people I wish it would come to them right speedily. They are such a loveable gentle people but at the present death rate will be extinct in half a century."[36]

Despite the fact that Moloka'i was known as hell on earth, or in the words of Jack London, "the pit of hell,"[37] Ida searched for beauty and curiously chose to describe the island to her sister as a place where the natives lived close to nature, in a veritable paradise.

> Molokai is wonderfully beautiful—a prison shut in on one side by the sea and on the other by a wall 1500 ft. high—covered with the softest green verdure leading into wooded vales—where the pandanus trees and guava bushes abound. There is only one trail over this wall—steep and precipitous—none but the strong ever attempt to scale it. The island is covered with grass. I had an idea it was a barren waste—but I think there is no finer scenery in all Hawaii than can be found in Molokai. A great many of the lepers were on horseback. They have fine horses and must enjoy them. They are very fond of riding and are never so happy as when in the saddle—white poppies meet one's eye at every turn.[38]

Ella Bridges

While the queen addressed her stricken subjects "in native," Ida and Helen began their search for Kawaiaha'o's former pupils. The first girl they located was Ella Bridges, whose older sister, Mary Ellen, back at Kawaiaha'o Seminary, sent a letter with Miss Pope to hand deliver. Ella, who had been on Moloka'i for three years, was found under the care of the Franciscan nuns led by Mother Marianne Cope in the village of Kalaupapa. "The Mother Superior greeted us most cordially and we were refreshed with coffee and delicious bread and butter. The Cottage where the sisters live is plain but neatly furnished and everything about the premises is immaculate. There is no ice manufactured on Molokai—and the water was so warm. Just before we started on our tour of investigation the Mother made us a delicious drink of acid phosphate [a dry, tart, tingly soft-drink ingredient]."

Ida described fifteen-year-old Ella Bridges: "She is a bright looking girl—and has no sores. Her left hand is diseased—partially paralyzed. A number of the school children were on the verandah. They all with the exception of Ella, showed marked evidence of the disease—faces swollen in bunches, many were distorted and looked like caricatures."

Reading the diaries of teachers can oftentimes foreshadow events that could have caused a girl like Ella to receive a diagnosis of leprosy. Helen Norton, once principal at Kawaiaha'o, wrote in her diary on June 28, 1881, of a "dreadful" experience visiting then-five-year-old Ella Bridges in the hospital. Ella contracted the flu and needed a nurse around the clock. The hospital was a good solution, or so it seemed at that time.

Helen recorded her horror that when she went to check on her pupil, Mrs. Mary Powers, newly diagnosed with active leprosy and mother of two other pupils, was found at Ella's bedside "acting as a nurse would."[39] Both were at the Kaka'ako Branch Hospital at the same exact time but for different reasons. A portion of the hospital served as a receiving station for leprosy patients but was loosely guarded. Mrs. Powers was the mother of Ella's classmates Maggie and Emma. A few months later, on November 10, 1881, Helen Norton ominously noted in her diary that she saw a suspicious spot on Ella's left hip and pleads, "Oh God, sustain me in these trials."[40]

Ida Pope correctly noted that "all" the children she saw at Moloka'i "showed marked evidence of the disease" except Ella. That is because she never contracted leprosy. Bridges' family accounts state that after the hospital incident, there was a "paranoia" that led to a close monitoring of Ella. Probable nerve damage to the arm from a severe "hot boiling water incident" instead of leprosy is likely what caused the medical error that sent twelve-year-old Ella to Moloka'i. In 1901, Ella Bridges' misdiagnosis was made public and she was released after a decade of isolation.[41]

What made a lasting impression on Ida was the loving care and management of the Bishop Home run by the nuns, in contrast with the horrors it sheltered. Besides the sad experience of visiting Ella, Ida reveled in the chance to witness good management—the sisters, "refined and elegant in appearance," not only cared for their island, their charges, and their garden but also "retained such sweetness and gentleness of manner amidst such scenes."[42]

We went into the dormitories. They are small cottages ten beds in each—neat and comfortable. In one dormitory three patients were in bed—one—the Sisters told us had been dying for several days—one of the Sisters went up and spoke to her. She seemed oblivious to all her surroundings. There was an unearthly pallor on her face—her lips were parted and her great black eyes were looking into the Great Beyond. At the foot of her bed was seated a little girl with one of her feet bandaged—the other one presented a horrible sight swollen twice its natural size and of a bright purplish color. A Sister said she had poulticed the foot and tried numerous remedies to no avail. Is it not wonderful that even in the most hopeless cases they do not give up trying to do something for them.[43]

And in a play on her own name, Ida passionately expressed what she would do with the powers of a real Pope in regard to Mother Marianne and her nuns.

Oh were I a Pope in the Catholic Church—the Sisters of Molokai should be in the front rank of saints. They may be the "little leaven" that will leaven the whole lump at Molokai. They are to me the grandest of loaves— and will remain to me as an inspiration. I don't see how I dare be discouraged when I think of them. That sweet serenity that rests so lovingly on lip and cheek and brow—can come but from heavenly inspirations—How the angels must love to watch over them—for they are meek and lowly and have learned of Him—They must love their duty for they do the most repulsive things with the same sweet grace that they proffered to us a cup of coffee. But when I think of the Sisters that have consecrated their lives to this work—what pigmies we ordinary folk are. Discouragements meet them at every turn—but yet they go on their way—pure and sweet as the lilies of the field—doing whatever their hands find to do—without a murmur. Subject only to our heavenly maker.[44]

Emma Powers

Ella Bridges lived in a degree of order under the nuns, despite her grim condition, and Ida found, at the settlement, a model of sorts for her own school, even as she was shocked at the suffering. She left the Bishop Home[45] to locate the second girl on her list, Emma Powers, where her estimation of lifestyles differed dramatically.

The Powers' cottage in Kalawao was three miles from Kalaupapa, but Ida stubbornly chose to walk because she refused to ride a horse "cavalier fashion." As she trekked the well-traveled road, she found the "views entrancing—a sight fit for the Gods" and the residents welcoming. "They were all out and greeted us with Aloha nui—we met many horsemen—who doffed their hats and smiled a greeting. I did not see an angry look or hear an unkind word the livelong day." Tired but invigorated, Ida found twenty-year-old Emma, "at one time one of the prettiest girls on the island, [who] married a leper and had a baby, now one week old. Both she and her husband had leprosy, in a very bad form. Emma's face is swollen and covered with bunches as large as a hickory nut. She has the softest black eyes and pearly teeth and uses good English."

Ida was then introduced to Emma's mother. The mother's grief, very apparent to Ida, undoubtedly stemmed from being permanently separated from her other daughter, Maggie, now in Miss Pope's charge. "I felt so sorry for the mother. She was much affected when we told her we were from Kawaiahao. Her grief was so silent and she looked so sad that my heart ached for her."[46]

Ida's experience reached an epiphany when she was introduced to others in the "family" and deduced that Emma was living in a plural marriage and had borne a baby by another's husband.

> Emma with the brightest of smiles said the woman was her husband's first wife and the little boy her son. If this Hawaiian people would but mend their morals—this terrible question of leprosy would be nearer its solution. I tried not to look shocked but I was sick to my very soul. It is not so that we are all born free and equal. When I looked into the face of that little babe and thought of its possible future, I felt like snatching it away. It looked so sweet and innocent—just like other babys!—And what will it grow up to be in such a household where no moral right is recognized.[47]

After leaving Emma, Ida went onward to visit Father Damien's one-year-old grave. During his life he was devoted to caring for the sick and dying on Moloka'i, and his story took on somewhat mythic proportions. However, some of the clergy in Hawai'i were highly critical of his life, and at this time he was a controversial figure. Reverend C. M. Hyde publicly described Father Damien as a "coarse and dirty man," intimated that the priest was "not pure in his relations with women," and argued that Damien's death from leprosy was due to "his vices and carelessness."[48] In response, Robert Louis Stevenson, who stayed for six days on Moloka'i in 1889, published a "heated and verbose and highly indignant defense of Father Damien."[49] Carrie and Ida both wrote letters home during the same month, and in them, they represent perfectly the two opposing views of Father Damien. Carrie was harsh and judgmental in her assessment of his reputation. "He was a man of very dirty habits, a coarse rough man who would do things that decent people could not think of doing such as eating from the same poi-bowl as the lepers etc. His having become a leper is considered almost proof of the immorality of the man and it is probable that the man never had any notion of noble self-sacrifice."[50]

However, Ida was not in the least convinced by such slander and appeared more compassionate in assessing his reputation. "Father Damien died a leper—He has been much criticized—He is said to have been unclean in his habits and morally impure—but this is but hearsay and he has gone to be judged by a more righteous judge than we are."[51]

After leaving the gravesite, Ida had an opportunity to see the devotion Lili'uokalani had for her young subjects, and they to her.

> The boys were out on the verandah when we came up. They stood up and bowed to us. Such a woeful sight. It will haunt me for ages! The boys are much worse than the girls. Some of the boy's heads were swollen to almost twice their natural size—their ears distended and swollen—nostrils enlarged and their lips were horrible—We went across the road to the Sister's cottage—and waited on the verandah for the Queen. She soon appeared and the boys marched over in lines—made their obeisance to their sovereign and formed in two lines on either side of the steps. They had composed songs in her honor—and their plaintive melodies and distorted faces will remain with me as long as memory lasts. The Queen was much affected.

There was no need for conversation with Helen, but much "reflection" as they passed numerous tombs on their way back to the dock. As the *Likelike* departed, one last dramatic incident took place. "We were all on board the steamer at five. Our boatload had quite an experience. A girl who had parted with her father became much excited and attempted to jump into the sea. It took three persons to hold her in the boat. I feared she would tip over the boat but we got on board safely—about half an hour after I saw her smoking a cigarette, with a youth apparently as happy as a lark."

Ida experienced many of the wretched scenes on Moloka'i entirely through her own perspective, of a young twenty-eight-year-old teacher, a long way from Ohio. It seems fair to say that she went to a place for which she had no reference—something totally outside her experience—and tried to make sense of it. And in doing that, she used the categories that were familiar to her. In the years to come, she would get closer to understanding the Hawaiians, and realize that her previously familiar categories would simply not apply. She would never forget Mother Marianne and the Franciscan Sisters' great personal sacrifices as they worked and lived among the most rejected of all people. Deeply inspired, Ida would use them as examples as she advocated for work among the disadvantaged in Honolulu.

Back at school, Ida took on more of a motherly interest in Maggie Powers and boasted to her sister that Maggie was "the brightest girl in the Seminary." Ida sent Maggie's school essay to an American periodical specializing in literature, and it was selected for publication. She wrote to Lois, puffed up with pride, "If you can get the 'Treasure Trove' for April read 'Margaret Powers—School Life in Hawaii.' It is the prize essay for the best serious essay. She wrote it in my room and I feel quite proud of my pupil."[52] Without a doubt, this news was relayed to the Powers family on Moloka'i, as was the bigger news that Maggie was made a public school teacher's assistant. Later in life, Maggie became the legendary and indomitable "Mother Waldron" with a playground in Kaka'ako named after her.

CHAPTER EIGHT

Prayer and Politics

The Revolution of 1893

A terrible homecoming awaited the new queen from her grand tour of the islands. She soon found her fifty-nine-year-old husband, John Dominis, on his deathbed. He ultimately succumbed to a severe bout of pneumonia on August 27, 1891.[1] In the midst of her sorrow, the new widow received a private warning: "Your Majesty will be able to draw conclusions for yourself, and realize that there is not only danger ahead, but that the enemy is in the household, and the strictest watch ought to be kept on the members of the present cabinet."[2]

Warnings soon became more specific when she was told that "the American minister, J. L. Stevens, with the aid of some of our residents" was scheming to overthrow her government. She admitted later that she "gave little heed to it at the time."[3]

Stop the Presses

Perhaps if she had heeded the warnings in a timelier manner, history might have turned out differently, because by the end of January 1893, it was widely known that there had been a revolution in Hawai'i. As soon as ships arrived at the dock in San Francisco with this stunning and inexplicable news, headlines around the world proclaimed that Queen Lili'uokalani was deposed from her throne. More shocking to the American correspondents was the news that their own citizens were the revolutionists who succeeded in overthrowing the government of Hawai'i.

The saga of the Hawaiian Revolution reveals a history full of paradoxes. After the benevolent works the missionaries accomplished in the first part of the nineteenth century, the schism between their descendants and the Hawaiian rulers had grown progressively wider and increasingly contentious. There is a well-known saying, with an unknown origin, in Hawai'i today regarding those early missionaries: "They came to do good, and they did right well." In fact, historical documents reveal that most came poor, lived poor, and died poor. But their children did much better. By the time Ida Pope arrived, many of the male descendants of those early missionaries were now the principal industrial leaders of the

Lili'uokalani, defiantly regal during the coup d'état. *UCSD Libraries.*

islands. Born in Hawai'i, they were bilingual and bicultural. Many of them had been sent to the United States for their education and returned as doctors, lawyers, merchants, and planters and amassed great wealth in the islands.[4]

In 1887 a group of them and their sympathizers formed a secret organization called the Hawaiian League. In the same year, they forced upon King Kalākaua a new, more liberal constitution. It became known as the Bayonet Constitution, because it was purportedly signed under a threat of force. This new constitution benefitted the businessmen's financial interests but eliminated every vestige of the king's monarchical powers, leaving him to reign but not rule.

Ida at the Queen's Prorogation

When Lydia Dominis succeeded her brother in 1890 and began her reign as Queen Lili'uokalani, she was determined to negate the constitution signed by her brother. She privately drafted a constitution of her own and waited for an opportunity to proclaim it and reclaim her sovereignty and the rights of her native subjects.[5] The date chosen for the proclamation was Saturday, January 14, 1893, and when this day was over, the Kawaiaha'o Seminary girls' lives would be irrevocably changed.

Carrie Winter's personal correspondence and published *Hartford Courant* newspaper articles as well as Lilla Appleton's unpublished diary titled

"Revolutionary" provide an intimate glimpse into what the residents of Kawaiahaʻo Seminary were experiencing during this uncertain time. Lilla's diary begins with a speculation on the queen's motives: "It seems the Queen had determined she should abolish the present constitution, obtained by the Revolution of 1887, and resume with slight changes. The object being to decrease the power of the foreigners and increase her own, to the extent of being nearly absolute in power."[6]

The queen's ceremony of proroguing the legislature would take place at noon with pageantry that Ida Pope did not want to miss. She, her sister Katherine, who was now teaching English at the Kamehameha School for Boys, and Carrie and Lilla quickly walked up the road to the government building to hear firsthand the much-anticipated proclamation. Lilla's diary entry revealed her feminine awe of the queen's "costume" and ceremonial pageantry.

> The Royal Band played in the Government Building Yard and when they struck up the National Anthem we knew Her Majesty was approaching. About a minute or two before twelve she entered. Four kahili bearers preceded her, carrying magnificent kahilis. They stationed themselves on either side of the throne. The Queen wore the most magnificent costume I have ever seen. Her robe was rich lavender silk or satin (I thought satin). She carried a long train probably about five (some say six) yards in length. She was gorgeously adorned with decorations and badges and the dress itself was trimmed with lace and ostrich feathers, short sleeves, low neck, white kid gloves, and a lovely coronet of diamonds in her hair. The Royal Feather Cloak was spread over her chair, a tablet was handed her from which she read her prorogation address first in Hawaiian then in English ending with the words "I now declare this Legislature prorogued."[7]

After the address, when the queen stood to make her way across the road to the palace with the intention of getting her new constitution signed, Lilla noted that the four of them, realizing they were witnessing something momentous, rushed to the steps for the best view of her departure back to the palace.

> The audience remained standing while the Queen was in the room and we made a rush for the corridor as soon as she went out. Our party took a stand on the stairs where we had a fine view of Her Majesty as she came out to the carriage. Her carriage was drawn up in front of the door. A rug in front of her seat, a strip of carpeting was spread down for her to walk to the carriage upon. Four stalwart men walking side by side carried her

train. The Royal Band played as they drove out of the yard. The Kahili Bearers walked beside the carriage and the show was over.[8]

Lilla noted the lack of representation for the queen's event: "Her Majesty must, I think, have been painfully conscious that not a white face showed itself among her legislators as she stood before them in all the splendor of her Royal Robes."[9] The strange absence of "white faces" would make more sense as the day unfolded.

The Queen's Betrayal

Historical documents reveal that once back at the palace, the queen summoned her cabinet ministers to sign the new constitution. They refused, and Lilla recapped this historical event.

> She summoned her new ministers whom she had evidently chosen because she thought they would be docile accomplices and commanded them to sign the new constitution. To her surprise and dismay they refused to do it. She urged, entreated and commanded but either because they did not wish to, or more probably because they did not dare to, steadfastly refused, and asked for fifteen minutes to consider the matter. Taking advantage of this brief release, they escaped from the palace and hastily went to some of the prominent men asking if they would be supported if they persisted in refusing the queen's command. Probably they were not only assured that they would be supported in that course, but also that every one of them might be expected to bitterly repent it if they did sign it.[10]

Queen Lili'uokalani's intentions in making her proclamation—and the turmoil that followed it—have been well covered by historians. In the views of most American businessmen living in Hawai'i, the act of reversing the constitution would be revolutionary in that it would hurt their business interests. The queen was ultimately coerced into a postponement and went to the Throne Room at 4 p.m. with the update.[11] By all accounts, she was defiantly regal as she passionately addressed the "Princes, Nobles and Representatives" in her native tongue.[12]

> The present constitution is full of defects. It is so faulty that I think a new one should be granted. I have prepared one in which the rights of all have been regarded—a constitution suited to the wishes of the people. I was ready and expected to proclaim the new constitution today as a suitable occasion for it, and thus satisfy the wishes of my dear people. But with

regret I say I have met with obstacles that prevent it. Return to your homes peaceably and quietly and continue to look toward me and I will look toward you. Keep me ever in your love. I am obliged to postpone the granting of the constitution for a few days. You have my love and with sorrow I now dismiss you.[13]

A few minutes later, she went out on the upper balcony of the palace to address the patiently waiting crowd, who were almost exclusively Hawaiians. Blaming her duplicitous ministers, she told them she was unable to give them the constitution and asked for patience, to which she received three cheers.[14]

After the teachers returned to the school, a neighbor soon arrived with the news that all women in town had been advised to stay inside their dwellings. Lilla, feeling that some excitement had finally begun to happen, would not be deterred by any such "request." After all, she "had an errand to do" and besides, "I wanted to see what was going on." Before she could leave to run her "errand," fellow teacher Margaret Kenwill ran into the room at 4 p.m., shouting that "the Queen was standing on the upper balcony leaning over the railing and addressing a great crowd of natives in the palace yard! Hurry up—go back!"[15]

Only Ida and Lilla ran up the road and pushed through the crowd, but "by the time we were back at the palace, the Queen had gone."[16] They encountered a great uproar among the throngs assembled. Antagonisms long held in check had reached the point of an outbreak. Lilla sensed "trouble was brewing" and noted the growing unrest "which betokened the gathering of a storm."[17]

Nonetheless, the ladies weren't leaving without a full report of the queen's balcony speech. They searched the crowd for witnesses. Ida soon found a fellow Ohioan, attorney Willie Whitney, who told them that what *followed* the queen's speech was more interesting than what she had actually said. He told them William Punohuaweoweoulaokalani White, who helped the queen draft the new constitution, had climbed the outside palace steps to give his own speech. He told his fellow Hawaiians that the queen had been betrayed and that instead of going home peaceably, as Her Majesty suggested, they should rise to her defense and "kill and bury" the traitors.[18]

The feeling of uncertainty and alarm was intense among those who defied the queen's authority. Soon, a group was organized to prevent any arrests made by the queen. This Committee of Safety, composed of thirteen men, strategized late into the evening on the best way to dethrone the queen permanently. Meanwhile, after the girls were sent to bed, the teachers dissected the events of the day, and Carrie wrote, "We are all so stirred up we hardly know what to think."[19]

Prayer and Gossip

The following day, Sunday, January 15, the teachers arrived early for church in order to gain the latest political news. Carrie sardonically stated that "prayer and politics" went together in Honolulu and "What was one to do if one is in a city where all the leading men attend prayer meetings and do some of their best talking there?"[20]

Meanwhile, the queen was having her own prayer meeting at the palace, where she "charged the native pastors present to pray for her, as evil-minded foreigners were endeavoring to deprive her of her throne."[21] The Committee of Safety members skipped church that day in order to strategize their next moves. They met at William Castle's home, formed committees, and decided to call a mass meeting of citizens on the following day in order to gauge their level of support for a proposed dethronement. Those loyal to the queen, the Royalists, caught wind of it, and planned their own counter–mass meeting at the exact time in the Palace Square. Posters were put up all over town on Sunday to publicize the Royalists' meeting.[22] Lilla noted the attempt by the annexation committee to minimize attendance: "The handbills have been pasted over the others."

That evening, after collecting more political news at an evening prayer meeting, Carrie heard that annexation was the only outcome that would be considered by the Committee of Safety. "It is late, but I cannot let the day end without a word on the latest rumors. I came for church tonight with Mr. Cooke [Charles Montague Cooke] He says the business men are determined now and that the outlook is that she will be deposed, a provisional government established, looking toward annexation. All the business houses are to be closed. No one knows what tomorrow will hold. We may have our hands full with the girls."[23]

Even though the queen had abandoned her idea of promulgating a new constitution and was going to make a proclamation to that effect, the committee, under Lorrin Thurston, the grandson of two of the first Christian missionaries to Hawai'i, would not relent. "What guarantee have we that this will not happen again? It is like living on a volcano, there is no telling when it will break out."[24]

Monday Mass Meetings

As the Kawaiaha'o schoolgirls were engaged in their lessons at 2 p.m. on Monday, January 16, the mass meeting at the Old Armory, virtually in their backyard, erupted into shouts to oust their queen. Mr. Thurston told his enthusiastic supporters that Lili'uokalani could not be trusted and there was no turning back.[25] The attendees at the "native" meeting were tame by comparison. A cautionary message had been sent by the queen with the directive to avoid violence or disorder,[26] creating a mood that was "constrained and unnatural."[27]

That evening Lilla recorded, "I can hardly compose myself to write. In fact, I can hardly get my own consent to stay in my room long enough to write for fear some additional item of news will come while I am up here which I shall miss."[28] She wrote, "The citizens are arming and news comes tonight that the marines have landed."[29] The marines numbered 160, and when they disembarked from the *Boston* in a show of support for the coup d'état, it was an intimidating scene. The Committee of Safety, purportedly out of fear for public safety and property,[30] implored their ally, American minister John Stevens, to order the disembarkation to assist in maintaining order as they officially deposed the queen and established a provisional government.[31]

At Kawaiahaʻo Seminary, everyone heard the marines marching in the night. Lilla recorded the tension that deprived the school of sleep: "They staid in town all night. The girls have been remarkably quiet through it all. The fire alarm rang twice during the night and it was rather noisy." Hearing rumors that missionary houses would be set on fire in retaliation did not worry Carrie, who felt "we at least are safe with all these Hawaiian girls in our charge."[32]

The Shot on Fort Street

On Tuesday, January 17, the school was awakened to news that something big was going to happen before the day was out. After breakfast, "several of the natives came for their children to take them out of school."[33] Defying another request that all women stay inside, Ida scurried to the center of the town in search of facts. After she heard a "man order two more rifle-guns, saw the marines around the legation and heard that much more was to happen," she returned to school to begin the structured schedule she felt the girls needed.[34] But Lilla didn't see why she should remain indoors and implored Annie Van Anglen, the sewing teacher, to accompany her to the post office, with the real intention of hunting down news.

> I had not fully realized how much the excitement had increased since yesterday and was surprised to find the streets lined with men for most of the way to the post office. If they had looked fierce or desperate or revengeful, I should have been frightened and turned back, but everything was quiet, and though I suppose many of the men must have been armed, the arms were not apparent. So we went on. There was somewhat of a crowd about the government building, but everything was quiet. We mailed the

The gun fired on Fort Street precipitated the revolution. *Library of Congress 3c04480u.*

letters, saw just one white woman there beside ourselves, and turned away feeling very much out of place.[35]

The two teachers decided to run another errand, down Fort Street, and witnessed the excitement turn to violence when it was feared ammunition was being taken to the Royalists.

We had gone as far as the Golden Rule Bazaar when a policeman darted from the sidewalk and tried to stop a man in a carriage going up the street with a load of ammunition. He declined to be arrested and the policeman blew his whistle for help. The driver urged on his horse. The policeman seized him by the bridle. The driver lashed him with his whip. The policeman held on. He reached his hand for his pistol. At any rate, the driver reached for his own saying "I must either hurt or be hurt," fired and hit the policeman. His horse then sprang forward and another policeman jumped into an express but the expressman religiously kept a block behind saying he "did not want to be shot." Almost instantly, a crowd had sprung up. In the midst of it, the sound of the shot was calling men on the run from everywhere. For a few moments, our way was blocked by men hurrying up to see what was going on. Miss Van Anglen was thoroughly frightened "O come! Come! Come!" She exclaimed. "Lets get out of this" "No" I said "Step in here and wait till the crowd has passed."[36]

Lilla made it back to the school to report on the day's "thrilling excitement" and growing tension on the streets. "Marines were stationed in the yard next to the opera house and near the palace. The houses of business have been practically closed. For the first time, the streets are almost deserted so far as women are concerned. The streets are lined with men who stand around talking or silent. 'Something will be done before night' was the word which came to us, and later, 'The blow will be struck at three o'clock.' Just what it would be we did not know."[37]

Diverting the Girls

Lilla's reports of witnessing a policeman shot must have seemed like the beginning of something terrible to Ida. As principal, it was up to her to be a stabilizing force and create a safe haven for the 142 girls under her care. Her job, as she saw it, was first and foremost to keep them as unaware as she could of the turmoil and confusion outside their windows. She knew that the girls would gain security from the predictability of routine, and she insisted that exposure to alarming information be limited, especially as it related to their queen, whom they revered.

Lilla recorded that Miss Pope, hoping to distract the girls from the frightening sounds on the street in front of them, wisely "turned back the clock to keep the girls in sewing longer for we did not know but firing might begin at any moment."[38] Ida did not want the girls to congregate unattended by an adult and made sure the teachers were on a rotation schedule. Then when the sounds on the street in front of the school became frightening, they all "met together for singing—to keep them from scattering in case anything should occur to frighten them."[39] That afternoon, they "could only wait with breathless anxiety for further developments."[40] They listened intently for "the sound of shots" and spoke in hushed tones, "lest the students should find what was going on and precipitate a panic."[41]

They soon found out what the big news was. At 2:30 p.m., on the steps of the Ali'iōlani Hale [former seat of government of the Kingdom of Hawai'i], a proclamation was made that the Hawaiian monarchial system was officially over and a provisional government would exist until terms with the United States could be agreed upon.[42] The queen, deserted by her cabinet ministry, was held in the police station during the proclamation.[43] At 6:00 p.m., with her head held high, Queen Liliʻuokalani, in order to prevent loss of life, officially surrendered her authority under protest. Carrie marveled at the queen's docility. "The Queen's party had an immense quantity of ammunition, had they just turned their guns, killed two or three of the leading men and roused the natives to deeds of violence all of which it is now known they had carefully planned—why one doesn't dare to think what would have been the consequences."[44]

Kamehameha School for Boys teacher Caroline Babb echoed Carrie's sentiments in a letter to her brother.

> We knew that the Queen's Party had such an advantage in ammunition. The Armory was full and the other side (whites) had very little. The suspense of those two days was awful—we can never be grateful enough that bloodshed was averted. After all the whites have done and are doing for the Hawaiians it would be a dreadful thing for one to spill the others blood—We all feel so thankful.[45]

That evening, martial law was ordered and the entire governance of Oʻahu was under total military control. All citizens were ordered to turn over any arms and ammunition in their possession.[46] These were tumultuous days for the occupants of Kawaiahaʻo Seminary, with teachers themselves taking different political sides. The children heard rumors and witnessed great turmoil taking place literally outside their school walls, but they were helpless to find the whole truth behind the filtered information offered them. However, Lilla notes the boys up at the Kamehameha School had their own sources and were not as easily diverted: "There have been various exhibitions of bitterness on the part of the boys at Kamehameha, and the feeling seems to increase rather than diminish. Fortunately, we have escaped much of it here. We have been very careful to speak guardedly before the girls and for the most part have spoken not at all. I wish the matter would get settled soon in some way or other."[47]

Lilla was right that things were not so quiet up at the Kamehameha School for Boys, as recorded by teacher Eleanor Little.

> All the boys were staunch supporters of the Queen, of course, and many tried to smuggle arms into the dormitories. Some tried to run away and join the rebels, but they were circumvented. The teachers all went armed and patrolled the grounds every night. You see, if the rebels had been successful, their plan was to seize the school, and use the brick buildings as their headquarters.[48]

Teacher Caroline Babb worried about the boys' increasing disdain over what they perceived as Christian hypocrisy.

> We hate to have our boys come back from town each week loaded with such sentiments as these: "White men come here; they say they love our people; they teach Christ's words: then they go down town: they hold guns against our people. We no believe them." It is so unfortunate a good many of our boys are surly over it.[49]

Charles Bishop, married into Hawaiian royalty, knew full well how the boys felt and said, "Whatever happens, whatever is the outcome of the present state of political affairs," the "Hawaiian flag would always be the flag of the Kamehameha Schools."[50]

The Queen's Girls

By Wednesday, January 18, Lilla noted that downtown was "quiet," with "no outbreaks or mobs."[51] This lull must have given the queen time to pause and wonder how she could practically and morally support Hawaiian girls in a school run by American trustees who played key roles in her dethronement. There were four pupils closely attached to her royal household, including her namesake, Lydia. The queen also contemplated how twenty-seven others might retain their royal scholarships, since her funds had been seized. Her first action was to send a message to Miss Pope that her four girls should pack their belongings and return to her side at Washington Place. They were Lydia Aholo and the three daughters of two of the queen's retainers, namely, Myra Heleluhe and sisters Nancy and Mary Ahia.

On Thursday, January 19, Lilla noted that Ida fearfully opened the letter. "The Queen gave notice that she should take out her four girls on Monday and would consider in regard to the twenty-seven paid for by the Liliʻuokalani Educational Society—it will be a heady blow to the school."[52] In a letter to her mother, Fanny, in Vermont, Lilla placed part of the blame for the predicament on Ida. "I have always advised Miss Pope not to take in so many of her girls, for it was likely something would happen to disaffect the Queen, in which case the withdrawal of her patronage would be a very serious blow to the school and now the blow has come."[53]

But something or someone changed the queen's mind, because the four girls were told over the weekend they could remain until the end of the school year. And then Mrs. Milania Ahia was personally sent by the queen to report to Ida that all her girls on scholarship would also continue with their education. Miss Pope thinks it almost too good to be believe and is "surprised with joy.[54]

Even though the queen found a way to pay for pupils' room and board despite her political predicament, William R. Castle publicly condemned her. Representing himself as a trustee for the school, he told readers of the *Boston Evening Transcript* that despite the queen's good intentions for native girls, her "evil" nature cost her the throne.

> Until her overthrow, the queen paid one thousand dollars a year of the expenses of twenty native girls in Kawaiahao Seminary. They were known as the queen's girls. She was desirous that the natives should get the best that education could give them. She has many good traits of character, curiously mingled with evil. Had she been content to reign as a constitutional monarch, she would have been queen today. But she determined to tread under her feet all constitutional principals and to regain the lost despotic powers of her heathen ancestors, and she dashed against the rock of nineteenth-century progress and fell.[55]

Her Ex-Majesty

A week after Lili'uokalani was ordered to remove the Hawaiian flag that waved over her private residence, she prepared to leave Honolulu for a few days. In a gesture that demonstrated no resentment toward the American teachers, she sent word through Miss Pope to "call on her when she returns."[56] Lilla wondered how to greet the woman who was no longer sovereign and who had indeed, in her opinion, never been ruler of American citizens in Hawai'i.

> We think it will be quite a lark to go visit her, but what can we say in the way of condolence and how shall we address her! We surely cannot longer say "Your Majesty." For that matter, however, I did not say it when she was queen. She descended upon us one day last year with her "ladies in waiting," and much to our consternation visited the school. We thought she would go after chapel prayers, but no; she visited every room. As my class was the oldest girls, she naturally stayed a little longer there than in the other rooms. I don't remember much about what we did. I believe the girls recited their Sunday recitation, but I did remember very vividly afterward that I never once addressed her as "Your Majesty," nor did I rise when she left the room.[57]

By Monday evening on January 30, reports of an uprising by armed Royalists caused fear and anxiety in Lilla. "The rumor is afloat tonight that attempts will be made between now and Wednesday to get possession of the government building by the Royalist Party. Two men with guns were seen Saturday night prowling around Kawaiahao church, or some say Kawaiahao Seminary. I shall feel like leaving a lantern burning for a good many nights yet."[58]

On Tuesday, January 31, Lilla recorded attempts to quell any subversion by those loyal to the queen. "Two new laws have been enacted: one against importing firearms except by permission of the government, the other against speaking or printing seditious matter."[59] She commented on what she perceived to be the response of the Hawaiians to the ousting of their queen: "So far they take it much more calmly than one could expect, but I do not think they fully realize yet what has been done. They have not fully comprehended yet that they no longer live in a monarchy. They still speak of their ex-sovereign as Queen, and in fact we all do. It is hard for ourselves to realize that there has been a complete and entire revolution not only in form but in name."[60]

Ida Gets a Paid Ticket Out

On the first Monday of February, Ida woke up to a broken window and her desk demolished. The *Advertiser* reported that the very day martial law was lifted, an "attempted raid on Kawaiahaʻo Seminary" occurred in the middle of the night.

> Entering by a window which had been left unfastened, the burglar proceeded to the desk of the principal, which was supposed to contain money. The desk was locked, and none of the keys from a bunch hanging near could be persuaded to fit. The burglar then hacked the desk pretty freely with a knife. The would-be thief got nothing for his pains, but carried off a door key, so that he evidently plans another visit.[61]

Ida wouldn't be around if and when the housebreaker made a new visit because she found a temporary way out of the mayhem. She told trustee J. B. Atherton that she would be the volunteer they needed to escort "insane" Eva Harris to a San Francisco asylum. Lilla wrote that it was necessary to get the hysterical teacher away from the children because "every indication is that she is much worse and will continue to grow worse, until she is hopelessly insane if indeed she is that already. It is too bad—so young, so pretty and so bright! She is determined not to go and we fear she will have to be taken by force, and it seems terrible."[62]

Katherine Pope stayed behind to teach at the school for boys while Ida went home to their family. Ida apparently kept it a secret from most that she had accepted another job offer, because her friend Caroline Babb seemed unaware that her time was limited at Kawaiahaʻo. "Miss Ida Pope, Prin. of Kawaiahao Sem. sails to take home a Miss Harris Sem. Teacher who is insane. Miss Pope will be at her

Ida, never an equestrian, holds the reins for sister Katherine in Kawaiahaʻo Seminary's school-yard, 1893. *Author's collection.*

home in Bucyrus, Ohio until next Aug. when she will come back to her old place for two or three years more. Wish you could see her she is a beautiful woman—sister to our Miss Katherine Pope and far more brilliant."[63]

Ida undoubtedly knew she would have her hands full with Eva, but she was homesick for her family and six months, an entire term, out of political chaos, all expenses paid, was just what she needed. After depositing her patient in a sanitarium, she would head to Ohio. As a favor to the trustees, she would also actively recruit and return in August with qualified teachers for Kawaiahaʻo Seminary, undoubtedly with an eye out for her new school's staffing needs.

The American Flag Goes Up

On the morning of February 1, Minister John L. Stevens raised the American flag in Honolulu and declared the existence of an American protectorate over the islands. On this same day he wrote to the U.S. State Department, "The Hawaiian pear is now fully ripe, and this is the golden hour for the United States to pluck it."[64] To make sure the "golden hour" would not be missed, three commissioners from the new provisional government arrived in Washington on February 3 to create an annexation treaty. One of those three commissioners was Kawaiahaʻo Seminary trustee William Castle, who regaled a large group at a Sunday picnic with his account of the adventure, as recorded by Lilla.

> "All the way over," he said, "we were hard at work getting things into shape for the American papers. By the time we reached San Francisco everything was all ready for the papers. We rushed to the office of the associated press and said "Can you get some more news into your paper this morning? There's been a revolution in Hawaii. The Queen is dethroned." The manager rushed to the telephone, pulled down [the] lever and roars *"Stop those presses!"*[65]
>
> For two or three days we were completely lost to the world. We actually had to buy papers to know whether anything was happening in the world or not. But long before we reached Chicago the fun began, we were besieged by reporters on every hand. When we reached Washington, we were surprised to look up and see the Hawaiian flag floating over the hotel. The flag remained there during our entire stay in Washington.[66]
>
> On our return, we stopped at Chicago to visit the cyclorama of the Volcano which is now being built for the World's Fair. Passing through one of the buildings I was surprised to see way up on one end, the Hawaiian flag. I enquired of one of the workmen "What's that flag up there?" "O" he said "I believe that belongs to that little group of islands we're going to annex."[67]

With delegations from both sides in or on their way to Washington, D.C., strange sounds on February 4 alarmed the residents of Kawaiahaʻo Seminary when they heard "two heavy volleys of cannon" but "were relieved to find that it was nothing more serious than the reception of President Dole on board the *Boston*."[68] As Lilla noted, the cannons proclaimed Sanford Dole, the son of missionaries, as the president of the provisional government. After this proclamation, Lilla seemed to have a change of heart towards the queen's circumstances.

> All is "quiet on the Potomac" politically. The American flag floats on the Government Building, although the Hawaiian flag still floats in the government yard. It seems very strange indeed that all these things could happen without the shedding of blood, but we are all very thankful that it is so. Personally I would rather see the Hawaiian flag floating here, than the stars

and stripes, except that I know it is better for the country under the circumstances to join the Union. Never-the-less, I feel sorry for the queen.[69]

Ida was in Bucyrus on February 16, when the news spread that President Har-
rison sent a dispatch to the Senate, formally requesting annexation of the Hawaiian kingdom. But incoming President Cleveland, following his inauguration three
weeks later, sent a message to the Senate, canceling all further talk of annexation.
In Hawai'i, John Stevens was disgusted and immediately resigned and prepared
to return to Maine. The annexationists, grateful for his role on their behalf, passed
the collection basket around in order to send him away with $1,000.

The American Flag Goes Down

March 29, 1893, was an important day for both annexationists and Royalists.
President Grover Cleveland sent James H. Blount on a fact-finding mission to investigate the true conditions of the coup d'état and the role Americans played in
the event. Lilla described the ostentatious patriotic efforts of the annexationists,
who hoped to portray Honolulu as an American town.

> The United States commissioner arrived unexpectedly. It was telephoned
> all around town that he was coming, and forthwith out came the red, white,
> and blue and up went the Stars and Stripes all over the town. Never before
> has there been so gorgeous a display on any Fourth of July in as that which
> greeted Commissioner Blount. Long before the steamer touched the wharf,
> a multitude of banners were fluttering in the breeze. On one street, a single
> flag (Hawaiian) was conspicuous among its foreign associates. On another,
> two large flags were suspended across the street side by side, one bearing
> the word "Welcome"; the other, "Aloha." Everybody's face wore a look of
> expectancy and everybody's neighbor was saying, "What's the news?"
> "Who's come?" "Where are they?" "Is it annexation?"[70]

The spring found politics virtually at a standstill while Commissioner Blount
investigated the situation. Both sides waited expectantly until July 17, when
Mr. Blount delivered his report to President Cleveland, condemning the actions
of the Americans who overthrew the monarchy. Given the power to reverse any
of the acts of the American military officers respecting the revolution, he ordered
the admiral, "You are directed to haul down the United States' ensign from the
Government building, and to embark the troops now on shore."[71] Lilla recorded
the annexationists' shock when the Hawaiian flag was re-hoisted: "Everybody was
surprised, native as well as foreigners, when a few days after his arrival the Stars

and Stripes were silently lowered from the capital building and the Hawaiian flag was silently raised in its place. Could Cleveland have heard the private howl which went up from many a throat."[72]

By the end of the year, President Dole had to respond to the demand of President Cleveland to return the government back to Queen Liliʻuokalani, abolish the Republic, and restore the monarchy. Dole brazenly declined to abdicate and told the president of the United States that he now had no right to interfere in Hawaiian matters.

Carrie Winter Goes Home

Soon after arriving with Ida in 1890, Carrie Prudence Winter wrote many special interest stories on Hawaiʻi for the *Hartford Courant* published under the byline "C.P.W." She had a gift with a pen and became a prolific contributor on all things "Hawaii." Lilla Appleton benefitted from Carrie's entrepreneurial spirit by taking the photographs for the articles and earned herself five dollars, exactly half of what Carrie made. As Hawaiian politics became increasingly tumultuous, Carrie was encouraged by the editor to switch from glorious sunsets over Diamond Head to the falling of the Hawaiian monarchy. While many newspapers in Hawaiʻi and in the United States questioned the legitimacy of the new government, Carrie's articles were outspoken in favor of Sanford Dole's provisional government.

As Carrie continued in Honolulu as a campaigning correspondent for annexation, Ida was thoroughly enjoying time with her family. She split her time between Bucyrus where her newly married sister Lois Prosser lived in their family home and in Chicago where her mother, sister, and brothers now resided. In her travels, Ida learned that America was evenly divided on the issue of annexing the Hawaiian Islands. Part of the division was party-political, with the Republicans in favor of annexation and the Democrats against it. Ida's father had been a staunch Democrat, her brother William edited a Democratic newspaper, and her brother Henry was a firm Republican. No doubt, the entire family had spirited discussions with her throughout the summer on the "Hawaiian Question."

As Ida was preparing to return to Honolulu, Carrie was preparing to depart. Carrie and Ida embarked on the journey together in the summer of 1890, never imagining they would witness the greatest political turmoil the Hawaiians ever experienced. As Carrie packed her memories after three exhilarating years to go home and marry Dr. Charles A. Kofoid, she wrote him, "I shall always have tales of that revolution to tell."[73] Ida, packing her own trunk, knew the political storm had just begun to brew, and she would collect even far more compelling tales in the years to come.

CHAPTER NINE

Endings

Kawaiaha'o Seminary, 1893–1894

When a startling five hundred citizens turned out at the Bucyrus train depot to wave goodbye to Ida and her recruited teachers from the community, it was newsworthy. In August of 1893, the *Bucyrus Journal* praised her as the "most efficient teacher ever raised in this community."[1] It was big news that Miss Ida Pope had recruited several local ladies to return to the distant outpost of Honolulu with her for two-year commitments.

Ida and her new staff of eight excited teachers left on the *Monowai* from San Francisco on August 17, reaching Honolulu eight days later. The journey was perfect, and Ida enjoyed the company of old friends from her hometown. One of those dear friends, Ida Whan Sturgeon, had brought along her ten-year-old daughter, Nora, who undoubtedly enlivened the group.

Ida was confident in her selection of handpicked teachers. She felt anticipation and a sense of well-being that she hadn't experienced in some time. She couldn't wait to get started. Even the *Monowai* cooperated by breaking her own record, and Ida, with her bevy of teachers, descended the gangplank on Friday morning, August 25, far ahead of the scheduled time, as reported in the *Honolulu Advertiser.*

Everything seemed to be moving according to plan. She was glad to be back in Hawai'i and anxious to get her new teachers trained for the upcoming fall term, which was only ten days away. The *Hawaiian Gazette* reprinted the *Bucyrus Journal* story in its entirety, and other Honolulu editors also found it noteworthy to report on the arrival of such a large contingency of American teachers from Ohio.[2]

Slander

Ida was delighted at the local interest until she picked up the newspaper the following morning. It had taken only twenty-four hours to remind her that she had returned to slanted journalism and horrid politics. Sereno Bishop, editor of *The Friend,* reported favorably on "The capable Principal's" arrival in "Kawaiahao Seminary"[3] and then astounded Ida by ending the story with disparaging words about the school's most loyal and ardent supporter, Queen Lili'uokalani: "Kawaia-hao Seminary would now be much improved due to the removal of the corrupt-ing influences of the Monarchy."[4]

In disbelief, Ida instantly sought an audience with the queen at her residence, in order to personally assure her that the annexationist slander in the article didn't represent her views. Ida found the queen infuriated and unsure of what to believe. Ida returned to school and fumed in a letter to Carrie Winter, now home in Connecticut, "The article was written with malice, and her late Majesty was incensed."[5]

In the seven months since the queen had been dethroned—six of which the apolitical Ida had gratefully missed—newspapers were looking everywhere for stories to fuel either the annexation movement or the restoration of the monar-chy movement. Nearly every newspaper published in Hawai'i had a libel suit against it. Ida would have to watch every word she said. As it turned out, even doing that wasn't enough.

Ida and Lili'uokalani at Odds

Apart from having her educational ally Queen Lili'uokalani now reduced to a citizen who went by "Mrs. Dominis," other changes soon became apparent. The most significant difference was the steep decline in enrollment. When Ida had left in February, there were 142 girls, the largest attendance in the school's history. In August, she returned to eighty-three girls, and many of them were there only because they were sponsored orphans.

The *Daily Bulletin* caught wind of the decline in school enrollment and re-ported that the sponsorship of twenty girls by the Lili'uokalani Educational Soci-ety had been revoked and that "many other girls have been withdrawn by parents and guardians" in a massive political protest.[6] Ida knew that this type of news could provoke a further decline in enrollment. She worried that if those twenty girls were indeed forced to leave, only sixty-three would remain, hardly enough to justify her newly recruited staff of teachers.

Shortly thereafter, the *Hawaiian Gazette* noted Miss Pope's movements around town as she sought donations from the wealthy missionary societies in order to maintain support for those girls in need.[7] She needed $1,000 to pay ex-penses for the coming year. To make matters worse, the revolution had destabi-lized the economy, and those second-generation missionary families who had kept Kawaiaha'o Seminary afloat over the past decades weren't inclined to con-tinue their benevolence. Ida's efforts were stymied, and the fate of the twenty girls who were orphans hung in the balance.

Lili'uokalani's private residence, Washington Place, fashioned after Mount Vernon, 1846. *Library of Congress 058017pu.*

Given the situation, Ida once again requested and was granted an audience with Lili'uokalani in order to discuss her continued patronage of the scholarship recipients, but to Ida's disappointment, the queen proved noncommittal. Then, as she was leaving Washington Place, Ida encountered Mrs. Cornelia Bishop on Beretania Street. It's easy enough to imagine the two women standing in the Hawaiian sun that day, exchanging what Ida thought were innocuous pleasantries about her meeting with the queen, but that brief conversation resulted in damaging consequences to her relationship with Lili'uokalani.

Cornelia relayed to her husband, journalist Sereno Bishop, that Miss Pope had exited Washington Place in a bit of a fluster, and speculations surrounding their meeting soon turned into "facts." Almost immediately, the *Hawaiian Star* slandered both Lili'uokalani and Ida in "The Ex-Queen Certain of Restoration, She Tells a Lady That Orders Will Be Received on Wednesday to Put Her on the Throne."[8] The "lady" in the headline is Ida. The editor then reported—most injuriously to Lili'uokalani—unsubstantiated plans to execute and imprison those who led the revolt against her. Ida, now thoroughly enraged, publicly confronted the editor of the *Hawaiian Star* and demanded that her rebuttal be printed. "The interview between the late Queen and myself was not a matter of public concern, and touched upon political affairs only as they might affect the Seminary. Her late Majesty has always taken a deep interest in Kawaiahao Seminary both by her good advice and material aid, and I deeply regret the publication of any article that will influence the natives against the school."[9]

The *Star's* editor, Walter G. Smith, published his own rebuttal with no real effort to apologize to Ida for falsely attributing harmful quotes about the queen to her name.

> Miss Pope:
>
> I have not the pleasure of your acquaintance, but I think it just to say that the information upon which the Star's report of your interview with the late Queen was based, did not reach us from you or with your knowledge. It came from sources which we have had reason to think were well informed as to the political views and sentiments of the ex-sovereign.[10]

Unfortunately, the damage to her reputation in the Hawaiian community had begun before the retraction was published. The *Hawaii Holomua,* a newspaper whose readers sympathized with the Royalist Party, attempted to portray Miss Pope, the authority figure mentioned, in a hypocritical light.

> The letters from W. G. Smith of the Star and Miss Pope, published in yesterday's issue, only serve to show that the same crowd who, during the past 7 or 8 months have been calling Queen Liliuokalani, in print and behind her back, a vile sensual degraded heathen. Just think of it, here on one side, are the authorities of the school trying to induce the Queen to send back to Kawaiahao those children who have hitherto been supported by her, while on the other hand, on the last page of The Friend for September, the bigoted editor of that paper states that Kawaiahao will now prosper because the "vile Queen" has ceased to have any influence or association with the seminary.[11]

It's easy to understand the outrage by many who had witnessed the queen's dedication to Kawaiahaʻo Seminary besides personally funding the education of many girls. When any fund-raisers were held, Liliʻuokalani with her full retinue arrived in grand style and liberally spent. The queen even had a standing order for the bread made by Kawaiahaʻo pupils for her personal kitchen in order to set an example in the community. When there were school musicals, she offered her own compositions and personally coached the school's music teacher and pupils. And when Kawaiahaʻo Church was being readied for a public event, she sent beautiful flowers and vines from her private garden to enhance the decoration. Her royal attendance at the yearly academic recitals made the events significant in the minds of the pupils. She had even honored the missionary teachers, offering her Waikīkī home for peaceful retreats, and included them in royal galas both at her home and at the palace.

Sadly, the slanted journalism about the queen attached to Ida's name soon caused a rift in their four-year relationship. The first hint came in a letter Ida wrote to Carrie. In it, she noted that the "Powers at Washington Place" were purposely going against fund-raising efforts for scholarship. "We rec'd the money from the Queen in payment of her last year's bill but she is using her influence against us."[12] It seemed slander had succeeded in forcing apart the two formidable women who had always felt only mutual respect toward one another. They had been close allies in the operation of the school and most importantly, in the joint parenting of Lydia Aholo, now fifteen. Lili'uokalani, out of funds, reluctantly withdrew her patronage, stating, "The education of the young girls of Hawaiian birth" since the "changed conditions of January, 1893, obliged me to live in retirement."[13]

It was up to Ida, once again, to carefully disseminate the information to the household of worried girls in order to maintain stability. It was a horrible start to what was supposed to be an exciting new school year. These were anxious days for the residents of Kawaiaha'o Seminary, and perhaps because of the stress, Ida came down with a severe case of the grippe that sent her to bed for weeks. Once she was able to resume corresponding with family and friends, she wrote to Carrie that being stuck in bed and out of commission wasn't all that bad considering the raging politics outside the school's doors. She even began to look at the reduction in enrollment as a blessing because her load had lightened considerably. She told Carrie that fewer girls made the school easier to work in and joked, "There is so little friction that I may continue on at Kawaiahao indefinitely."[14] But Carrie, more than anyone, knew that nothing would keep Ida from opening the new Kamehameha School for Girls, which had already broken ground, two and a half miles away from the epicenter of revolutionary activity.

Public Outcry

The word soon got out that the demise of Kawaiaha'o Seminary was imminent. Many in the community speculated that the school would transition into the planned Kamehameha School for Girls, despite Charles Bishop's word to the contrary. Ida's recruited teachers fed the community gossip by openly advocating for a takeover, as it would be in their own best interest to remain under Miss Pope's leadership. Due to the Bishop Trust's endowment, they saw relief to the endless and exhaustive fund-raising efforts that Kawaiaha'o Seminary depended on. Miss Pope even petitioned Mr. Bishop to adopt it as a "companion school" as a preparatory for Kamehameha.[15] The request angered Mr. Bishop, who wrote to trustee Carter that the idea "should not be entertained" and more pointedly, but privately, marveled why "Miss Pope 'cannot see why' this and that new thing, all costing money, cannot be undertaken."[16]

Worse yet for Kawaiaha'o, a provision in the new constitution of 1894 eliminated all appropriations to religious or private schools after the end of 1895.[17] The school's future was grim, and the public outrage among the Hawaiian citizenry was published in *Hawaii Holomua*.

> The prospect of the Kawaiahao Seminary being obliged to close its doors for lack of funds is a little short of a national calamity. The school has for years been instrumental in preserving and building up the Hawaiian race. Private schools like Kawaiahao Seminary are more than schools, they are homes. It is a great pity if the government cannot see its way to assist the Seminary. If the school is forced to close, the girls now there will be thrown on their own resources and brought under the often pernicious influence of their homes. It appears Kamehameha Girls School now under construction will interfere with the work of the Kawaiahao Seminary. It may be an unpleasant fact, but it is true that when it was under the patronage of Queen Liliuokalani the Seminary flourished; under the republican government this school for the daughters of the People is threatened with ruin.[18]

The indignation in the Hawaiian community was justified when considering Kawaiaha'o's three-decade history of alliance between the monarchs and the American missionaries. Many remembered that when the annual examination of the missionary school took place in 1888, the Hawaiian government adjourned for the express purpose of attending the public academic examination of ninety-three girls. Alumna Princess Likelike; her daughter, Princess Ka'iulani; nobles; and representatives of the Legislative Assembly all showed up in full support to view the end-of-the-year public exhibition of Kawaiaha'o's pupils.

Kawaiaha'o Seminary's Destiny

As Ida was preparing to leave for Kamehameha in the fall of 1894, a newly formed Board of Managers was put together after all the former trustees resigned during

The youngest pupils pose on the school porch for picture day. *Lilla Estelle Appleton private collection, Betsy Lang.*

the summer. Financially, the school was barely getting by. During the summer, Hiram Bingham II, as manager-in-chief, was called in to provide an "inspection of the general conduct of the school; its receipts and expenditures, the course of study being pursued in it, the developments of the Industrial Department by the teachers and the general moral and physical training of the pupils."[19]

Revenue was now urgently needed to keep the school afloat. Mr. Bingham couldn't retain the academic direction in which Ida had taken the school, and moved quickly to undo her advances in curriculum and instruction. The board informed the newly installed principal, Miss Florence Perrot, Ida's former Bucyrus teaching colleague, that the Bible would now be returning as the primary textbook. Disregarding the library established by Miss Pope with the queen's help, Mr. Bingham stated, "We do not recommend the study of algebra, geometry, trigonometry, botany, geology, French and English literature as these would take too much time from Industrial work."[20] The new board's bylaws, which he quickly put into the hands of Miss Perrot, clearly stated that books were pointless because "the educational work of the Seminary must be clearly auxiliary to the preaching and teaching of the gospel."[21]

Staff and students were soon informed that they would be laboring harder than before with a "view to increase the revenue of the school by the sale of articles made."[22] It appears that Mr. Bingham was making sure every pupil, regardless of age, would be earning her keep, as he proudly noted that two new arrivals at the school, children aged four and five, "were found knowing on which finger to put their thimble, how to thread a needle, [and how]to knot their thread."[23]

Other rules informed Miss Perrot that she would be micromanaged and inspections would occur on a regular basis. Not surprisingly, her first year would be her last. Ida quickly worked behind the scenes at Kamehameha to influence the recruitment of Florence Perrot and others.

The Slow Demise of the Queen's Beloved School

Thus, the light that many teachers had sparked over the years and fanned into a flame by Ida Pope had dimmed and flickered out with her departure. And the once proud Kawaiahaʻo Seminary, a representation of the old alliance between the monarchy and missionaries to promote the education of Hawaiʻi's daughters, began its slow decline. The school exceptionally loved throughout the decades by Queen Liliʻuokalani simply could not survive without her.

Even though Charles R. Bishop and many others donated sums in an attempt to keep the school running, its endowment income never equaled its operating expenditures. At the end, Kawaiahaʻo was obliged to frenetically raise even more funds through concerts, fairs, and the work of its industrial departments than they did in years past. Those fund-raising events are scattered throughout many teachers' correspondence as exhausting affairs. Principal Christina W. Paulding, who succeeded Florence Perrot, fought the trustees over the fund-raising issue, claiming that the activities diverted both staff and students from the educational program. Principal Katheryn McLeod led the students and teachers through another hard period, when repairs to the buildings were severely neglected. She wrote to the Board of Managers that the high attrition of her "faithful and hardworking faculty" supported the school's "established reputation as a woman-killer."[24]

By 1901, Ida, burdened by the school's deterioration, again asked the trustees of the Bishop Estate if they would "consider taking over the Kawaiahao Seminary."[25] Mr. Bishop responded directly to Miss Pope and told her while he was "sorry to see it fail," it should move to a better place. Four years later, it did just that.

The Hawaiian Evangelical Association decided in 1905 to solve two overcrowding problems by merging Kawaiahaʻo Seminary with the Mills Institute for Boys and relocating them with the intention to unite them into a single, comprehensive educational organization. Three years later, the historic Kawaiaha'o Seminary on King Street was sold to the Castle Estate and the new Kawaiaha'o moved up to the beautiful Mānoa Valley. The Mission Memorial Building, built in 1915, still standing today, sits on the previous site of the original Kawaiaha'o Seminary as a memorial to the early missionaries.

In 1908, the first group of girls moved into their new home and classrooms. While the institution was theoretically and logistically united under the name Mid-Pacific Institute, the reality was that Mills and Kawaiaha'o retained their respective names and operated quite independently for many years. In 1923, the names Kawaiaha'o and Mills were dropped as a "partial step toward the creation of an integrated institution."[26] The stately lava rock building is forever memorialized as Kawaiaha'o Hall and remains today a prominent feature on the Mid-Pacific campus in the Mānoa Valley. Ida's records show she actively maintained a strong collaborative relationship with the new Kawaiaha'o Seminary throughout her lifetime.

CHAPTER TEN

Beginnings

The Kamehameha School for Girls, 1894–1897

It was the beginning of the end of the Hawaiian monarchy the year the Kamehameha School for Girls came into being. Several weeks before the first term, Hawai'i had officially become a republic. Sanford Dole and the provisional government declared Hawaiian independence and gained U.S. recognition on July 4, 1894. Ida knew her pupils would be emotional and confused over the recent state of events when they arrived for school. With no other choice, it would be up to her to calm their fears and usher them into the "new Hawai'i."

Lili'uokalani Shunned

With all the political uncertainty in the air, the school swung open its door without fanfare on a bright November day. The real pomp and ceremony were delayed to coincide with Princess Bernice Pauahi Bishop's birthday, December 19, 1894. The Hawaiian community, eager for distraction and celebration, came out in droves to witness the dedication of the new school for Hawai'i's daughters, held in Bishop Hall. It is certain that many Hawaiians expected to see Lili'uokalani in attendance.

Instead, Mrs. Amoe Ha'alelea, a prominent figure in the royal court of Kamehameha IV and a close friend of the late princess Pauahi, stared deeply into the faces of the new pupils and told them in their native language that they now had "advantages and privileges your grandparents never dreamed of seeing—be it yours faithfully and make the wisest possible use of these rich provisions for your preparation for life."[1]

It's easy to imagine Miss Pope's head nodding vigorously when Mrs. Ha'alelea added, "Be diligent in study, faithful in work, neat in your person."[2]

Trustee Reverend C. M. Hyde then delivered the dedicatory address by expressing his confidence in the selection of Miss Pope, whose "love for Hawaiian children was deep and sincere."[3] The portion of Pauahi Bishop's will bequeathing her property for the schools was then solemnly read and the school

For its time, the "A-shaped design" was modern and beautiful and "views from the windows—more beautiful than any picture from any artist's hands, that adorn the abodes of royalty." *Kamehameha Schools.*

keys ceremoniously handed to the beaming Miss Pope, who, as Lydia Aholo remembered, "in her usual happy way, accepted the keys with a few impressive words."[4]

Yet the dedication—this vital moment in the school's beginning—was marred by controversy. *Ka Makaainana,* the Hawaiian language newspaper, speaking for its citizenry, pronounced its outrage over the opening day ceremonies in "A Hypocritical Remembrance." The publisher articulated the Hawaiian community's indignation that the royal Queen Lili'uokalani, still living and breathing, was literally shunned by the Founder's Day ceremony, while the royal Pauahi Bishop, deceased, was disproportionately worshipped.

> The girls knelt before an image of the Alii, and placed flowers upon that picture. This is not a good lesson for the children. Pauahi has died, she has gone, she is no more in body—For here is the Queen, still living, and she is not honored by those missionaries for her good works. She took up the Liliuokalani Educational Society, its funds from her own earnings and property. There were many girls who received an education because of this society. She is still living and yet these haughty missionaries of her days

don't at all remember her great deeds. Aye, she is still living, and now she sees clearly those who are steadfastly loyal to her and those who are traitorous, abusive, and speak badly about her.[5]

Many others denounced the school's hypocrisy and failure to honor its living, if dethroned, queen over a deceased princess. Ironically, Loring G. Hudson, the Kamehameha Schools' historian, in years to come, would also defend and advocate for Ida in a manner strikingly similar to the defense of Liliʻuokalani. Hudson compared Ida, as the "real and living ideal," to the "sanctified ideal" of Pauahi Bishop. "The Chiefess Pauahi was a revered memory, and almost sanctified ideal, through her saintly life and full-hearted devotion to her people. But 'Mother' Pope was a real and living ideal to these young Hawaiian women, a living Alii, whose life left an ineradicable imprint on scores of new generations of Hawaiians."[6]

Ida, more than any other in attendance at the opening ceremony, knew firsthand that many of her pupils were there because the queen paid for their foundational education in the elementary years. Her absence at the opening ceremony, particularly since she was the *hānai* sister of the schools' founder, Bernice Pauahi, would have been felt deeply by Ida and her pupils.

Walking a Fine Line

Ida soon learned that she was still in the middle of a tug-of-war between two warring factions, the Annexationists and the Royalists, both camps represented at Kamehameha Schools. After the queen's dethronement, William Brewster Oleson, the principal of the Kamehameha School for Boys, had been targeted in the native community as an antiroyalist to the point of bodily harm. Concerned for his safety, he had resigned during the summer of 1893.

His replacement, Theodore Richards, was much more sympathetic to the Hawaiians. He pointed out to Mr. Oleson, who took up arms against the queen in the revolution, the hypocrisy of supporting those who would fire shots at Hawaiians and then turn around and teach their children.[7] Ida, becoming politically astute, was learning to walk a fine line between supporting her pupils, who were adamantly loyal to their queen and culture, and maintaining fealty to those who paid her wages, many of whom favored the 1893 rebellion.

After the passing of his wife and the monarchy, Charles Bishop's heart was no longer in Hawaiʻi. At the age of seventy-two, he moved to San Francisco on March 2, 1894, but *out of sight* did not mean *out of mind*. Even though he relinquished his trustee status, he controlled the big decisions, especially the financial ones of the estate, from his residence, the Occidental Hotel, where he entertained

Charles Reed Bishop. *Kamehameha Schools.*

"visitors travelling to and from Hawaiʻi; royalty and commoner, businessman and planter, teacher and student, trustee, scientist, and author."[8] Ida often made it a point to visit Mr. Bishop prior to boarding the train for her visits home. During those visits, she lobbied hard for improvements that she deemed necessary for the school.

Soon after the school opened, the trustees, impressed with her administrative abilities, privately submitted her name as a possible replacement trustee for the school. But Mr. Bishop's concern over her ideas "all costing money" made him "doubt her fitness for the position of trustee."[9] He even went one step further to squelch any future proposals of any female: "Do not think of appointing a woman as a Trustee. It is not necessary nor would it be wise or right to do so."[10]

As Ida was outlining procedures for the school, she soon learned firsthand that Mr. Bishop was very frugal and had strong views in how the Bishop Estate money would be spent. As a small example, he asked her to consider future water usage: "Only a small quantity is necessary for a single bath, and teachers and scholars should know that fact and be required to act accordingly. There is no utility in soaking one's body in fresh water."[11] Miss Pope kept a daily bathing schedule for each of her first sixty pupils and apparently dismissed that advice, generously allowing each girl thirty minutes throughout the day. The male-dominated world that controlled the school was another line that Ida had to straddle, and though she complained bitterly about it in private correspondence, the trustees would have never guessed her dissatisfaction with them until much later in her tenure.

The Building

The Kamehameha School for Boys had already been established on eighty-two acres of land that the Bishop Estate owned at the foot of Kalihi Valley. Although the exact location of the new school for Hawaiian girls was not prescribed by the will, Charles Bishop honored his wife's wishes that the school for girls also be built on land belonging to her estate. Thus, a site was found in a suburb of Honolulu "between King Street and the Oahu Railroad."[12] Even though Trustee Hyde had publicly advocated for a wider geographical separation from the boys, his recommendation was overruled so that the girls could mingle together under "proper social conditions."[13] The principal for the boys' school, Uldrick Thompson, felt the girls shouldn't be too widely separated, or they wouldn't be able to find a future Hawaiian husband among the boys.[14] Trustee Hyde partially got his way when the girls' school was erected across the thoroughfare of King Street. But in fact, it was only a "three or four minutes' walk away."[15]

The school's courtyard was lush, colorful, and fragrant. *Kamehameha Schools.*

For its time, the new school building was modern and unique in its A-shaped design. The *Gazette* reported it had "views from the windows more beautiful than any picture from any artist's hands."[16] But the trustees, almost defensively, wanted it known to the readers that they "seduciously avoided making it elaborate in its ornamentation"; instead, "it is a plain building for ordinary folk; not a decorated extravagance for girls set up to be pampered or coddled."[17] Someone, however, added an addendum—likely Ida Pope, who maintained that while the girls would not be living in the lap of luxury, they were, however, worthy of the beautiful boarding school: "Woman is not regarded as a drudge or a plaything, but as a co-worker with man in building up human society after the divine law."[18]

Indeed, the girls' rooms were modest and each given "a bed and mattress, bedding, a dresser, a washstand and an enamel set consisting of a washbasin, water pitcher, soap dish and mug."[19] But Ida knew from traveling around the islands to the homes of her students that this would have been more luxurious than most had ever had. She would see to it that they took great pride in their personal space.

With the royal mansion Keōua Hale about to be sold, Charles Bishop invited Ida to select freely from the furniture and items that had belonged to Princesses Ruth and Pauahi for use in the new school.[20] Because of his generosity and the

Kamehameha Schools

The school lānai and all common rooms were filled with beautiful ferns and flowering plants grown by Ida and her girls. *Kamehameha Schools.*

donations of other wealthy people in the community, the school received museum-quality furnishings, including a beautiful polished table of koa wood formerly owned by King Kamehameha the Great, placed in a central position of honor. It seems as if Ida might have had free rein with the selection, because influential guests who visited the school down the years noted Miss Pope's gifts of rare and historical significance that dated from the Kamehameha lines.

Respecting Mr. Bishop's mandates to keep the girls' private spaces simple and sparse did not mean that common areas could not be warm and elegant. It didn't take long for Ida May Pope to turn a building into a home and dirt into a garden. She was known for her artistry in Ohio, and this extended to landscaping. She saw splendor in nature and made sure all the classrooms, patios, common rooms, and the very grounds were filled with beautiful plants and flowers grown by Ida and the girls. "We cannot make farmers of Hawaiian girls, but we can train them to beautify their homes and supply their tables with flowers, fruit, and vegetables raised by their labor; and we can give them an insight into the keeping and caring for well-ordered homes and grounds."[21]

Mr. Bishop knew the land was bad and worried about water usage on the "poor and rebellious"[22] soil and that water should only be "just enough for instruction-object lessons."[23] Disregarding that mandate, Ida put students on a daily rotation in the "yard." Soon, she acquired a fountain for the courtyard from Charles

Gardening was a daily event. *Kamehameha Schools.*

Montague Cooke, and before long, the beautiful grounds of the new Kamehameha School for Girls were the talk of the town.

She no doubt remembered the ruffians who threatened the girls at the Kawaiahaʻo Seminary, and to keep a watchful eye over who came and went at *her* school, she strategically designed her space. Her office and private room were just left of the main entrance, while the classrooms were on the right. Nobody would escape her watchful eye. Her staff of teachers and the older girls resided on the second floor and the younger girls on the third floor. She had visited some impressive schools throughout her travels with an eye out for necessities, and was ready for pupils with "the best modern conveniences, scroll-top desks, typewriters, ready reference file, and so on."[24]

The First Pupils

The trustees gave Ida sole power to determine who should be admitted, but Mr. Bishop represented his late wife's preference in the will: "Only those having native blood are to be admitted at present."[25] This meant some of the capable girls she had come to care for deeply over the last few years didn't meet the heritage requirement. Unfortunately, she had to leave them behind at Kawaiahaʻo Seminary. One full-blooded Hawaiian girl was temporarily left behind in a huge predicament. With the queen deposed and her finances confiscated, the education of Lydia Aholo had been uncertain. The girl fell into deep despair during the first part of 1894. One mother figure, the queen, was in political turmoil, and the other, Miss Pope, gone to Kamehameha.

Once Ida moved to the new school, however, she sent for Lydia with the full intention of obtaining a work scholarship for her. Mr. Bishop had allotted $250 to Miss Pope to use at her discretion for five scholarships for the first year.[26] But to Lydia's joyful surprise, she was able to continue as a royal scholar at Kamehameha without working for her tuition. At ninety-two years old, Lydia proudly remembered her relief: "When I went to say goodbye to the queen, before I went to school, she said, 'Now remember, you ask Miss Pope to send all your bills to Mr. J. O. Carter."[27] Ida instantly made Lydia her office assistant, which relieved her of manual chores.

This moment seemed to mark a symbolic passing of the maternal torch from one educational leader to another. Liliʻuokalani was indisputably the first guiding light for the education of Hawaiian girls, and now Ida Pope would need to take the full lead. No matter the political outcome for her country, the queen knew an education under Miss Pope would give Lydia a full advantage in the new unfolding economy. Hawaiian parents were eager to follow her lead, and the applications for admittance grew long. With all of the best students from Kawaiahaʻo who qualified for admission and her reputation on the line, Ida took the job of recruiting girls from the community very seriously. She had clear admission requirements, and during her in-depth interviews with each applicant and family member, she shared her mission statement.

> The object of the school is to furnish a carefully arranged, practical education to Hawaiian girls of twelve years of age and over, qualifying them for service at home, for wage-earning in some handicraft, or as teachers in the government schools. So far as we are able to train these girls to meet the conditions about them, so far shall we be able to send forth a body of students with moral fibre to resist temptation, with minds trained for skilled labor, to enter home or trade, with bodies strong for physical endurance and the enjoyment of good health. Hasten the day when we may be able to meet these requirements![28]

Toward fulfilling this mission at the outset, Ida handpicked thirty-five pupils, who were to pay $50 a year, and as the *Gazette* noted, most of the girls came from Kawaiahaʻo Seminary.[29] By the end of the first school year, her numbers were up to fifty-nine students[30]—all of whom were put on notice that each of them was to be on a year's probation. At the same time, she instituted an application examination that tested the potential student's ability to read and write selections from the Gospel of John, in English. This requirement alone would rule out most girls who received a public school instruction from Hawaiian speaking teachers. A prospective student was also required to have knowledge of fundamental arithmetic, common fractions, Hawaiian history, and geography, as well as positive reports from reputable professionals as to her health and moral character. If admission was gained, the student's progress in her studies and moral development would determine whether she would pass the probationary year.[31]

The Teaching Staff

The majority of teachers Ida had encountered working in the islands were New England Congregationalists.[32] In fact, this denomination dominated all the mission work, which often gave Hawaiʻi the name "tropical New England."[33] Ida met many teachers who were full of puritanical religious zeal but had little or no practical experience or love for children. Because of this, they seldom lasted. When it came time to recruit teachers, Ida desired to leave as little as possible to chance. She looked for an educated, experienced, and stable teaching force for the school.

She wanted to surround herself with women she both respected and liked. After all, this was to be more than a boarding school—the Kamehameha School for Girls was to be a home for her and the girls.

So, with complete autonomy from the trustees, she began creating a teaching family for herself with familiar women with shared experiences from her home state of Ohio. A few[34] migrated with her from Kawaiahaʻo Seminary, revealing her selection of teachers may have been strategic when they were recruited a year earlier. Seven of them were instantly hired on her recommendations, including the widow Ida Sturgeon, who brought along her daughter Nora. Mrs. Sturgeon, not qualified to be a teacher, became the matron of Kamehameha and supervised the domestic department. Her daughter resided with her and attended the exclusive Punahou School daily (the school was founded in 1841 for American missionaries' children). Young Nora would unknowingly be the one to reinitiate the social relationship that had been politically severed between Ida and Liliʻuokalani.

Every day, as precocious Nora trod back and forth between the schools on Huapala (Sweetheart), she paused outside the walls of Washington Place hoping to catch a glimpse of the queen in her garden. Nora at age ninety-six recalled one afternoon in particular when she was nine. After signaling to her friend Lydia Aholo, who was spotted with the queen, she was invited to leap over the wall to join them. Lydia at age ninety-two recalled the same incident, adding that Nora, nervous about protocol, first asked her, "What shall I do when I come before the Queen?" to which Lydia responded, "You pay your obeisance and the Queen will do the rest."[35] The ice was broken when the queen asked, "To whom does the horse belong?" Apparently, Liliʻuokalani was "sufficiently impressed with the little girl"[36] because shortly, Ida Pope and Ida Sturgeon were invited to a party at Washington Place and were specifically told to bring the child. Nora remembered they were conspicuously the only haoles, or white people, present.[37] This event welcomed Ida Pope back into the queen's inner sanctum.

In her choice of staff, Ida was naturally guided to hire teachers similar in sensibility to herself. She had been raised by a democratic father whose death announcement in the paper noted his goodness despite the fact that he "was not a member of any religious denomination."[38] It is apparent that Ida's progressive, break-the-mold mindset was clearly shaped by her childhood home's open environment. That mindset guided her choice of teachers, sensible Presbyterians like she had become, not Congregationalists. This was encouraged by Mr. Bishop, who reminded employees that his "wife was a liberal Protestant"[39] and hoped "the teachers will be sufficiently liberal and reasonable to worship together without raising any question as to denomination."[40]

When she arrived with her new recruits in October of 1894, Ida had a little over a month to fully prepare the school for the eager pupils. Even though this must have been a daunting and exhausting experience, records show that she was in her element, micromanaging every aspect of the school, inside and out. Her notions of perfectionism, combined with her pleasing qualities, elated the trustees. At age thirty-two, she youthfully tackled the enormous job of mentoring and supervising her new teaching staff on how she believed the school should be conducted. Later, these personal traits—her drive for control and inability to delegate—would take their toll on her health.

The Curriculum

The trustees promoted a separate and distinct education, which was fine for Ida. She didn't desire to follow the established boys' school curriculum; in fact, she wanted complete autonomy in outlining the course of study for her girls, which would mirror the most successful U.S. institutions of her day. During her teacher recruitment trip, she took the opportunity to visit some top industrial schools. The school that impressed her the most was the Pratt Institute in New York. She saw in its technical and mechanical training a potential component for her curriculum. Pratt's progressive curriculum distinguished itself by moving from the podium to the laboratory. It differed from vocational training by its advanced level, providing for specialization in occupations that required skills more demanding than purely manual labor.[41] Ida could envision a whole new field of nursing for her girls based on the Pratt model. In Ida's mind, a hospital on the school grounds would be an excellent laboratory, and she was naïvely certain Mr. Bishop would support this.

When Ida began to amass literature to supplement the formal school curriculum, Trustee Hyde curiously let her have her way, perhaps overruled by Charles Bishop, who like Ida was an avid reader. In the past, Reverend Hyde hadn't seen the need for textbooks and was on record for dismissing with textbooks, except as a reference, because "the main feature of instruction is *language*"—and, further, the boys' school had been doing fine without them.[42] Hyde's views presaged the official rejection of the Hawaiian language. Incredibly, in 1896, Act 57, Section 30, of the Laws of the Republic of Hawaiʻi would ban the Hawaiian language in all public and private schools and render Hawaiian a foreign language in its own country. The reasoning was that even though the missionaries had translated many textbooks into Hawaiian, to continue that daunting task was impossible. To offer an advanced education, it would be easier if all pupils were taught English from the time they entered school.[43] Sadly, this law began the decline of the melodious Hawaiian language.

The first scope and sequence of the school curriculum covered a three-year "English Course" format.[44] Ida's academic program was developed around four major branches: elementary science, literature, history, and mathematics. Calisthenics, reading, geography, drawing, and vocal and instrumental music supplemented the curriculum. Ida wanted her girls to have a rigorous curriculum but also to be accomplished in what were considered genteel talents at the time, such as fine sewing, music, and art, and, because they were necessary and mandated by Mr. Bishop, cooking and laundry. Beyond the academics, Miss Pope reported, "The general housework of the school is done by the pupils. Games—tennis, croquet, basket and tower ball, afford ample relaxation and recreation. Mondays are holidays. Saturday evenings the pupils gather in the assembly hall or gymnasium for literary or social entertainments. Committees are formed in every department and encourage the development of Christian character."[45]

Fraternizing with the Boys

Ida certainly learned the hard way at Kawaiahaʻo Seminary that she could not keep boys away from her girls, so she arranged for a day when the boys were welcome under her supervision. One aged alumna remembered Mondays with a giggle because the boys were allowed to visit "some of the lucky girls": "I can still remember how we used to sit on the sofa; we were so shy and bashful. There used to be a space of about two feet between us, and we never even thought of holding hands!"[46] Those who had no suitors among the Kamehameha boys were released to "go to town" if there were "no black marks for misbehavior."[47] Lydia Aholo humorously expressed wonderment that any of her classmates ever found a husband due to the fact that "our good old teachers used to guard us very well indeed."[48]

While the two schools were placed near each other for the sole purposes of social interaction, in reality, there was very little contact with boys in the first years except for those Mondays, church on Sundays, and the occasional social event. To the casual observer, the girls' core experience was seen as that of a well-rounded but feminine community in which domesticity was seen as the central goal. In contrast, the boys' school was known as a "semimilitary" institution. Most school photos of the era reveal the boys in a marching line in their immaculate gray uniforms, contrasted to Ida's feminine lines of girls in their white dresses, white hair bows, and polished shoes. At first glance, the differences in dress and demeanor between the two schools sent a message to the society that the girls' place in the world was, first and foremost, inside the home. But Ida had big plans for her pupils that were not limited to lives as domestic housekeepers.

The masculine Kamehameha boys in their immaculate gray military uniforms contrasted starkly with Ida's "virtuous" feminine girls in white. *Kamehameha Schools.*

As the first school year began, Miss Pope put the Kamehameha boys on notice that her girls would be respected as fellow scholars and given the full standard of respect that she herself expected. Principal Thompson remembered the day they were taught that lesson. Miss Pope and her girls visited the campus for a coeducational opportunity. When her girls were "whistled and called to" by boys hanging out the windows, Miss Pope immediately returned her girls back to their school, to the astonishment of all.[49] In a school-wide meeting, the boys were told that unless they acted like gentlemen, Miss Pope would forbid all intercampus visits. Mr. Thompson quickly reported that "the results were entirely favorable, as the boys soon learned to treat the girls with due respect."[50] This was the beginning, as Mr. Thompson later noted that Ida's dominant and respected views were so "trusted that her judgments were accepted without question—by pupils, alumni, teachers, and trustees."[51]

It wouldn't be long before Ida was able to convince the trustees to allow dancing under her "control and supervision" to "relieve the monotony" and to teach "social graces." Mr. Thompson was both incredulous and pleased that Miss Pope gained approval for this formerly taboo activity and expressed awe that she got her way with the trustees and would soon "revive the ancient Hawaiian dances and customs."[52]

A Firm but Gentle Hand

Ida's often-reiterated philosophy, as she created the culture of the school, was to instill a sense of dignity in each of her pupils. Since each girl would be involved in several types of housework throughout her enrollment, a good attitude was a must. In multiple documents, including the first official catalog, trustee reports, published articles, and more, she declared there would be no whippings and that all discipline would be "maintained by refraining from force as a corrective,"[53] and in its place,

> the design of the School is to make it as home-like as possible, while securing good discipline by appealing to the honor of the pupils. A system of demerit marks for laxity in deportment, disorderliness, untruthfulness and other serious offenses had been adopted with some degree of success.[54] We are endeavoring to train the pupils to form habits of thrift and economy, to return gratitude for favors, to pay debts, to earn a little, to spend a little less, to put beauty in homes, and morals in living.[55]

Ida had "basketball fever." *Kamehameha Schools.*

It's clear that Ida left all the inhumane discipline she witnessed at Kawaiahaʻo Seminary behind and, with the autonomy given her, created the management of the new school based on her good instincts and love for children.

Ida had also come to understand the importance of play and that both team and individual competition were historically important to Hawaiians, especially young growing ones.[56] Most importantly, she came to realize that youngsters needed healthy outlets to combat the structure of the boarding school, and recreation was a sound defense against misbehavior. Ida's school scrapbook soon overflowed with newspaper clippings of her girls' baseball and basketball matches. Ida, never physically fit, nonetheless embraced basketball with passion and fervor and had many professional photos taken of her girls in their uniforms. Soon, her competitive nature took over, and she formed a girls' basketball league composed of high schools throughout the island, justifying it to the trustees as "beneficial to all concerned," since the "friendly competition" bonded the girls to each other in rich ways when they went out into the community.[57]

In just a few short years, Ida knew she had landed the career of a lifetime. Her sister Lois and her husband, Joseph Prosser, sold The Vatican in Bucyrus, and there was now very little reason to pine for a home that no longer existed. The Prossers relocated to Chicago to join the rest of the Pope clan in business at the Paramount Knitting Company. Ida would soon look for an opportunity to get her youngest sister, Anne, to join Katherine and herself in Honolulu. She had fallen deeply in love with Hawaiʻi, and this would be the Pope sisters' permanent home.[58]

CHAPTER ELEVEN

The Foundational Years

The Queen under Arrest

The entire school population was shaken to its core when a January 1895 attempt to restore the queen to her throne ended horribly with the mass arrests of Royalists, including the queen herself. Liliʻuokalani was charged with treason and imprisoned in a small room on the second floor of ʻIolani Palace. The girls were deeply affected by this arrest, but none more deeply than seventeen-year-old Lydia Aholo. Losing access to the queen was devastating, and at age ninety-two, she emotionally recalled this time.

> They just came and took over—I don't know how they did it, but they did. She was taken to the Palace and they imprisoned her in there. And one of her ladies-in-waiting was with her. The woman who did her washing, she would have to have a pass. And they always examined that bundle of clothes to see if she was carrying anything that she shouldn't. We always wrote to her and asked how she was. We couldn't go to see her. And they would read our letters before she got them.[1]

During the eight months of her lonely imprisonment, while the royal prisoner worked on her famous love quilt and composed wonderful melodies, Ida kept a watchful eye on Lydia. During the political upheaval, Ida probably thought it best to keep the sensitive girl out of the political commotion, safe and secure within the school. The queen's love for music had been instilled in Lydia early, and she had received private vocal and piano lessons at school from the time she was a small child. Lydia recalled the queen had been lenient with everything except piano practice. "When I was home, I had to practice like I practiced at school—one whole hour. And when she was in Washington, I thought, I didn't have to go practice. I was going out one morning and the housekeeper came out of her room, clapped her hands, says, 'Come back and practice, come back and practice.' So I *had* to go back and practice."[2]

Practice paid off. By the time she was a young adult, Lydia was an accomplished pianist with a rich contralto voice, often compared to the queen's own style.[3] At Miss Pope's urging, Lydia became much in demand as a soloist in the school and in the community. Ida noticed that the shy and serious girl showed confidence while performing in musicals and made sure her talents were showcased. Shorter than average, Lydia surely reminded Ida of her favorite younger sister Anne, who was also soft-spoken and petite, and only a few years older in age. Ida's preference for Lydia during this time is highlighted in the pupil's work schedule. While others worked in the kitchen, yard, and washing house, Lydia assisted Miss Pope with her office duties. All the favored time slots for bathing, work, and leisure went to Lydia.

With their queen in custody, Ida had to keep a more watchful eye on the psychological states of all of her pupils, ever loyal to the monarchy. Given the unprecedented political turmoil under which Ida worked that first year, it had been an especially taxing beginning. Even during calmer times, establishing new routines and school regimens would have been hard work. If there was a silver lining to her educational work, though, it was the promise of a summer vacation in one of the most beautiful places on earth. At the beginning of summer in 1895, Ida, exhausted from the tough first year, immediately took off for the Island of Hawai'i to rest and recover with her sister Katherine in the plantation home of her Oberlin classmate Helen Hoppin Renton. In a letter to Lilla, she covered some highlights.

July 29, 1895

Dear Miss Appleton.

My sister and I are in the cool bracing air in our old clothes. Mrs. Henry Renton very kindly invited us to spend the summer with her in Kohala. We left Honolulu the sixteenth of July—had a most miserable night on the Kinau and were very happy to reach the hospitable home of the Rentons the afternoon of the seventeenth. The Rentons furnished us with a guide, a pack mule and saddle horses and on the morning of the nineteenth we mounted our gallant steeds and started for Waimea. I managed to keep in my saddle. You know I have sprained both of my ankles and once I managed to escape accident and reached Waimea safely, we were treated to a wonderful sunset glow on Mauna Kea. Tuesday we went to Waipio Valley. We had a unique experience and had a taste of native life and customs that are enjoyable once in a lifetime. I have visited the natives in their homes. Tonight we called on two girls who go to Kohala Seminary. Their garden was beautiful and well kept, but the house was an old thatched cottage of one room and a family of eight. Three young men of seventeen were about the place and all under the influence of liquor. We have seen so much of the curse of liquor and laziness that the task of elevating them seems well nigh hopeless. Ah me! Who will riddle me the flow and the why?[4]

Lilla received this letter in New York, where she was furthering her education at Oswego. Ida thrived on learning new educational strategies and expressed a yearning to join her at the "Mother of all Normal Schools."[5] Oswego was based around the theories of Johann Heinrich Pestalozzi. Ida's own philosophy was already aligned with the core of the theory that stressed the dignity of children while creating an "emotionally secure learning environment."[6] It was said that Oswego's founder, Edward Sheldon, was "Pestalozzian in spirit" because he loved children and had the "sympathetic insight into the child-mind."[7] He created a hands-on curriculum for young children under the name of "object teaching,"[8] a concept that Ida had intuitively embraced in her first years at Kawaiaha'o Seminary. Oswego was unique for its time, and so it became a Mecca for educators. Ida hated to miss out on any program that might enhance teaching and learning at Kamehameha, but her contentment is obvious as she ends the letter: "The school year has on the whole been satisfactory. We have had fifty-three pupils gathered from public schools and seminaries. With so small a number much individual work could be done and effective work too. How I would love to go to Oswego and study."[9]

All in all, Ida's first year presented a mixture of challenges that required much of her. Her dual allegiance—to her native Hawaiian pupils and her missionary benefactors—was a tension that would persist throughout her career. But even early on in her tenure as head of the girls' school, her strength of character helped her to find a balance between the two camps. Her satisfaction with the first year's progress seems more than merited.

The Cholera Outbreak of 1895

Ida returned to Honolulu from her carefree summer vacation on Hawai'i Island to a full-blown cholera epidemic, which delayed the opening of the school year once again. It was such a serious issue that the recently inaugurated president, Sanford Dole, told the people "the Board of Health is the government now."[10] The board acted swiftly, sealing off businesses within the affected districts, banning church services and public meetings, and closing all schools in an effort to contain the situation.[11] Many Kamehameha girls had no homes to return to in the summer and were lucky, as it turned out, to be confined to the school.

During the height of the cholera epidemic, many in the community were in dire straits, unable to work and feed their families. Among many volunteers, the principals and teachers of Kamehameha Schools answered the call for help by building a food station in the disadvantaged Pālama neighborhood.

Meanwhile, Ida, used to many crises by this time, used creative methods to keep her quarantined girls in good cheer, as Lydia Aholo recalled.

> School did not begin again until October 15, 1895, on account of cholera. I well remember the girls who came back to school from the other islands because their clothes and the girls themselves were fumigated before they were allowed to go around with the girls who had remained in school all summer. The Honolulu girls who were out of school for their vacation were put into quarantine in what we called "the tank house." The place had been fitted up very comfortable and the girls with Miss Pope in charge, did not suffer very much from lack of ordinary comforts. Their meals were taken to them from the main building and in the evening the girls who were not in quarantine went to serenade them.[12]

When the school year finally began, it was not the effects of cholera that kept away thirteen girls, but conduct and aptitude. Ida reported to the trustees in the fall of 1895 that some of the girls were "of so little promise" they had already been expelled. In what was perhaps a wake-up call to the student body and a testament to Miss Pope's exacting standards, she reported to the trustees that discipline was now more easily maintained "and on the whole, [students] dwell as a large family should, in unity."[13]

The Queen Is Released

The brightest spot in the fall semester of 1895 was the day Lili'uokalani was released from her imprisonment and allowed to return to Washington Place. When she arrived home on that warm September day, she encountered a touching homage. A pathway to her door had been formed on both sides by a guard of honor made up of native Hawaiians in full dress. This ceremony, traditionally given for public figures fallen in war, would only empower Lili'uokalani in the days to come to fight back. To have her back home greatly eased the minds and hearts of the Kamehameha girls and their principal. Over seventy-three years later, Lydia remembered that the subject of her dethronement was "never" a topic for discussion. "She never—just to mention of the name—we have to be very careful what we say, you know, about that dethronement. At Washington Place we used to go

The kitchen had every modern convenience for its time. *Kamehameha Schools.*

White linen tablecloths and napkins required etiquette. *Kamehameha Schools.*

out and play croquet, and she'd go with us. We never talked about those things in her presence. Never. I was old enough to know, you know. Oh, but it was sad."[14]

With the success of the first semester year behind her, Ida, feeling established and perhaps a bit entitled, formally requested from the trustees numerous wants, which included a carriage house, a dairy, playgrounds, and garden plots. She also invited the trustees to enjoy a refined dinner party on December 19, 1895, entirely prepared and served by the girls. Lydia humorously recalled the celebration designed to showcase the domestic department.

> We celebrated our first anniversary at the School for Girls. A dinner was given to which a large number of friends of the school came. Nine courses were served, I was one of the waiters at the first table where sat the Trustees and their wives and Miss Pope. I had on new shoes and they fitted pretty snugly and after I had been on my feet for more than two hours I began to think that the Americans ate more than the Hawaiians, although the common saying is that the Hawaiians eat a great deal. I wondered how the guests could eat everything that was placed in front of them. But, of course, if my feet had been comfortable I would have thought that was a very grand dinner.[15]

After her release, Lili'uokalani, in her words "with a long breath of freedom," left for Washington, D.C., the first of seven such voyages to continue pleading the "Kingdom's case."[16] Lili'uokalani may have lost her royal title and status as a head of state in Hawai'i, but she was a celebrity everywhere she went in America. Newspapers across the land reported on her every move and nuance, including what she wore, when she wore it, and where she wore it.

Lofty Expectations

As the world watched Lili'uokalani's every move, many watchful eyes were also on Ida, particularly those who held the purse strings of the Bishop Estate, and the trustees scrambled to meet her ever-increasing demands for the new school, believing her indispensable. Knowing their scrutinizing gaze was upon her, Ida made sure her high expectations were followed by pupils, teachers, parents, and herself. She required faculty meetings every Tuesday night, no matter how exhausted the staff undeniably was, and all were required to formally report on the monthly progress of their classrooms. Since Ida taught in addition to running the operations of the school, none of the other teachers could easily complain about the meetings. Lydia recalled that Ida "did everything."

Our principal, whom we honored and loved, did everything. She had a class in history, she kept her own books, paid the bills incurred by the school, did the shopping for the school and girls too, and last but not least, she was our nurse. Every morning, noon and evening the patients gathered in a big hall which had been fitted up for bedrooms. Here you would find her as regularly as the tick of the clock looking after the girls' needs. I recall the time when one of the girls was taken seriously ill with pneumonia and Miss Pope stayed right by the girl for many days until the doctor pronounced her well again.[17]

During the 1896 school year, Ida informed the trustees that one more year would now need to be added on to the three. She cited the future need for teachers for the new government schools being established all over the islands. Teaching would be a great employment opportunity for her graduates, and she wanted them to be hired as soon as possible. To focus on the Normal Training, she beseeched the trustees to employ Lilla Appleton at $200 more than her other teachers received. Mr. Bishop instantly turned her request down at the dollar amount requested. He felt that female teachers were already getting a fair wage due to their room and board, and were not entitled to the same salary as male teachers. Outraged, Ida expressed a clear feeling of gender inequality to Lilla.

April 1, 1896

Dear Miss Appleton:—

I sent your letter to the Trustees, with as strong a plea as I could write, urging them to offer you the assistant principalship at a salary of eight hundred. To say that I am cross is "putting it mild"—I think it outrageous—It is one of the indignities that womankind suffers in the business world—in competition with mankind. I have done my level best and am only sorry that it was of so little avail. I do so want you at Kamehameha. I will send a contract—with faint hope that you will sign it. I am writing this hurried note tonight for the steamer tomorrow. Pray pardon the scrawl. In the native vernacular, will you make me a reply soon?[18]

Lilla refused what she viewed as a stingy offer but feigned health over budget issues in her April 21 regret letter to Dr. Hyde: "Knowing the boarding-school work as well as I do, it does not seem just either to myself or your school to enter upon that work until health is fully restored."[19]

To appease Miss Pope, Mr. Bishop reluctantly approved an extracurricular teacher trainer. He didn't see the need for a dedicated teaching program, as it would keep girls boarded longer, minimizing space for new pupils. But Ida pushed forward. Her urgency was that the Honolulu Normal and Training School had just started up. Ida, highly competitive, wanted to beat this "formidable rival." Nobody should surpass her girls. She begged Lilla to search on her behalf for an exemplary teacher trainer with "sympathy" for the Hawaiians. All these issues and more began to sap her strength, and Ida expressed a weariness so severe that it had begun to cloud her thinking.

June 23, 1896

Dear Miss Appleton:—

Your expected answer has at last reached me. I am very much disappointed. And now you will think that I am taking advantage of your kindness— secure some one for me. You know so well the requirements of the place that I will have the utmost confidence in your decision. I desire a thoroughly trained experienced teacher in the Normal department, some one that has go, pluck, and will have sympathy for these people. We will have a formidable rival in the Honolulu Normal School and we must do good work. I could never ask you but for the sake of the native work, for Kame-hameha, I will do and dare much. I am very much worn out. I am writing very hurriedly and I fear not satisfactorily but I am really not able to think clearly. I am so tired and weary.[20]

Lilla was unable to secure a teacher, and Ida resorted to a teacher's agency. In the fall of 1896, Ida shared the exciting news of her new teacher trainer, Helen Harding. She sounds encouraged that she was attracting young, high-caliber, trained educators for Kamehameha and refers to Miss Harding as an "acquisition." Helen had already published a paper on the Froebel methods espousing her views that education must not be narrow, unyielding, and formal, but liberal in scope, respectful of the idiosyncrasies of every individual, and prolific of the most free and complete development.[21] She seemed a perfect fit.

October 15, 1896

My Dear Miss Appleton,

Fisk Teachers' Agency in Chicago sent us—a Miss Helen Harding—a graduate of Terre Haute Normal School. A woman of charming personal appearance, twenty-five years of age. Thus far all is well and I believe she will be an acquisition at Kamehameha—she has from the start taken a decided interest in the pupils and all her suggestions have not only been sensible but practical.[22]

Ida was crestfallen when her new recruit resigned after only a few months and grimly informed the trustees, "Miss Harding was not able physically to cope with the work and was obliged to resign at the end of six months."[23] She then recommended her old friend Frances Lemmon from Oberlin as a replacement. The Fisk Agency might attract talent like Helen Harding, but Ida knew that only she alone could recruit for Kamehameha. An older and hearty Midwesterner like Frances, who had been an assistant principal of an Ohio high school for six years, could be more easily retained, and this proved true for the next thirty years. Miss Lemmon substituted as principal for Ida quite capably during Ida's sabbaticals.

The fact that Helen Harding could not be retained was not surprising even in the well-equipped Kamehameha School. Living and working around the clock with a school full of girls, no matter the beauty of the school or the islands, was an unanticipated hardship for even the hardiest of souls. Many of the teachers quickly found it necessary to purchase a horse to have the freedom, adventures, and exercise they craved to relieve tension. But Ida had never had much luck with horses in Ohio or Honolulu and even feared them after several ankle-twisting incidents recorded by Carrie Winter. When she finally learned to ride a bicycle, she boasted to Lilla,

> The bicycle fever is upon us. I thought I should never learn but after much practice and several falls I mastered the situation and can ride without fear. The teachers of the three schools have the use of a little cottage at the beach near the Bishop place and two weeks ago we had a picnic supper. Some wheeled down, others went in carriages or on horseback. The wheelers though, I think, had the best time. I was one of them and so speak from experience.[24]

In Ohio, Ida never had time to learn to ride a bicycle. She was both her mother's and father's assistant in raising her five younger siblings and helping with the family business. Of the four Pope sisters, only Lois married, and the little Prossers were adored by their Aunt Ida.

October 10, 1896

Dear Ruth and Tom,

Last night I began a letter to you little people but the mosquitoes almost ate me up—so I went to bed and tucked my net in so the bloodthirsty mosquitoes could not find me. I have your picture in my bedroom—and look at you often and wonder how much you will grow before I do see you. Someday I hope you can come and see me. I will take you to the beach and you can play in the biggest sand pile you ever saw, and learn to swim in the salt water—and then I would put you in a little canoe with a big native man and send you out for a row.

I send a load of kisses to my dear little nephew and niece.[25]

Much later, when Ruth Prosser was in her early twenties, the "big native man" who took her "out for a row" on behalf of her Aunt Ida was none other than 6'1" Olympian and surfing legend Duke Kahanamoku. Ruth Prosser recorded in vivid detail the afternoon spent at Waikīkī in 1918, with "the magnificent Hawaiian who had made a clean sweep of Olympic swimming events."[26] Duke, who attended the Kamehameha School for Boys a short time, felt honored to "take Miss Pope's niece out in an outrigger canoe beyond the reef" and to teach her to catch a "cresting wave" and paddle vigorously to ride it "just ahead of the curling wave."[27] It seemed that everywhere a family member of Ida Pope went in Hawai'i, someone wanted to extend a courtesy on her behalf.

The First Graduating Class

Finally, on June 29, 1897, Ida would see the first fruit of her labors. Nearly two thousand onlookers crowded inside the walls of Kaumakapili Church, with accommodations to sit only eight hundred, to see the first graduating class of fifteen girls receive their certificates.

It was, as many papers noted, a "historical event" and a "triumph for Miss Pope."[28] To show the Hawaiian community a broad spectrum of their education, Ida required capstone projects from her graduates that reflected their particular interest. The program revealed a variety of themes surrounding Christian ministry, education, nursing, and music. But one reporter aptly discerned, "The leading idea throughout the graduates' essays seemed to be that it was time for Hawaiian girls and women to come to the front and take part in the training of their own race."

"The Teacher and Trainer of Hawaii's Little Ones"—Lewa Iokia
"My Life at Kamehameha"—Aoe Wong Kong
"The Servant of the Soul"—Elizabeth Kahanu
"Wake the Divine Within"—Elizabeth Waiamau
"A Bit of Clay"—Kalei Ewaliko

Miss Pope's first graduates holding their cherished diplomas in 1897. *On the top bannister from left to right:* Kalei Ewaliko (Lyman) (1879–1959), Louise Aoe Wong Kong (McGregor) (1881–1969), Elizabeth Waiamau (1877–1913), Harriet "Hattie" Kekalohe (Hanakahi) (1876–1910), Lydia Kaonohiponiponiokalani Aholo (1878–1979), Elizabeth "Lizzie" Keliinoi (Keawe) (1877–1915). *Below the bannister, left to right:* Keluia Kiwaha (Kini) (1878–1916), Jessie Mahoahoa (Horner) (1878–1902), Julia Lovell Kahaunani Imaikalani (Bowers) (1878–1938), Helen Kahaleahu Kalola (Kinney) (1879–1920), Miriam Agnes Hale (Auld) (1877–1939), Lewa Kalai Iokia (1874–1913), Elizabeth "Lizzie" Holoaumoku Kahanu (Gittel) (1878–1932), Julia Mahealani Akana (Tavares) (1878–1919), Malie Kapali (Trask) (1876–1919). *Kamehameha Schools.*

"A Plea for the Children"—Malie Kapali
"Domestic Sciences"—Jessie Mahoahoa
"The Use of Music"—Lydia Aholo
"A Practical Art"—Julia Lovell[29]

Most of these girls had been "mothered" by Ida for over seven years. Therefore, the day was bittersweet. The commencement occurred while Lili'uokalani was politically occupied in America, but her thoughts were on her adopted daughter Lydia as well as Myra, the daughter of her retainer, Wakeke, and stepdaughter of her secretary, Joseph Heleluhe. Ten days prior to the ceremony, she sought to free them from the structure of school in a letter to her adviser, J. O. Carter.

Ida Pope with ever faithful
Lydia Aholo by her side.
Author's private collection.

> Will you have the kindness to write to Miss Pope and say to her that I
> would like to have Myra Heleluhe and Lydia Aholo come out and spend
> their vacation with Akana at Waikiki. It has been customary for Miss
> Pope to keep my girls during vacation time and they need all the
> change they can get after a long confinement in school—it is my wish
> at least.[30]

Lili'uokalani referred to Lydia in this letter as "her girl," but the reality is that
she had become Miss Pope's girl by this time. When the class of 1897 left school
to explore a variety of possible life directions, Lydia chose to stay behind at Kamehameha to live and work in a paid position. She had grown very close to Ida
emotionally by this time and was easily persuaded to stay at the school as Ida's
office assistant and bookkeeper. She told the queen, "I wanted to earn my own living, you know, see how it would be to work."

Lydia's life choices may indicate that she preferred Ida's steadying influence
and the structure of the school life she had known since she was five years old.
She had spent her entire childhood shuffling back and forth between boarding
schools and the queen. Torn between two cultures, she may not have been eager
or even equipped to embrace her dual identity at the time of graduation. Lydia
clearly remembered the queen's offer to return home with her at the same pay
Miss Pope was offering her.

> Oh, she was kind. I sent her an invitation to my graduation. And at the
> same time I wrote and told her that I had been offered a job at the
> school in the office—twenty dollars a month and board and lodging. So
> she wrote back, congratulated me, and she said, "Come home, and I'll

give you twenty dollars a month." Oh, but I didn't go home. And when she came home, I went down to see her. I told her I was going to stay on, and I wanted to earn my own living, you know, see how it would be to work.[31]

Working long hours at Kamehameha prevented Lydia from frequently visiting her *hānai* mother at Washington Place. Thus, Lili'uokalani visited her "all the time," as student Joanna Niau Wilcox remembered.[32] When the queen's carriage pulled up in front of the school entrance, Joanna recounted how she and her classmates darted to the railing hoping to catch a glimpse of the royal personage. They waited expectantly until "the carriage door opened. And Lydia Aholo would come from the office and get in the carriage with the queen and sit down and chat with her. Then she would go back and the queen would go off."[33]

Although Lydia did join the queen once in Washington, D.C., her act of independence was a regret that can be clearly heard in her voice years later.

Two years after she refused her *hānai* mother's offer to live with her as a paid companion, correspondence to J. O. Carter from Lili'uokalani revealed the queen's lonely state of mind: "For myself, a sense of loneliness comes over me, without a kin in this wide world."[34] It is well known that the queen, surrounded by many, actually felt quite alone in her last years and wrote about this isolation in her diaries. Looking back, Lydia called herself a "fool"[35] for allowing herself to be diverted from the "only mother I had."[36] She wished she had acted more assertively when others, including Miss Pope, kept her from the queen's side, when she was needed the most.

For Ida, however, who was in constant contact with her family and had her sister Katherine a few minutes away and a school full of girls who loved her, her state of mind was better. Since Lydia would remain by her side, there was also a hope and a promise for relief of the ever-increasing and demanding administrative responsibilities. Ida wrote glowingly about the 1897 school year and proclaimed to the trustees, "It has been the most satisfactory year in the history of the Girl's School. There have been discouragements sufficient but there could not be found the world over a more industrious, willing band of pupils."[37]

Asserting Herself

Just as they were making plans for an island vacation following the graduation ceremony, Ida and Katherine were summoned to Chicago. Their mother, Cornelia, was sick and feared near death. Ida's beloved father died while she was away, and Ida was not going to take any chances with her mother's situation. Once in Chicago, she found her mother's health stabilized.

At her mother's bedside, Ida had time to reflect, and she decided the time was right for her to ask for an increased salary. Ida had a known knack for advancing her causes with the trustees while still maintaining the delicate balance of propriety that wouldn't threaten their leadership. She understood they would not accede to her wishes if she got outside the bounds of their understanding of appropriate female behavior, and thus she carefully pressed her cases within those bounds. She outlined an extensive list of her duties for the trustees, knowing that it was far and above what her ever-changing male counterparts did. Given the era she lived in, she would never have dared to ask to be granted the same salary as current principal Uldrick Thompson, but she told the trustees in a letter dated July 28, 1897, that she would like a raise to be at least on par with a male teacher. "Comparisons are odious, but the position is one of sufficient responsibility to receive a salary equal, at least to that paid one of the men instructors at Kamehameha—I have not written this letter impulsively, but after much consideration, and believe the request a fair and just one."[38]

The trustees forwarded her request for a salary advance to Mr. Bishop, to which he responded on September 2: "I came near overlooking the letter of Miss Ida M. Pope. She is an able woman and I have great respect for her, and would be willing to pay her fully as much as has been paid to any other female teacher, and a little more, though I think that her duties now that the school is organized and fairly under way, are likely to be rather lighter than heavier."[39]

Ida immediately sent a separate letter requesting a $200 yearly salary increase for her staff: "The work is specialized and demands instructors skilled and trained above the average teachers."[40] The request for an increase in her salary would be granted because he felt, "Not one in fifty good teachers are competent to fill the place of principal."[41] Her salary was elevated to $1,200 and that of the three teachers from Ohio who opened the school with her also advanced to $800, but Mr. Bishop denied the $200 increase for the four others. One year later, she again advocated for those four teachers, who, unlike the teachers at the boys' school, had college degrees and a longer tenure than their male counterparts. But Mr. Bishop responded, "It will never be possible to adjust salaries exactly according to merit. There will always be jealousy."[42] He privately told his agent that Miss Pope and her teachers should not ask for any more salary increases because they "are furnished with good lodgings and board and do not make due allowance for what they receive."[43]

While Ida was nursing her mother in Chicago, the whole of Honolulu society was debating annexation. The Hui Aloha 'Āina (Hawaiian Patriotic League) organized and mobilized a mass petition drive with the hope that if the U.S. government realized the majority of native Hawaiian citizens opposed annexation, it could be stopped. Women had no voting rights, but they were still allowed to sign a separate petition, and while Lydia prepared to settle into the secretary role at Kamehameha, her stepmother, Lilia Aholo, was traveling to five islands, encouraging Hawaiian women to join the movement. Her signature as the recording secretary is on the top of every petition against annexation. Today, the petitions, holding twenty-one thousand signatures of both men and women, provide an important historical accounting of a people who were not passive, as some have stated, but intent on fighting for their nation.[44]

CHAPTER TWELVE

Outside the School Gates

Pālama Settlement

Most of Miss Pope's 1897 graduates had been together since early childhood. Kamehameha had been more than a school; it had been their home, and their classmates were like sisters. It's not known what the girls felt at the point that their graduation sent them out into the world, but it's easy to imagine the psychological impact of leaving a boarding school environment for the first time. Miss Pope's feminine society was virtually isolated from the Hawaiian community in the early days. Girls returning home would probably have felt alienated as they reencountered cultural practices and beliefs so long denied to them. For those with no home to return to, this exodus from school might also have rekindled an earlier sense of helplessness. At Kamehameha, they were told what to do and when to do it. Now they would need to make these decisions on their own, something they may not have been prepared to do. The sudden loss of routine might have made them feel very vulnerable.

Though the departing girls' feelings are unknown, Ida's feelings about losing them were transparent. She was not ready to cut ties. She felt a deep responsibility to the girls, many of whom she had raised from childhood. This made it hard when she learned her first graduates faltered on the job market. The goal of giving them a high standard of education did not seem to be translating well into actual jobs. Curious at this point as to why her education did not adequately equip the pupils to support themselves, Ida wrote, "It would not be just to speak of the Girls' School either as a success or a failure. Who will riddle me the how or why of any problem in three short years?"[1]

Like a Worried Mother

More than a principal or teacher—more like a mother—Ida began to worry about the quality of life for her next cohort, and she wrote freely about it. Her lengthy editorial "Within and without the Gates at Kamehameha" spanned the 1898 March and April issues of the school's newspaper, *Handicraft*. Many Hawaiian communities at the end of the century had been left behind in the industrialization

Overcrowded conditions and hastily built frame tenements created grave sanitation problems in the Pālama neighborhood. *Pālama Settlement.*

of Honolulu. They had fallen into unsanitary and impoverished conditions. Native Hawaiians often lived in tenements alongside immigrant workers, who had become disconnected from the society. She worried about the girls who would return to these neighborhoods.

> My girls love fun. I have gone pleasuring with them when it has been pure joy, not an ugly word or sound all day. They will seek for this fun after school days are over and not in places for their edification. In this land where it is always afternoon, it would be pleasant to dream and muse and picture all things fair. The glimpses I had of the homes from whence come some of the best girls at Kamehameha has oft times marred the pictures Nature gave of sea and hill and sky. In the majority of cases are there safe and sheltered places for these girls? Are you familiar with their homes? Do you know of the temptations they are constantly meeting?[2]

Ida wondered if the girls could endure on their own after years of a cultivated home and school life, and worried that their souls would starve without the refined cultural environment she created. She had tried to give them the materials of what she, along with many of her contemporaries, considered a more "elevated" life. "The pupils are surrounded by much that is elevating. Their rooms are tastefully furnished and all the pupils take much pride in their arrangement. Books, pictures, and games are at their command. In the majority of homes, what do you find to content these school girls?"[3]

This view, while it failed to account for the social and economic stresses hindering Hawaiian families, was nonetheless unusual at a moment when the general idea was, as Charles Bishop believed, that the natives should not get above their station. He was firmly against educating "the natives into habits that they cannot afford" or "maintain" once they left school.[4] While Ida's perceptions might appear to imply that she thought little of Hawaiian culture, she was afraid that if Hawaiian women did not keep moving along with the larger pace of history, they would be left behind and fall into poverty.

In contrast to Charles Bishop's viewpoint, Ida asked the question, "Is it better to educate girls for the old conditions or to train them along the march of civilization?"[5] It was her goal from the beginning to put a love and desire into her girls that would make them hunger for music, poetry, art, and literature long after they left school. She publicly rebuffed the "criticisms galore" regarding her methods of acculturation and "social elevation"[6] of her pupils.

> A short time ago I was accosted on the street by this remark, "You are too fine at Kamehameha, Miss Pope." Too fine! What does this mean? Are the

common decencies of life too fine? I wish that the Bishop Estate was so unlimited in its resources that it could appeal to every thing fine and beautiful in human nature; to the head, hand and heart. Is it not for the nourishment of the soul that we purchase books, pictures and statuary? How far reaching is the influence of a good book or a good picture? How much sweeter life would be for people in moderate circumstances? What an uplift it would be at Kamehameha to exchange the rocks that cumber the ground for a Diana or a Venus.[7]

Ida deeply believed that people's behavior was shaped by their circumstances and that by being surrounded by beautiful things and words, people could rise up from even the most impoverished circumstances. She asked for community intervention to make the society her girls entered more genteel and safe: "Is there not a duty that the community owes the daughters of Hawaii? Can you for a moment conceive of placing your children in the environment by which these girls are surrounded? How far is the community responsible for these conditions and what can be done to mitigate the evils that are prevalent? What efforts are made for their social regeneration, to keep them up to the standard they have received in school? Pleasant associations and refining influences are necessary, or retrograde is the motion."[8]

Understanding that her students' fate was intertwined with that of their community, and seeking solutions that could aid both at once, Ida turned to a new method being used to assimilate immigrants—a type of institution called a social settlement. She imported a hybrid of the concept and hoped to establish a social settlement right outside the gates of Kamehameha because "they must be shielded, sheltered, and guided until developed into self-respecting, self-supporting womanhood. Individual interests and responsibility, clubs and social settlements are the ways of the day. I favor social settlements, especially in crowded parts of Honolulu."[9]

The Social Settlement Model

Creating a social settlement—somewhat akin to a community center—in a down-trodden section of Honolulu was seen as a dubious experiment by many, but not by Ida Pope.[10] The working-class neighborhood of Pālama, close to the school, became home to one of her first community projects. She had traveled through the multiethnic neighborhood countless times, and worked at a station offering relief during the cholera outbreak. She asked her readers to consider the desperation in their midst: "Have you driven down King Street, on a Saturday night, across the Nuuanu Bridge, where lurk germs as deadly as cholera and watched the people? Oh for something pleasant to give these people that will make life sweet and worth the living! What a God's acre is lying waste in that neighborhood for men, women, children and babes."[11]

Ida believed the settlement model was the solution. The settlement movement had begun in England to meet the practical needs of unemployed immigrants and was replicated in Chicago by social workers Jane Addams and Ellen Gates Starr in 1889. Their settlement, housed in a former mansion, was dubbed Hull House. The main purpose of this and other settlement houses was to help immigrants assimilate into both the culture and the labor force. The Hull House, for instance, provided courses in art, history, and literature as well as a myriad of social services for Ellis Island immigrants. Personal stories of Jane Addams' success in gaining employment for the Hull House residents were legendary. After an in-depth observation, Ida felt that Honolulu should have its own Hull House.

> I had the great pleasure of visiting Hull House, and my heart was glad for the beauty of it. Chicago gives of her best to this work: It sits down in the midst of its humble neighborhood with the idea of sharing the influence of its large opportunities with those whose lives are defrauded of the light and beauty that belong equally to all. It has no cumbrous theories to which it is bound to conform, but is ruled only by a loving intelligence that constantly seeks the best of the community.[12]

While the settlement movement's logistics were rooted in philanthropy, its philosophy was self-sufficiency—and this was right up Ida's alley. Like the South Side of Chicago, the neighborhood of Pālama was packed with immigrants. In Ida's view, the sanitary and health conditions were dire. A mission-centered community complex with organized support consisting of a library, social training, Bible studies, medical care, childcare, and social clubs would be one way to improve neighborhood conditions. And if cottages for her graduates could also be constructed alongside the center, even better.

Spreading the Vision

As early as 1895, well before the first graduates left, Ida began sharing her vision for a settlement with a Christian emphasis among her fellow Central Union Church members. They were no doubt eager listeners on how to improve the neighborhood, especially as it related to unsanitary conditions among the children. They had all lived through the horrors of the cholera crisis that shut down all operations in Honolulu.

To garner financial support, Ida circulated in the community to present her case. She prepared a detailed report of her vision and presented it, no doubt enthusiastically, to fellow members of the Hawaiian Mission Society on May 31, 1896. She titled her report "Palama Hull House," hoping in vain that the name would stick. At that meeting, held at Charles Montague Cooke's home, an impressive $51 was deposited in Ida's collection plate, and she was off to a good start.[13]

That same evening, she formed a group with Judge Lyle Dickey and former Kawaiaha'o Seminary teacher Margaret Brewer to collaborate with a "similar committee from the Central Union Church to iron out the practical details of establishing social services at Palama."[14] With the two committees in charge, things went quickly. A building campaign began, and the wealthy Peter Cushman Jones, deacon of Central Union, funded the bulk of the money for the building campaign. In 1896, a "small building" was soon "dedicated to the worship of God and the service of their fellow men,"[15] and Pālama Chapel (later renamed Pālama Settlement) became a reality.

Miss Pope in Charge at Pālama

Miss Pope nonchalantly reported to the trustees in January of 1896 that she would be heavily involved in the establishment of Pālama Chapel.[16] It's unknown how the trustees or Mr. Bishop reacted to the fact that she not only donated money but also signed on to become the superintendent in charge of the Sunday school curriculum and instruction for Pālama Chapel.

With Lydia Aholo by her side, Ida worked the neighborhood, distributing hundreds of gift bags to encourage attendance at the Sunday school. Within a year, Pālama Chapel's minister, Reverend John Lewis, reported that the once-dubious experiment was now an established mission "rooted in the life of the community," crediting "Sunday School Superintendent, Miss Ida M. Pope."[17] He wrote that "due to Miss Pope's efficiency, the Sunday School, under her direction, increased the attendance of children in the neighborhood to seventy -five."[18]

As the numbers swelled, Pālama soon became the training laboratory for Ida's older girls. Several were gaining teaching experience by delivering Bible lessons to the small children on Sundays.[19] Unfortunately, Reverend Lewis didn't stay long, and as 1898 began, Ida was recruited, along with a few others, by Central Union to assume leadership of Pālama until he could be replaced.[20] She didn't seem worried that her employers might not understand why she was spreading herself so thin, but Pālama had become her practical ministry.

Pālama, a Practical Ministry

When Ida went to Moloka'i with the queen in 1891, one of the highlights of her journey had been meeting Franciscan nun Marianne Cope, whose dedication to people sick and dying from leprosy made a deep and lasting impression on Ida. She told the trustees that she was going to look outside the comfort and beauty of the school gates and begin to meet the needs in the community in the same way Mother Cope was. Kamehameha pupils, who had been given so much, needed to

> look beyond the scarlet of our own hibiscus hedges into the strange and unfamiliar hedge rows of our neighbors. Love was the secret of the Master who toiled by the Sea of Galilee and made the disciples fishers of men. And we are his avowed disciples and here by the Sea of Hawaii would we toil and be fishers too. Not for a faith to remove mountains but for a faith to see a way in each of our own particular problems, and a charity for all in the carrying out of them, a feeling for the brotherhood of man for all sorts and conditions. Nor can we fail to help a weaker

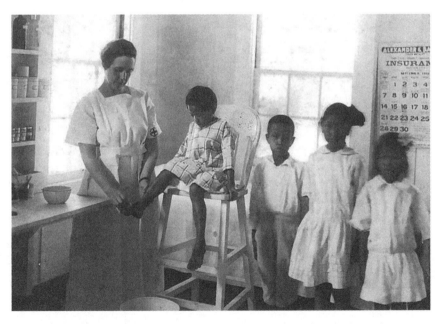

Health, hygiene, and most human services were unavailable to most of the underprivileged on O'ahu until Pālama Settlement stepped in to provide public health visiting nurses. *Pālama Settlement.*

sister whose feet falter; slip and oftimes fall, because the pathway is beset behind and before.[21]

Her next graduates would not be graduating without practical life experience. She would see to that. She justified supplementing the school curriculum with social work in a rough neighborhood as both necessity and ministry. She believed that her Hawaiian pupils could bring others "out of the darkness into the light" and that the only way to do this would be to "supplement the schoolwork by organized social help."[22] Before long, the Pālama Settlement was teeming with Kamehameha girls. Pupils who wanted to be nurses were observing, assisting, and training alongside the Pālama nurses in their ministrations. In the evenings, girls taught sewing skills and lace-making to the women in the neighborhood. Ida felt that nobody knew the community better than her Hawaiian girls, and she soon put seven of them in complete charge of Pālama's Sunday school program.[23]

The Free Kindergarten Association

In Ida's view, settlement houses and progressive education went hand in hand. Significantly, John Dewey, the great proponent of progressive education of the time, whom Ida deeply respected,[24] had served on Chicago's Hull House's first board of trustees. The Free Kindergarten Association, supported by private contributions, was established throughout America as a result of the late-nineteenth-century "child saving campaigns."[25] The association provided a basic education as well as social services for impoverished children and their families. The major focus of the progressive kindergartens was to teach youngsters habits to ensure their future health.[26]

In Honolulu, the movement began in 1895 by the energetic Harriett "Hattie" Castle sustained by a gift of $10,000 from Mary Tenney Castle.[27] Without hesitation, Ida donated to her friend Hattie's fund-raising efforts.[28] This union of five kindergartens was segregated by race throughout the island. It became apparent that a sixth kindergarten was desperately needed in the Pālama neighborhood. A perfect solution was to house it in Pālama Chapel, but in view of the multicultural neighborhood, it would be integrated. A trained kindergarten teacher was soon recruited for Pālama but would last only seven months. Ida immediately stepped in to solve the problem.

A Sister by Her Side

Ida was strategically placed to see that her younger sister Anne, trained in the famed Chicago Kindergarten Training School, would fill the teaching va-

Anne Elizabeth Pope
(1871–1933). *Author's private
collection.*

cancy. Ida's sister Katherine had temporarily left Hawai'i to help with their
mother's increasing medical problems, leaving Ida bereft without a sister by
her side. But Katherine had always been more of a free spirit than Ida; Ida was
closer to Anne, who was "similar in temperament and natural bent."[29] Nine
years older than Anne, Ida had always felt maternal toward her. Anne had
weighed only three pounds at birth. When she was seven, she fell from a hayloft and severely injured her hip, which caused her lifelong discomfort. Despite the pain, she was known as "jolly and endearing" and won the hearts of
all who met her.[30] While sturdy in spirit, she remained physically small and
frail into adulthood. Knowing that Lili'uokalani and "little Anne" each wore
a lift in one shoe due to an accidental fall would have certainly created another
bond with the queen for Ida.[31]

Anne was twenty-five when she boarded a steamship to join her big sister
in Hawai'i. As she would discover, she was to be more than a teacher. Ida
had seen to it that Anne's position was upgraded to director of the Free
Kindergarten.

Anne in Charge

Even though her last name was Pope, Anne was still a malihini (stranger) and was not easily accepted by the community. Pālama Chapel also provided free medical care, and children were treated by two nurses biweekly who treated "all the cuts, thorns and sores."[32] At first Anne "labored against a tide of prejudice and suspicion." Parents were especially reluctant to "trust the ministrations of doctors and nurses" in what was viewed at the time as an "experiment."[33] Anne recorded that mothers often scrutinized the nursing procedures out of fear for their children. She would need to work hard to prove to "seven nationalities" of parents that her objectives with the little children were "friendly of intent."[34] To meet that challenge, she soon boasted that she had learned "Hawaiian Pidgin," a conglomerate of languages, well enough to communicate with the different nationalities.[35]

And after a hard day's work, the Pope sisters walked through the tenements of Pālama to establish personal connections with the parents. Daughters of a doctor, they kept a sharp eye out for illness. "Miss Pope went to the trouble of making a personal visit to each home. One of these visits some months ago saved the eyesight of a child. The little one fair-haired and cute and bright was suffering from an eye trouble that with a few weeks more of inattention would have meant blindness for life. This baby is now one of the happiest and healthiest of the lot."[36]

Even as Anne ministered to the poor, she, like many of her time, perceived their poverty through the lens of morality. "The parents of my native children quite often do little work; they fish, string leis, smoke and gamble. They eat when they are hungry and happen to have food. They live out of doors most of the time, their housework is almost nothing. Many have not beds or tables. They eat and sleep on the floor."[37]

Apparently, her displeasure in their lifestyle was undetected, because parents soon embraced Anne and began bringing in food to supplement Pālama's meager but healthy meals. Anne also began a little garden to teach her children how to grow vegetables.[38] She seemed dedicated to helping the children and their parents become self-sufficient in terms of their food provisions in order to combat hunger in the tenements.

By all accounts, Anne was deeply committed to the children, not just with regard to their health and education but also in preserving their childhoods—making sure that they had fun. And she seemed to have a real connection and rapport with the kids, one that led to a rapport with their families. The local newspaper reported on her innovations in gaining support of the parents who had in some cases strenuously opposed the intrusion.

A little while ago Miss Pope undertook the direction of this kindergarten, and immediately began visiting and working among the families of her charges. The result is that not only are the children themselves greatly improved, but the sympathy and interest of many parents have been won. The children had a tree at Christmas, to which they invited about 100 friends and parents. Every mother was given presents done by her child, and the pride exhibited by the recipients of these gifts was in itself a guarantee that a friendly feeling existed toward the kindergarten.[39]

In her teaching, Anne learned to be indulgent of the easily distracted child. She wrote her friend Emma Cross in Chicago about cows that were herded by her playroom every afternoon. Since the herd "cleared the room instantly"[40] of curious youngsters despite her pleas, she just made the cow parade visit a regular festive event. By spring, Anne had fifty-two children, and the *Advertiser* reported, "Miss Pope is heart and soul in the work and is familiar with the most modern and latest approved methods. She knows the name of every member of that motley crew of babydom and is simply idolized by the little ones. She teaches them singing and motion songs and games and shows them how to play with sand and clay and blocks and how to plant flowers and treat pets and sew in a small way."[41]

Dozens of nurses made house calls throughout Pālama neighborhoods, helping with laundry and providing sick care, education in nutrition, hygiene, well baby care, and childcare. *Pālama Settlement.*

All four Pope sisters had been taught that a subdued, well-regulated pattern of speech represented "good breeding." It seems as if this was also a trait of Queen Lili'uokalani, as remembered by Lydia Aholo: "There's one thing I learned from her. That's talking out loud. You never heard her yell at anybody. If she had to—if she wanted to reprimand us for something we had done that she didn't like, it was always in the same low soft voice."[42] In the classroom, this marker of status became a key tool for Anne to connect with the very young children. "One would think that to handle a corps of half a hundred young-sters, the voice at least of a general commanding divisions would be a requisite. Miss Pope's voice is low and sweet and gentle and she can get the attention of any child about the place in an instant. In the early days of the school it was necessary to keep the doors closed to hold them in the house. Now they are quite under control."[43]

Anne's "Unflagging Efforts"

By all accounts, Anne proved equal to the demands of the pioneer effort. But after two years of "unflagging effort," she had to return to Chicago.[44] At home her dis-ability was a manageable matter, but in the rough conditions of the islands, it was too much. Ida didn't want her to go, but was too worried about her pallor and weight loss to allow her to stay.

Central Union Church members voted unanimously to pay her steamer pas-sage to San Francisco out of gratitude for her hard work. As Anne prepared to leave, in the summer of 1899, a group of grateful parents met her at the dock to present her with a "princely gift" of a "giant old calabash bearing a silver plate engraved to *Anne Pope from the People of Pālama*."[45] Accompanying the calabash was a card bearing forty-eight parents' signatures expressing their appreciation. She treasured these two objects for the rest of her life.

Weighing less than eighty pounds when she arrived back in Chicago, Anne was immediately entered into a "rest-cure." This was a treatment for nervous ill-ness popular in the nineteenth century that included "rest, a fattening diet, mas-sage, and electricity."[46] After six weeks at the Christina Forsythe Rest-Cure on a "diet which included six eggs a day, much cream and butter in addition to meat," Anne weighed 126 pounds.[47] Of her Pālama experience, she wrote in her journal, "I would not have lost this experience for years of experience in the states. It is full of richness for me, and I hope there is something in it for the children and mothers."[48]

The newspaper reported on Anne's departure as if Hawai'i were losing two Popes in one fell swoop: "The service of these two sisters will always be a bright memory with us."[49] For Ida, however, it was only the beginning of her service to the community. She was heavily involved in the life of the Pālama Settlement until her death.

An Unchanged Mission

A year after Anne left, the management of the Pālama Chapel was transferred to the Hawaii Evangelical Association with the intent to become part of the American Settlement movement.[50] In 1906, Pālama Chapel became "Pālama Settlement," to reflect the growth and development of its programs.[51] The new Pālama Settlement became a chartered, independent, nonsectarian organization headed by social worker James Arthur Rath Sr. and his teacher wife, Ragna Helsher Rath, who arrived in 1905.

Ida became great friends with the Raths and worked closely with them on social issues in the first decade of the twentieth century. By 1910, the settlement, now incorporated, was pulsating in the community. Mr. Rath reported that its social services included an "employment bureau, day camp, clinics, visiting nurse service, milk depots, religious service, library and reading room, gymnasium and baths, kindergarten, adult school including English, history, arithmetic, sewing and music."[52] During the early 1920s, the settlement moved to its present location where it continues to thrive as a community center, maintaining its long tradition of being integral to the neighborhood. The Raths' granddaughter, Paula Ragna Rath, is still active today at Pālama, a living legacy to their hard work.

CHAPTER THIRTEEN

The Turbulent Ending of the Nineteenth Century

Boys in Blue

On February 15, 1898, the sinking of the USS *Maine* in Havana Harbor set in motion a series of explosive events that led to the United States declaring war on Spain. Many Americans assumed that the Spanish were responsible,[1] and in the late spring of 1898, patriotic Americans gathered at Fisherman's Wharf in San Francisco, ready to fight for their country. It was said that almost all of the young volunteer soldiers, the "boys in blue," were seeing the ocean for the first time and were ill prepared for the misery that followed their departure. The crowded conditions, the seasickness that kept them hanging over the railing, and the lack of fresh water and food even took lives. Every soldier highly anticipated the moment when he could put his boots down on dry land in the tropical paradise of Honolulu.[2]

What they did not expect was the patriotic carnival atmosphere among the throngs of citizens in the new Republic of Hawai'i welcoming them ashore in the summer of 1898. To the sounds of cheering and a band's playing "The Star-Spangled Banner," they caught fresh tropical fruit in midair. The American flag flew from virtually every visible building. Every horse tram was placed in service so that the weary soldiers could take in the sights of Kapi'olani Park and Waikīkī Beach free of charge. Though the citizens meant well, most of the soldiers were in too poor of a condition to enjoy the festivities.[3]

Many of the younger soldiers, homesick boys between the ages of sixteen and eighteen, were directed to the Kamehameha boys' campus to be housed. Principal Uldrick Thompson remembered feeding and housing some downhearted boys for their three days in port. Other soldiers were not so lucky as to have such clean and sanitary lodgings. Many camped out in Kapi'olani Park, and Mr. Thompson lamented that the "officers knew less of sanitation than a child of ten years."[4] Because of this, a typhoid epidemic soon filled the hospital. Red Cross work actually began in Hawai'i during this time, in tending to the needs of the sick sol-

Thousands of young patriotic "boys in blue" were ill prepared for the miserable shipboard conditions. *Library of Congress 18983b26167u.*

diers. Hundreds of women, including Princess Kaʻiulani, worked tirelessly to aid the sick as they came and went from the Philippines. Kamehameha teacher Cora Albright commented on the sad condition of the soldiers as well as the vast sums of money spent on them, in a letter to the alumnae of her college: "We have seen much more of the signs of war here than you in America. Thousands and thousands have passed through here, and fourteen thousand dollars have been spent for their entertainment. Many have been left here too ill to go on, some have returned home and some have died."[5]

Despite Liliʻuokalani's best attempts, Ida's first graduates would never see their nation returned to them. A multitude of boys in blue were in the port of Honolulu on July 7, 1898, when the news came that President McKinley had signed the resolution annexing Hawaiʻi. On top of Punchbowl, a great bonfire of timbers and tar barrels was lit to relay the news to all the other islands.[6] The proponents of annexation were jubilant. They looked forward to the official ceremony, making it final, which would take place in August. Among the Hawaiians, there was nothing but devastation. Passionate speeches had been given, debates held, articles written, and petitions signed so that the native Hawaiians could show their opposition, and now all appeared to be lost.

With emotions flying high on both sides, Ida planned to escape to the island of Hawai'i for her summer vacation. Just before she left, Ida wrote to her sister Lois that on her thirty-sixth birthday she had received a surprise from Ohio, when two of their hometown's soldiers showed up at her school.

Dear Prossers.

Honolulu is infested with "boys in blue"—I was called into the Reception Hall to meet two soldier boys—who said that they were from Bucyrus. I did not recognize them as former acquaintances. We asked them to stay for dinner. They did ample justice to the fare. Uncle Sam is not doing much credit to the U.S. by the manner in which he is feeding the soldiers on the transport ships. The fare of necessity is simple—but is neither sufficient nor well cooked. On the Pennsylvania there was almost a mutiny— there was no bread and the hardtack was mildewed—the doctor found a cook washing his shirt in a coffee pot.

We are all awaiting the arrival of the Philadelphia—and the raising of the American flag when we become a full-fledged American Territory. The American politicians have already begun to canvas the situation for governorship and our local magnates may not find it so easy to secure office as heretofore. I hope that Pres. Dole will be Governor. He has had a bitter fight and given us a clean government and deserves the glory of it, if there is any.

Thank you so much for the lovely ring—I have it on now and wore it to dinner—where it was much admired. Thirty-six—what an old maid I am.[7]

At Washington Place, Lili'uokalani also entertained uninvited boys in blue. One friend, Bernice Pilani Cook, recalled being with her on a Saturday morning, when a frantic servant entered the room with the news: "Your Majesty, there are a number of American soldiers in the garden picking flowers and fruits. Some have even come up on the lanai and are taking maiden hair ferns and peering into the rooms."[8] Bernice was astonished that the queen's response to the Americans "who had deprived her of her throne, rank, power" was to direct her to "go out and pick some flowers and give them to the men."[9]

The Flag-Raising Ceremony

On August 12, 1898, gunfire echoed throughout Honolulu. It was not a battle but a twenty-one-gun salute announcing the annexation of Hawai'i by the United States and therefore the end of independence for Hawaiians. Years of arduous debate in the American Congress over the advantages and disadvantages of the annexation of the Hawaiian Islands had quickly ended when the Spanish-American War began. Honolulu's strategic value as a midway coaling station between San Francisco and Manila virtually guaranteed its annexation.

Days before the ceremonial raising of the American flag, Mrs. Frances Parker of the Chicago Normal School made an observational visit to Kamehameha. She was also the president of the Political Equality League of Women, and a good friend of Susan B. Anthony. She was interested to see what a heavily endowed private girls' school looked like. Her husband, Colonel Francis Parker, was a pioneer of the progressive school movement and the director of the school of education at the University of Chicago. Frances Parker was a renowned teacher of the Delsarte method, a system of expression that brings to mind the melodramatic poses of the silent film era. Miss Pope asked her to demonstrate the value of good elocution to her pupils, and after a "sumptuous dinner, cooked by the girls,"[10] Mrs. Parker demonstrated the method by reading a book. Ida's girls were soon known for their public elocution and projection.

Afterwards, the girls reciprocated by passionately singing "royal songs" to Mrs. Parker in their native language. Mrs. Stewart, struggling during her visit with a cancer she would soon succumb to,[11] privately wrote to a friend that the girls were "intensely loyal" to their queen and "greatly aroused over" the imminent flag ceremony. She told her friend that the schoolgirls sang with sadness, and much "emotion and expression."[12] Mrs. Parker remembered that the principal was as melancholy as the girls. This might have been Ida's personal and private rebellion, to encourage her girls to boldly sing their kingdom's patriotic songs in their native tongue on the very week their flag would be removed.

Mrs. Stewart was later present at the official flag ceremony and reported that when the Hawaiian flag was slowly and solemnly lowered, to the notes of the Hawaiian national anthem, "Hawai'i Pono'ī," "it was as still as death, and tears on the eyes of nearly everyone present."[13] She related that when a cheer went up following the raising of the American Flag, it was quickly "hushed out of respect for the feelings of the natives."[14] Historians have confirmed that the flag ceremony had the tension of an execution.

Teacher Cora Albright reported that the committee for this historic ceremony attempted to recruit twelve Kamehameha girls to assist in the lowering of the

Hawaiian flag. Out of a student population of eighty, not one Hawaiian girl would participate.

> They tried to find twelve Hawaiian girls to lower the flag preparatory to raising the stars and stripes, but I do not think any one was surprised to find that no Hawaiian girl was willing to do it. I think it would have been hard to find that many American girls willing to pull down their old flag. There were many tears shed as Hawaii's flag came down, not only by the natives but by some of the men who have worked hardest to bring this about. Old natives even sat and sobbed as they realized that their last hope of a Hawaiian monarchy was gone.[15]

Miss Pope clearly supported her pupils' decisions to decline the invitation to the flag ceremony. However, Lydia Aholo and a few friends were curious enough to try to get a view from the sidelines. It was widely reported that Hawaiians shunned the ceremony out of disgust, but Lydia, a full-blooded Hawaiian, known as

A proud Hawaiian family with their flag. *The Huntington Library.*

attached to the royal family, clearly remembered being denied access. "I remember the day they were going to raise that American flag—I forget how many there were of us. Stupid enough, we were going to see the Hawaiian flag lowered and American flag going up. And the—police at the gate asked us where we were going. Said, 'You don't go at all. You stay right here.'"[16]

Annexation was a divisive issue at the school; it placed Ida on one side and the parents on the other. Whether they favored annexation or not, the entire faculty at Kamehameha Schools was American, including the trustees. Ida, while deeply sympathetic to the plight of the country and the Hawaiian culture she had come to love, was well aware that this year she would need to teach her girls more than history or literature; she would have to teach them to be Americans in Hawai'i. Like the girls, Ida had torn allegiances and conflicting emotions, but it would be up to her to motivate the girls, despite their collective sadness over the demise of their sovereign nation.

Preparing the Girls for the New Economy

Since the recent graduates were not reporting successful transitions into the job market, Ida told the trustees, "It is of grave concern to me that the industrial education at Kamehameha does not better equip the pupils for self support when they leave the school."[17] The basic education coupled with domestic training surrounding keeping a well-ordered house apparently did not provide her first graduates with the right specialized skills for the changed marketplace.

Around the period of annexation, tourism was at an all-time high. Hotels and restaurants were going up. Office and retail buildings were being built. Banks were opening and government offices were being established. In 1898, Ida's educational goals would center on offering training for these new trades. Ida reminded the trustees that the money that Bernice Pauahi Bishop had bequeathed for the education of her race should support without hesitation the new frontier of opportunities for her girls in the newly unfolding economy.

The trustees fully agreed to formally extend the school program from three years to four. Ida would need to work hard to ensure that this fourth year would foster greater success among future graduates. She shifted all efforts to ensure jobs, and in 1899 she urgently appealed to the trustees for a revamping of the curriculum to include the trending, domestic science. But she had to educate the trustees on the difference between learning to cook and clean in the home and the far more complex training that would ensure jobs. These girls would need to learn the advanced domestic skills needed to work in the new hotels, restaurants, and tailor shops that were opening up throughout the community.

In the training that she wanted to offer, the girls would learn to become refined waitresses, dressmakers, and proficient seamstresses for delicate undergarments, lace, and table linens. Typewriting, bookkeeping, and stenography were also high on her list. With these secretarial skills, coupled with their bilingual abilities, her girls would be highly sought after in the new government offices and in the burgeoning business community.

Tragedy at Kamehameha

As the calendar turned to a new year with the hope and promise of transformation, tragedy struck. On January 21, 1899, Grace Beckley Namahana Kahea, then in the last year of her education, jumped to her death from a third-floor window.[18] *The Friend* reported that Grace was "insane," but details on the front page of the *Hawaiian Star* told a different story. It was reported that Miss Pope, who witnessed the jump, was interviewed by a jury and testified that her pupil had been under great pressure. The eighteen-year-old had "studied especially hard in order to pass the teacher's examinations"[19] due to a promise of a teaching position. Miss Pope reported that "the strain was too much" and that Grace was sent home two days before Christmas "in the hope of restoring her strength." But once she was there, her concerned family decided that Grace would be better off at home indefinitely. Grace disagreed. When she went back to school to secure her belongings, she took the first opportunity to jump from the window. "Miss Ahia grasped frantically after her and caught her dress but the weight of her body plunged her to the ground, causing her neck to break while scores of schoolmates and teachers screamed."[20]

And just eight weeks after Grace Beckley's suicide, the beautiful twenty-three-year-old Princess Ka'iulani, heartbreakingly, reportedly died from cardiac rheumatism.[21] The princess had been a role model to every girl in the school, and her beauty and grace were envied and emulated throughout the islands by young women. Many girls hung photos of her in their rooms, and Miss Pope displayed her portrait at auspicious events. While Princess Ka'iulani lay in state, it rained for six days as if God Himself were crying. But on the day of the funeral, "the sun broke through the clouds."[22] Thousands of mourners who lined the street hoping for a glimpse of their fallen princess watched Miss Pope somberly lead her girls "all dressed in white, with black hat bands and a knot of black, yellow and red ribbon on the left shoulder,"[23] in a solemn line to their assigned seats in Kawaiaha'o Church.[24]

The Kamehameha girls had experienced far too many losses in their young lives, beginning with the loss of their monarchy. The tragic deaths of their young classmate Grace and Princess Kaʻiulani must have gravely threatened their collective state of mind. They were fortunate they had each other to console. Miss Pope knew the best way for all of them to cope with this terrible grief was to stay busy focusing on their futures.

Pressing for a Hospital and a Home

After her forays into teaching and specialized industrial work, Ida's ambitions reached further. She proposed that a hospital be built on school grounds, plus a dormitory to house her nurses in training. She reasoned that the hospital would create jobs and give the pupils a natural laboratory for practical nursing experience. She noted that in a boarding school of eighty girls living, working, and learning together, there was enough illness to demand a hospital. To support her requests, she carefully enumerated the thirty-eight maladies that had stricken her girls in a single year. They included rheumatism, whooping cough, malarial fever, dyspepsia, and even leprosy.

> Hawaiian girls, if properly trained, will make excellent nurses or assistant nurses. Why cannot these girls have the advantage of training under the shelter of the Girls' school, where they can have the home life they so much need? I believe it would be a practical thing if a hospital for women and children could be established on the grounds of the Bishop Estate. It is a much needed institution. Such a hospital would furnish employment for numbers of our girls and give them related hospital practice. Why not take the initiative? Kamehameha is the last hope of the Hawaiians.[25]

She postulated that a hospital for women would mitigate the racial extinction of the Hawaiians. "The mortality among Hawaiian infants and children is alarming as shown by the reports of the Board of Health and comes largely from unintelligent care in infancy. A Hospital for Women and Children would help eradicate this evil, which threatens the extinction of the race."[26]

She pointedly told the trustees, "When I think what there is for the girls outside of this institution, I have little cause for encouragement." Ida found that her unmarried graduates faced pressing housing needs. Even for girls with marketable skills, there was often no safe place to live. Ida directly urged Mr. Bishop to consider building a residence on campus so that graduates could be assured safety, security, and the domesticity they were used to. She included two pages of data to support her request, as well as letters from community members, all offered in the firm belief that he would ultimately see the need as clearly as she did.

The trustees willingly sent her request to Charles Bishop. Perhaps because he did not have to look straight into her piercing blue eyes and was not willing to bend as easily as those who worked with her daily, his answer was no. Multiple letters followed from Charles Bishop to the trustees reminding them that the school's principals should not anticipate spending freely from the estate. In one such letter, Mr. Bishop indirectly told Miss Pope to be patient: "There are many things which may be desirable, but which under the circumstances could be waited for. Many of the great schools of the world have been built up gradually, and it was never expected that the Kamehameha School was going to be perfected in a few years."[27] He wrote more directly, "I am thankful that the trustees have not undertaken to carry out all of Miss Pope's recommendations as to expenditures."[28]

Charles Bishop, an orphan raised by his grandparents who became a self-made man, told trustee J. O. Carter in May of 1899, "Young people should learn to help themselves. In Kamehameha there is too much giving away."[29] With this in mind, he ordered an accountant to thoroughly examine Miss Pope's financial ledgers. The auditor reported on June 30, 1899, "I have much pleasure

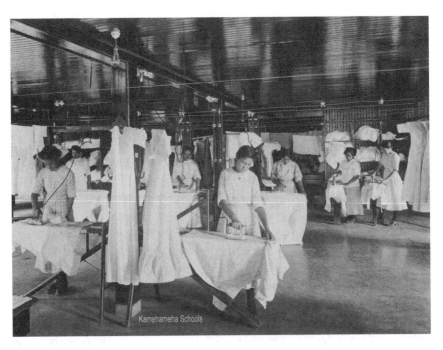

Laundry and ironing were labor intensive. *Kamehameha Schools.*

in reporting that the books are very neatly kept, the entries made in a most careful and legible manner, there being but two or three erasures apparent for the entire year."[30]

Perhaps as a response to the audit, or to the denial of the hospital as well as the home for alumnae, Ida implemented new rules for the 1899 fall term that would appeal to Mr. Bishop's requests for stringency. As a response to the "growing taste for luxuries among the pupils," she told the parents and patrons not to send any money to the girls. "The extravagant spending of money for perfumes, jewelry, and laces is forbidden," and further, all money spent on luxuries would need to be earned in a "manner satisfactory to the principal." She also told the girls that "no photographs shall be displayed unless they are of family, public persons, and places" and that they would all wear prescribed "simple white dresses and sailor hats trimmed with bands of white ribbon to all Sunday services."

The year before, she notified the trustees that laundry was too difficult for her girls due to their feminine fragility and that outside help was needed, but the new rules stated, "Everyone will now do their own washing." It appears that she was imposing something closer to Mr. Bishop's vision of hard work and frugality, all the while continuing to foster big, new plans for the school.

Seeking Inspiration

With these new rules in place, she boldly asked for the opportunity to visit the States to observe innovative programs aligned with her mission. Sounding strained but empowered, she told the trustees that her responsibilities had drained her and that she needed inspiration from outside sources to inform changes to her curriculum that would ensure wages for her graduates.

The Hull House in Chicago appealed to the social worker in Ida. Miss Addams had recently created the Jane Club, a "cooperative boarding club for young working women."[31] Innovative for its time, it offered young disadvantaged women a home where rent, food, and utilities could be had for small weekly dues. There were also clubs within the club, for social and intellectual purposes.[32] Ida would look deeply into the structure of this model for the future housing plans of her graduates.

The Hampton-Tuskegee model of industrial education was at the top of her list to observe for vocational training. At this time, black colleges were very dependent upon philanthropic funding, and to increase donations they found themselves reluctantly putting aside the liberal arts curriculum in favor of vocational education. General Samuel C. Armstrong, the son of missionaries to Hawai'i, founded the Hampton Institute in 1868. Booker T. Washington, the founder of the Tuskegee Institute in Alabama, was schooled at Hampton University in Virginia. He found that donors were more inclined to give to a college that provided an education that ensured employment for its graduates.[33]

Hampton's domestic science department was revolutionary for its time, and Ida could not wait to replicate its success at Kamehameha with the end goal of meaningful employment for her graduates. She pitched her plan to the trustees and reminded them that Princess Pauahi would have approved.

> I have worked eight years in Hawaii for Hawaiians but I cannot go on conscientiously on past ideas. Will the Trustees give me an opportunity to do better work? After careful consideration, I have this plan to offer. I would like to become thoroughly cognizant of work done at Hampton, Tuskegee and Hull House. Could I manage four months of careful study of problems in these schools? The domestic science department and department of agriculture at Hampton and the social schemes of Hull House I wish

Lois Pope-Prosser
(1860–1932), ca. 1898.
Author's collection.

to study specially. I do not hesitate to bring this scheme before you. I believe it practical and necessary for the good of the work.

As director of this school I find the detail work has consumed time, strength, and energy, and all thoughts of leisure for new schemes and enterprises. It has been somewhat of a strain to equip the school, find suitable pupils, have an oversight of all departments, keep the books, care for the sick, directly and indirectly superintend the grounds and to formulate a course of study—and now is the time ripe for new life, plans that will meet new conditions. There must be a place for the Hawaiian girl. She has it by right of inheritance and the bequest of Bernice Pauahi Bishop.[34]

Given that Mr. Bishop had squelched Ida's hospital idea, the trustees could not reasonably deny her far more modest request to take this four-month research trip on behalf of the school. Ida, feeling a little bit in control of the trustees, excitedly wrote to her sister Lois in October of 1899,

Dear Lois,

It is really decided that I go home and now it seems almost impossible to wait until February. My poor head fairly spins with schemes for Kamehameha. I want to do so much in four months. Please do not urge me to visit you before summer. It is going to be hard to work first and visit my family last, but that is the way that it must be, otherwise I would not have been granted so long a leave of absence.

The next five years will see many changes in the school, and I want to be the one to initiate the new things. The Trustees are lovely to me and I am getting spoiled and arbitrary, but yet I rather like it. My plans are not fully made but will be something like this—leave here the last of January or first of February. Spend some time in San Diego, Cal. looking into the silk worm culture, then to Chicago—then Hampton, Tuskegee—back to Chicago—visit Hull House. Chicago Commons—Prof. Dewey's school— Public Schools and then home in the summer. It will be hard on my clothes and purse—but my blank vacuum will have a little needful filling and I will escape the routine and responsibility of School—which will be refreshing.

The clothes question bothers me considerably. I do not want to spend any money and yet I wish to go home arrayed decently. It perplexes me much. I am thinking of getting a black broadcloth skirt for a traveling skirt and a silk waist—a thick waist will be of no use visiting schools. I will be obliged to have good clothes too. I have about decided to have things made here. I do not think that I will be so entirely out of vogue if I do. I am more than anxious to see the children. They will have changed much but they are all in an interesting age. Love to all.

Lovingly,
Ida[35]

As the turbulent nineteenth century ended, Ida was excited about her future and all she would soon learn and implement. As she enthusiastically planned her journey, she had no idea that her January 1900 voyage would be postponed by the worst civic disaster in Hawaiian history.

CHAPTER FOURTEEN

Up and Away in the New Century

Plague-Stricken City

Ida's joyful anticipation of going home to see her family was swept away when, in mid-January 1900, bubonic plague struck Honolulu in a trickle of cases that rapidly grew into a swelling wave. Ida wrote to her sister Lois,

Dear Lois,

There has been great excitement in Honolulu today—four cases of plague—consternation reigned. I have spent the day finding out where our eatables come from and placing orders in the country—out of this plague stricken city. We are all well, not a bit of sickness anywhere, and all of the carriers are watched now, I can assure you. I am sorry that my going home will be delayed, but if we can keep well, I can be thankful. There are seven cases of fever, of typhoid and malarial fever at Punahou. I wonder when I will see you all. Life is full of such strange experiences. I am tired and sleepy and will hasten to bed. Good night.[1]

As it had in the cholera outbreak five years prior, all business in the city came to a standstill. Public gatherings of every nature, even church services, were prohibited. With no public transportation available, some of Miss Pope's pupils could not return to school from their holiday break. The swiftness and indiscriminate nature of the plague must have left many people anxious and helpless as they contemplated whether they might be next. But Ida had hungry children to take care of, so while others waited helplessly for the Board of Health to provide aid, she located food sources for the school that were far away from the "plague stricken city."[2]

She soon informed her sister that she had proactively fumigated the school herself. It's possible this involved the very dangerous cyanide gas, used at that time for the extermination of rats.

Dear Lois,

The plague is on the increase and the most stringent measures are taken
and I hope it will soon be stamped out. Have been fumigating this morning to get rid of rats. The death of Mrs. Boardman, a white woman, has
caused consternation. Am glad we are all well. It seems rather selfish to
think of my own special plans at such a time, but I wonder much when I
can get away—I fear not before March.[3]

In an effort to stamp out the spreading disease, the Board of Health had a
policy of purifying buildings in the quarantined area of Chinatown with controlled fires. They were operating under the theory that "fire would destroy the
plague germs, kill rats, cleanse soil and open it up to the purifying influences
of sun and air."[4] While that theory was being put into practice on the morning of
January 20, 1900, a freak wind whipped one of those small fires into an out-of-
control inferno. In a single afternoon, more than six thousand people lost their
homes. All of Chinatown was wiped out, as was the historic Kaumakapili Church,
where Ida had enjoyed many services and celebrations. Kawaiahaʻo Church was
pressed into service as the town's shelter for five thousand evacuees. Many, mostly
the Chinese, were marched under armed guard to detention camps.[5]

The Chinatown fire was the worst civic disaster in Hawaiian history. Estimates
of the eventual death toll range between forty and sixty. The quarantine regula-
tions were not rescinded until April 30, but Ida somehow departed for home in
February, before the city was officially declared free from infection. *Handicraft* reported an emotional scene: "Miss Pope departed from us last Tuesday. She has
gone back to the States for six months. All the girls wept at her departing."[6]

Centralized Management

Upon her return to Honolulu for the fall term of 1901, Ida found her authority
and autonomy were now threatened. Charles Bishop decided during the summer
term to centralize the management and fiscal control of the schools, which had
previously operated independently, by naming Charles Bartlett Dyke as principal of Kamehameha Schools. Ida, one of three principals who ran their schools
independently under the Bishop Trust, was forced into a subordinate role for the
first time. The other two schools were the Boys' Manual School and their "feeder
school," the Boys' Preparatory School. All three schools functioned as separate
entities, as stipulated by Princess Pauahi's will, a fact that Miss Pope probably re-
iterated to Mr. Dyke multiple times.

There was some speculation that the trustees were weary of dealing with three strong-willed principals who were constantly pushing their separate agendas.[7] Charles Bishop and the trustees reasoned that if Principal Dyke could run the boys' school as well as prioritize the needs of Alice Knapp, the principal of the younger boys, and the formidable Ida Pope, their lives would be much simpler. Charles Dyke attempted to unify the educational activities of the three different schools by requiring structured collaboration, but he wasn't very successful.

He didn't last more than three years, and it was rumored that Ida had had a hand in his departure.[8] It's easy to understand how intolerant Ida would have been if he had espoused some of his views on race in her company. Charles Dyke's educational agenda following his years at Kamehameha Schools, much like those of William Brewster Oleson, the first principal of the boys' school, is rife with racialist rhetoric. In 1909, at the National Education Association conference, he shared his low expectations of nonwhites: "It is absurd to theorize about the propriety of a college education for the mass of Negros, or Indians, or Filipinos, or Hawaiians. They lack the intellect to acquire it."[9] Besides, he said, "for economic reasons, primitive man must be trained on vocations that fit him for life in the white man's world. This is a fundamental requirement in the education of primitive races."[10]

Realizing the Importance of Cultural Identity

Racially prejudiced men like Charles Dyke surely kindled the need in Ida to reconnect the Kamehameha girls to their inherited culture. A further impetus was provided by the real-world situations of her students. In one summer, Ida visited the homes of fifty pupils, and saw that a Hawaiian way of life differed vastly from the "culture" she created inside the school. She saw in a very personal way that parents were engaged in cultural practices that had become foreign to their daughters. Miss Pope's progressive approach of having pupils actively engage in the world around them omitted a crucial element, Hawaiian culture. At Kawaiaha'o Seminary, Queen Lili'uokalani had provided the Hawaiian cultural balance, now void at Kamehameha Schools.

Almost as an apology for nine years of forcing Hawaiian girls into a mold that did not fit, Miss Pope went into the new century at full steam, making sure her pupils knew they had a distinct cultural identity, one that must be acknowledged, respected, and enabled to flourish in the midst of the Americanization of the islands. She required the girls to research every aspect of their Hawaiian culture. Now for the first time the subject of Hawaiian history was a curricular offering.[11] The school newspaper began printing articles highlighting or explaining

Hawaiian music and legends to the students so that they could get reacquainted with, or in some cases introduced to, their heritage. Miss Pope was excited to showcase the results of the yearlong cultural revival at the 1901 commencement. The event was so unusual that the *Honolulu Republican* reported on it.

> Quite an interesting departure was made in the Fifth commencement exercises of Kamehameha School for Girls given yesterday evening before a large throng of admiring friends. In the place of the usual prosaic and stereotyped school essays which has been done at graduations from time immemorial, the exercises assumed an entirely different aspect. The legends as related by the young ladies showed a most careful and painstaking preparation upon the part of the individual as well as the Instructors. Each represented a vast amount of historical research, assisted by a wise and judicious selection of the material. After a careful digest of the efforts of the graduates in their recital of historical lore, the visitor became immediately impressed with the idea that throughout the early ages of Hawaiian history the people who occupied these Islands possessed a rare knowledge of astronomy. They had a good working knowledge of the rudimentary elements in mechanics. The weaving of feathered leis and capes, the carvings and wood-working achievements were admirably brought out in story in a manner that made the receipt of the knowledge imparted all the more pleasant and agreeable.[12]

To ensure that the audience knew that Hawaiian girls from a bygone royal era were entertaining them, they closed the ceremony with royal chants and music from the days of the monarchy. The name song of King Kamehameha V, "He inoa no Kamehameha," was delivered by chanting in both the language and the spirit of old-time Hawai'i.[13] Composed long before the girls were born, by "an old Hawaiian woman in the train of Queen Lili'uokalani,"[14] the song was known to "tug at the heartstrings."[15] The *Republican* told its readers of "the fifth commencement exercises of Kamehameha School, one of the most successful in its annals."[16] The commencement ended with the singing of "Hawai'i Pono'ī,"[17] the kingdom's national anthem, composed by King David Kalākaua, whom Ida had respected.

Honolulu, a Town on the Move

One reason for Ida's commemorating the past seemed to be the radical pace of modernization, rushing Hawai'i forward into a technological age. The first year of the new century brought about changes that preoccupied the school. The first gasoline-powered automobile arrived in the islands in 1900. The city had new electric trolleys, public parks, first-class hotels, newspapers, social clubs, fraternal orders, public utilities, a one-mile racecourse, and a thriving red-light district.[18] The long-anticipated Pacific Cable was completed at about the same time that Pearl Harbor was completed. These were two events of massive importance to Hawaiʻi in the early twentieth century. Yet as technology progressed, and a massive building campaign got under way, Ida and her girls retreated to the beach and to nature.

The boys had been participating in extracurricular opportunities in the countryside for a few years, and now it was time for the girls to enjoy the great outdoors as well. Though never an outdoorswoman by choice, Ida now deemed it critically important for the girls to learn the fundamentals of camping next to the ocean. On these off-campus excursions, out in nature, girls could recover the home craft skills that boarding school had taken from them. Ida saw that many of her girls' families maintained a strong sense of identity with the sea and land, and it was time their daughters did the same.

During the camping trips, Ida revealed another "fault in the life of the school." She noted "narrow chests, faulty respiration and many flabby, unused muscles. The lazy, logy, indolent bodies should be transformed into bodies alive, alert, energized." She recommended a physical education teacher because

> when our children enter school, *routine* possesses them. Work is the hourly slogan and regular, persistent work in class room and about the house pursues them for forty consecutive weeks. Like the proverbial "dumb, driven cattle" they follow their leaders with little outcry and rebellion. A certain amount of drudgery is needed for the fittest, but "why" make of life so solemn a thing and "why" in the setting of the Paradise of the Pacific with a people born for *do's* and not so many *don'ts*.[19]

Ida decided that the girls also needed to get out from under books and learn how to build and repair "useful articles" in the same way the boys did. She soon commissioned a workshop to be built for her girls. She felt it important to "enable the girls to accomplish their work in comfort" and rebuffed criticisms that she might be defeminizing her group. "We have not the slightest idea of making carpenters of these girls; we are simply striving to prevent the usual waste of material seen in many houses. If these girls are taught to drive a nail straight, to repair the many broken articles around a house and to convert soap boxes and useless bits of waste into useful and pretty things, we shall have accomplished some good."[20]

Evidently, the new century was unfolding with some mixed feelings expressed by Principal Pope. These are reflected in her 1901–1902 annual reports, which

Ida Pope seated in a chair, unwell and squinting in the bright Maui sun, where she hoped to recuperate during summer vacation. Lydia Aholo is seated at her feet and Katherine Pope is holding the guitar in 1902. *Bishop Museum.*

began with a "backward glance" and posed the question wondering if Bernice Pauahi would be pleased with the educational results, and "is the school carrying out the will of the founder?"[21]

Professional results for her students were mixed. When twenty of the thirty-eight students who had graduated by 1902 arrived for an alumnae meeting at the school, one observer noted that the ones who were "self-supporting" or who were "wives and mothers" were unselfishly "assisting in the support of the others" who were in need.[22] This undoubtedly evoked both pride and dismay in Ida. Though she was grateful that her alumnae were taking care of each other, she was frustrated that her repeated requests for an alumnae boarding home had not borne fruit. With renewed passion, she pleaded for those alumnae who found themselves at the mercy of charity.

> The large majority [of alumnae] are making a brave fight for self-support, but positions that ensure sufficient income, for decent living, are difficult to find. The proposed Home for Hawaiian girls under the protection of

this school would tell more for success for our pupils than any another one thing could possibly do. Thousands of Dollars are spent on the education of the girls. And then at a most susceptible age they are turned from this sheltering roof into conditions most deplorable. Case after case comes to our observation of the signal failure of girls, due to overwhelming temptations. A Home would tide them over this period and build up a band of self-supporting Hawaiian women. Cannot such a home be instituted in the near future at Kamehameha? It can be filled with Alumnae who clamor for help and protection. Are we in any measure their keepers?[23]

Becoming Known

At Kamehameha, Ida was an activist, complaining that not enough was being done, but abroad, she acted as an ambassador for the school and the success of its programs. When Ida made her observational visit to the Hampton Normal and Agricultural Institute in 1899, it had been her intention to learn as much as possible to take back to her school. It appears that they were impressed enough with her accomplishments to solicit an essay outlining her work. In 1900 the *Southern Workman,* a magazine published by the institute, featured her long article "The Education of Hawaiians at the Kamehameha School for Girls."[24]

Ida's essay described much more than her educational mission with Hawaiians. She succinctly covered the line of the five Kamehamehas, from 1782 to 1893, and then took the reader through the extraordinary political changes she personally had witnessed up to the date of publication. She described former religious practices and specifically addressed cannibalism, a prevailing myth in America at the time: "No laws were known to the Hawaiians in the early days but the will of the chiefs. The common people were victims of a taboo system and the temples were ruled by priests. Many gods were worshiped and heathen practices observed. Human sacrifices were offered and infanticide was not uncommon, but the Hawaiians were never cannibals. Their gods were represented in images of stone and wood, grotesque in the extreme. There was no marriage rite."[25]

Her empathy and love for the Hawaiians are evident as she reveals the degree to which contact with Caucasians decimated their population and culture.

When Captain Cook came in 1778 there were several hundred thousand Hawaiians. The last census gives less than forty thousand, including half-castes. The Hawaiians are of Polynesian origin and are often called "dusky blondes." They are an amiable, pleasure-loving people, physically superb in youth but in middle life given to obesity. They are musical, lovers of flowers and nature, generous, hospitable, with few wants and those easily supplied, taking little thought of the morrow, receptive alike to good and evil influences; they are born fishermen, at home in the sea, in canoe, or on surf-board, and are expert horsemen. Like the American Indians, they have been taken from a free and untrammeled existence into a civilization that taxes the powers of industrially trained races.[26]

She saw these tensions—of history, industry, race, and culture—coming to a head in the first years of the twentieth century. "The stress of the new century is felt in this sylvan spot. The land is invaded by the march of civilization. Native and Celestial, Japanese, German, English, American, Norwegian, and Portuguese touch elbows. Amid the clash of nationalities and of religions, a great problem is to be worked out. Such is the problem that confronts the Kamehameha Schools."[27]

Ida cited a portion of Princess Pauahi's will to make the case that moral character was just as important to the founder than merely reading, writing, and arithmetic. By her will her estate was placed in the charge of five trustees to establish two schools, one for boys and one for girls. The plan, as she stated it, was to "provide first and chiefly a good education in the common English branches and also instruction in morals and in such useful knowledge as may tend to make good and industrious men and women; and I desire instruction in the higher branches to be subsidiary to the foregoing objects."[28] To that end she cited the Christian activities her school was engaged in: "The religious life has been awakened by the formation of a Young Women's Christian Union and is a prominent factor in the school. Committees for religious, missionary, and social meetings, membership, and athletics are formed in every department and encourage the development of Christian character. Church service is held every Sunday morning in the Bishop Memorial Chapel."[29]

She proudly boasted that after five years of adjustments to the curriculum and training, results were evident.

Three classes have been graduated from the school. One of the young women completes a Normal course in Milwaukee in June, and will return to Hawaii and teach. Several graduates are teaching in the government schools. One is an assistant in a kindergarten and two are receiving kindergarten training. One is doing general housework, another is assistant in the Hilo Hospital, and one is office assistant in the Boys' Preparatory School. A number are married, and one is filling the position of bookkeeper very acceptably in the Girls' School.[30]

Lewa Kalai Iokia was the young woman in a teaching training program at the Milwaukee State School. Lewa earned the first teaching certificate awarded by the Kamehameha School for Girls in 1898. Miss Pope mentored her first trained teacher, an orphan, very carefully. She arranged college admission for Lewa. When Lewa returned to Hawai'i, she had multiple offers for employment. She might have been the first Hawaiian girl from the islands to attend graduate school on the mainland—but sadly, would die in the prime of her life of a condition or incident lost to history.

The bookkeeper mentioned with pride is Lydia Aholo, whose own abilities increased after Ida sent her to Oberlin College for business coursework in 1904. Lydia stayed, as did Lewa for several weeks, with Ida's family in Chicago. The Pope family history book noted "Queen Lili'uokalani had entrusted Lydia's care to Aunt Ida" and she was welcomed into "our home as family."[31] Ida's Memory Book holds a 1907 newspaper clipping from Ohio, obviously cherished, titled "Oberlin Business College." The news is that "Miss Aholo has become one of the best stenographers in the Hawaiian Islands" and that "her services are eagerly sought at sessions of the legislature and other important conventions where accurate work is required."[32] Oberlin was proud to boast that they were educating for lands afar.

The more Ida wrote, and traveled throughout America, and visited educational intuitions, the more people heard about the Kamehameha School for Girls. She was proud that influential people began to look to it as a prototype. One such visitor was the wealthy California philanthropist Ellen Browning Scripps, who on a visit to Hawai'i in the spring of 1902 observed the operation of the school. Miss Scripps' extensive philanthropy was largely confined to California, but her travels were newsworthy due to her wealth. On April 22, Miss Scripps recorded in her diary that she found Miss Pope's school "exceedingly interesting, well conducted, and beautifully equipped. Teachers showed us great kindness and cordiality."[33] The following Saturday, Ida hosted a reception for the Scripps delegation, and that day's entry recorded, "Girls sang, refreshments served. Everything pretty."

It's not known whether Miss Scripps toured the school for inspiration or a prototype, but soon after leaving Hawai'i, she donated land and money to establish the famed Bishop's School, a girls' boarding school in La Jolla, California, that was named for an Episcopalian bishop. In San Diego, Ellen Browning Scripps met Carrie Winter's scientist husband, Dr. Charles A. Kofoid. Miss Scripps ultimately funded what would become the world-renowned Scripps Institution of Oceanography, which was cofounded by Dr. Kofoid. A hundred years later, the material and inspiration for this book would come from the archives of that institution.

European Voyage of 1906

Even as more people reached Hawai'i through the era's increasing ease of travel, Ida herself was journeying farther afield—not only throughout the United States but also to Europe. In the beginning of the twentieth century, travel abroad was a mark of high status. Passenger ships catered to these clients by creating luxurious steamers providing extravagance on a par with fine hotels and restaurants.

Ida was invited to join an organized tour group of American educators in the spring of 1906 on a grand European tour. The timing was right. There is a smattering of references in family documents that indicate she was fatigued and her health was in decline. Her siblings thought the tour was a good idea. A long trip away from everything familiar, to the land of romantic images, magnificent castles, and glorious cathedrals might be just what she needed to recuperate. Travel brochures promised renewed health and vigor due to "constant motion" of "the bromine and ozone contained in sea air."[34] Brochures also tantalized prospective passengers with the possibilities of a shipboard romance under moonlit nights. Ida's brother Henry's wife, Adele, advised Ida to be receptive and "agreeable" to any single men's advances.[35]

From Hawai'i, Ida went straight to Bucyrus and began the journey on April 4, by placing violets on her father's grave. Ten days later, she left from Hoboken, New Jersey, on the steamship *Königin Luise,* one of the swift and lavish steamers from the North German Lloyd Line. This first leg of the trip took her to the Mediterranean ports of Gibraltar, Naples, and Genoa. She then, by train, small ships, and other modes of transportation, traveled to all the major cities of Europe and returned in July on the *Bremen.*

Her travel diary consists of hundreds of pages filled with insightful and humorous observations of people and places.[36] In the course of the journey, she read travel books to better understand the places to be visited next. In the main, the diaries reflect, as would be expected, the thoughts of a history teacher granted sabbatical by the trustees, the serious purpose of her travels, and her desire to learn something of value to take back to the classroom in order to share her experiences as fully and as promptly as possible with her Hawaiian girls. The first page of her diary begins buoyantly with a quote from one of the twentieth century's most acclaimed female novelists, Ellen Glasgow[37]: "It is not the moving about, the strange places one sees, or the people one meets that really counts. In life, you know, I think it is the things one *learns*, the places in which we take root and grow, and the people who teach us what is really worthwhile, *patience* and *charity* and the beauty there is in the simplest and most common lives when lived close to nature."[38]

The SS *Bremen* at the Hoboken, New Jersey, Pier 1905. *Library of Congress 4a12543a.*

These early diary notations indicate Ida quickly sized up the passenger list for marriage prospects, heeding her sister-in-law's advice to look out for love: "Good for me to follow Adele's advice and be agreeable and get to know my fellow *man* better. But somehow I do not progress very rapidly. All comments should be reserved until a later date to deepen or change first impressions. There is one love lorn widower a congregational minister by profession whom I do not think there will be heart burning over among the various spinsters in the party. There is time enough for all sorts of developments."

The "love lorn widower" was Reverend William Edgar Wolcott from Lawrence, Massachusetts, whose onboard preaching instantly turned her off. "He gave a good talk on prayer but it was long and rather heavy. I felt in a cheerful frame of mind and wanted some praise and not so much piety—Afraid I am not addicted to ministers and they return the compliment."

She soon squelched Adele's suggestion, because "the passenger list has not revealed anything particularly illuminating." It's hard to know if Ida longed for love or not, but one early hint comes from Carrie Winter's correspondence fourteen years earlier.

Mr. Walsh is a self-made man, a lawyer, worth a million, a widower and looking for a wife. There are some good points about him but still I think he would be very distasteful to me but for one thing. I think Miss Pope has quite a little leaning toward him. It seems she met him last summer at Mr. Castle's and I believe if he would pay attention to her she would be glad of it. I know she would like to marry. It seems a little horrible to me that she should fancy such a man, but when a woman is towards 30 she isn't so particular as when she is 20.[39]

In Ida's shipboard diary, she noted that her partiality for people had nothing to do with their status or wealth: "Good taste and breeding are in evidence but not distinction—still want to meet men and women big in thought and mind. I want to be lifted out of myself and touch great things—I am dreaming dreams and seeing visions that may someday be real and vital—anyway it does no harm to idealize the commonplace and seek for the larger view."[40]

Bad News in Gibraltar

Ida had been four days at sea, when in the early morning of April 18, 1906, San Franciscans were startled awake by a tremendous shaking. A 7.8-magnitude earthquake drove them from their homes by the thousands. Soon fires sprang up everywhere that would burn for the next seventy-two hours. The loss of life and property made this the greatest disaster an American city had experienced up to that date. Ida was shaken to her core by the shocking news in a cable message that greeted the passengers in Gibraltar on April 25. "I wonder if sad news always welcomes a crowd of wayfarers. The shocking news of the earthquake and subsequent disaster at San Francisco greeted the California members of the party. The London newspapers gave a bad enough account—and we all await with anxiety the news that greets us from Naples. I will be rejoiced if Mr. Bishop is spared—but fear that the old Occidental was not a stable structure."[41]

Charles Bishop was "spared" but, as Ida had feared, not the Occidental Hotel, where she had begun her journey with Carrie Winter as a young twenty-seven-year-old. Now, forty-four years of age, her travel diary makes it clear that Hawai'i, not Ohio, was the home she pined for: "By noon we were approaching Gibraltar—The graceful pepper tree was common in gardens and along the streets and I saw an arbor with bougainvillea in bloom and it carried me across the Pacific to Hawai'i."[42]

Besides familiar foliage, Ida also missed the flavors of home. She became so weary of the monotonous continental breakfasts served in hotels that she penned a humorous poem titled "The Continental Roll" on the long-established European custom of rolls and coffee for breakfast, which met her at every city.

"The Continental Roll"

The Continental Roll
I have walked in dim cathedrals,
Viewed the pictures, old and new
Sailed upon Venetian waters
Neath Italian skies so blue.
But the thing that haunts my slumbers,
And that lingers in my soul,
Is not palace, church or pictures
But the continental roll.

When it greeted us in Hamburg,
We were quite inclined to smile
But we did not know the future
Could not see the after while.
So we ate of it in Berlin,
And on Dresden's "china plate"
Till we wondered if that breakfast
Were our everlasting fate.

The Venetian rolls were bolder
Harder, too, as we all know,
But there was no escaping
From that bunch of sour dough.
There the coffee, too was blacker.
Butter extra, and no cream.
For all the cows give scalded milk.
Wherever rolls are seen.

We braved the heats of August
Pompeian sights to see.
But the roll was there before us
By, perhaps, a century.
We chewed them amid the glory
Of the castles on the Rhine,
And on the steeps of Switzerland
Where only goats can climb.

In aristocratic Paris
We thought they'd change the style
But they only served them warmer
In a somewhat smaller pile.
And in Austria we ate them
Mid the frozen peaks of snow.
They thought it was emotion
That made us tremble so!

With joy we hailed the windmills
That dot the Holland shore
But we found the cream still lacking
Though the rolls were there galore.
The clatter of the wooden shoe
Was drowned by groans of pain,
When we saw the breakfast coming,
And the rolls appear again.

Raphael's grace and Titian's color
Even now are not quite clear,
We'll forget the Campanile
Pisa's tower, too, I fear,
But that continental breakfast
Haunts us like a nightmare yet.
Yes, the continental breakfast
We shall never quite forget.

In her diary, Ida commented on fellow passengers who did not seem content or fulfilled in their lives, and expressed sympathy for them: "Happiness must have its seat within or there is little to be found seeking it elsewhere." She witnessed opulence and grandeur in many places throughout her grand tour. But she was ultimately affirmed by the sentiment of the poem that began her diary: True contentment is found not in having everything you want but in not wanting to have everything. Ida felt it was vitally important to just bloom where one was planted. And where she was blooming was in Hawai'i, at the Kamehameha School for Girls.

CHAPTER FIFTEEN

A Dream Realized

The Kaʻiulani Home

Pleading Her Case

After investigating the "Jane House" in Chicago, Ida clearly envisioned the ideal group home she desired for her alumnae. A facility built near the campus was a perfect solution for her unmarried graduates. These young women could work in the community and then return to the familiar boarding home atmosphere they had known for their entire childhood, only now they would live fully independent. She decided to name the proposed home after Mr. Bishop's favorite royal niece, Princess Kaʻiulani, but he was not entirely favorable to the concept, as indicated by his 1900 letter to Trustee Carter.

> In referring to the Kaiulani Home for Girls—The girls and their relatives should do all they can in taking care of themselves. While I desire that the Home should have a fair trial and wish it success, I am not disposed to help healthy people to an easy or too cheap living. To provide a safe and wholesome home for good industrious young women is the purpose as I understand it; and while I would prefer to favor those for whom so much has been done at the Kamehameha School, I would not like to give them the impression that they are always to be protected. The world does not owe any (able-bodied) person a living.[1]

When Mr. Bishop's response to her through Mr. Carter failed to generate a favorable support of the venture, Ida, once again, turned to the town's philanthropists. As a member of many women's benevolent and charitable organizations, she was strategically placed to campaign among them. She immediately recruited her friend Ida Waterhouse to be the "front person." On her 1893 teacher recruitment mission to Ohio for Kawaiahaʻo Seminary, Ida discovered her childhood friend Ida W. Sturgeon, in dire straits, with her ten-year-old daughter, Nora. Ida immediately recruited her as the matron for the seminary. Before long, Mrs. Sturgeon caught the eye of widowed Henry Waterhouse, and they were married in 1900. By 1904, Mr. Waterhouse had died, and Ida's old friend found herself in comfortable circumstances. Mrs. Ida Waterhouse was delighted to help Ida convince the community to join her efforts in housing the growing number of homeless alumnae.

The impassioned campaign generated healthy financial pledges for the structure to be built on school property. At this point, Ida felt confident enough to implore Mr. Bishop to reconsider, since the costs would be now substantially defrayed. It was also important to let him know that she could easily run the school and oversee the alumnae home herself. The best way to do this, she surmised, was through a man. Prior to Principal Dyke's departure, Ida was able to convince him to advocate directly with Mr. Bishop for the home with the assurances she knew were important to him. The letter reads as if Ida were hanging over the table as he wrote.

March 12, 1902

My dear Mr. Bishop:

In no other city that I am acquainted with, is it such uphill work for girls to remain industrious and virtuous. There are no decent boarding places at moderate prices. The girls are thus obliged to live in debasing and often immoral surroundings exposed to the greatest dangers. All of these young women work on small wages and must live on very little. Cheap living in Honolulu in nearly all cases means to live among the corrupt and immoral.

Now it has been proposed by a number of people in Honolulu to establish a home under the best conditions in charge of a competent preceptress and matron where these young women, graduates of Kamehameha and other schools, may live within their means; do the work of the home and pay the cost of their living in the home.

The young women in the home must be self-supporting. The cost of living must be kept within their means and no one must be allowed in the home that is not of good character and who is not regularly employed. No one in this city has so strong a hold on Hawaiian girls, nor, in my estimation, is better qualified to make this work a success than Miss Pope.

The home must have no organic connection with the school, the condition of the estate would not permit of that now, nor would it ever be right to load down the estate with this kind of work. The finances must always be entirely separate.

Yet, if Miss Pope is to undertake the responsibility of managing such an institution, under a competent board of trustees, the home must be located at or near the Girls school under Miss Pope's immediate direction. I believe the necessary funds for building, equipment, and the necessary fund for endowment to secure the financial success, can be secured from interested people in Honolulu.

I wish to add no additional work on Miss Pope, but she feels that she can manage such a home in addition to her present duties, and it would be a real labor of love with her; in fact the proposition first came from her.[2]

Mr. Bishop quickly responded to Charles Dyke, tentatively approving the Kaʻiulani Home, but only if it did not cost the estate a single penny. For the very first time, hope began to stir within Ida.

March 21, 1902

Dear Mr. Dyke:

Your letter of the 12th came to me yesterday and I was glad to receive it. I agree with you entirely in what you write about the peculiar difficulties, exposures and trials in which many of the Hawaiian girls are ushered on graduation from the boarding schools; a situation which has been much thought about and talked about, and has excited the sympathies of teachers and other friends of the Hawaiians during many years past. I am afraid to encourage a new effort, great as the need is, because I know of the large and *constant* expense of *maintenance* and that people become tired of contribution, or discouraged as to results. And I am particularly afraid of favoring anything that may interfere with the plain object and duties of the Kamehameha schools.

If such a home as you and Miss Pope have described to me can be established on the terms stated in your letter, with the hearty approval of the Trustees, I can hardly disapprove, because I hope that would supply a great want without any cost to the Estate and by furnishing an outlet for some of the girls quite prepared to leave school and go to work, who now hold on because of no safe place to go, and thereby prevent new girls from entering the school.[3]

But just six weeks later, Mr. Bishop had a change of heart and informed Trustee J. O. Carter that he flatly refused to support the endeavor with estate land, money, or personnel.

May 9th 1902

My Dear Mr. Carter—

Much as I would like to see more done for Hawaiian girls after they finish at school, I know that the Estate cannot contribute at all, and I have come to the conclusion that it would not be prudent to allow a "Home" to be located on Estate land near the Kam. Girls School or to have it under the care of the principal or teachers of that school. There would be great risk of its falling into financial difficulties and of annoying efforts to get support or aid from the estate. The Trustees have their hands full now, so full that I am anxious.[4]

Circumventing Mr. Bishop

After learning that Mr. Bishop had changed his mind about sponsoring the home on the estate property, Ida began to survey her options. First and foremost, she needed money. She began by using what resources she had at her fingertips: her girls. She had learned how to fund-raise effectively at Kawaiahaʻo Seminary, but this time she would not have Queen Liliʻuokalani's generous support. Along with the music teacher, Ida organized a fund-raising operetta at the school to benefit the proposed home. It was a resounding success financially, and she was on her way.

When Mr. Bishop learned that the establishment of the Kaʻiulani Home was proceeding without his approval or the support of the Bishop Estate, he directly but carefully warned Miss Pope to turn over the administration to others, and return to her own administrative duties: "Your advice and influence will be of much value but they should not expect any considerable active service from you. Your hands and heart and time are fully occupied with girls already; many others need to be and should be in the service for their own good and the public good."[5]

However, Ida resolutely carried on and soon informed the trustees of her year-long fund-raising success, proclaiming her dream for an alumnae home was now a reality. Charles Bishop magnanimously congratulated her on the success of her efforts and acknowledged that it was "a need which has given you much thought and great anxiety."[6] In June of 1903 she assured her managers that her efforts had not been wasted: "The conditions of life which our young women meet in the community makes the graduating of pupils a serious one. The establishment of the Kaiulani Home will, in a measure, mitigate this and afford a sheltered home for deserving young women, earning a livelihood in Honolulu."[7]

On July 11, 1903, the community learned for the first time that an "organization of ladies"[8] had leased the former Salvation Army home to use as a boarding home. Mrs. Susan Dorcas Heapy was placed as "matron and manager" of the home. Ida Waterhouse was identified as the president of the organization, and Ida Pope as the treasurer.[9] At the proper time, those roles would switch. The *Advertiser* shared the mission: "The Kaiulani Home for Girls is intended as a place of abode for girls who otherwise would be without homes. The home is not endowed

Ida Pope and her fund-raising friends. *Author's private collection.*

and the money for its support is being raised in the community by a board of ladies who have the matter in charge. It is not a charity home nor is it to be sectarian. It will be independent in every way, simply a boarding home for the graduates of Kamehameha particularly."[10]

Gathering Them All Together under Her Wing

At long last, on September 1, 1903, Ida's dream became a reality. The Ka'iulani Home for Girls was established adjacent to Kawaiaha'o Seminary, near the palace, on King Street. For Ida, it was returning to the location she had arrived at thirteen years earlier. Twenty-six young women soon moved in. Ida encouraged local women to help furnish the home, and soon nice things began arriving, such as plants, pictures, and rocking chairs for the parlor.[11] Ida's personal gift to the home was magazine subscriptions to *Review of Reviews*, *Harper's Weekly*, and *Week's Progress*.[12] In Bucyrus, all of the Popes sat around by the fire at night reading magazines and discussing their contents. Her young women would soon do the same.

Initially, the home was promoted for women with Hawaiian blood, but admission requirements swiftly changed to accommodate all ethnicities. It was soon reported that the new home "domiciled a number of the graduates of Kamehameha and Kawaiaha'o Schools."[13] Miss Pope had successfully brought all her girls together under her maternal oversight once again.

By 1906, the waiting list was so long, the need so great, that a larger facility was envisioned. The home exceeded everyone's expectations, even Ida's, and the waiting list had "58 applicants for admission, and there is room for but 26 or 27 at the most."[14] Another massive fund-raising effort began, to build and construct a more spacious home.

Charles Bishop had always felt that Kamehameha's graduates should take responsibility for their own futures. Ida, on the other hand, thought it was the Bishop Estate's moral responsibility to take care of the female graduates. But somewhere along the way, he was swayed—because in a complete reversal from his previous attitude, he quickly moved to support the expansion effort with the assurance of Miss Pope that the management of the home would be in the hands of others.[15] To generate matching income, the *Advertiser* proclaimed on its front page, "Money for the Kaiulani Home from C. R. Bishop": "The well-known philanthropy of C. R. Bishop of San Francisco, whose wife was the late lamented Princess Pauahi Bishop, has come with an offer to give to the Kaiulani Home for Young Women the sum of $5000. The purpose of the fund is to purchase a site for a permanent Home. The Kaiulani Home is one of the local institutions that has thrived without the flourish of trumpets."[16]

The New Ka'iulani Home, 1906

In February of 1906, the *Hawaiian Star* assisted in the fund-raising efforts by describing the unique concept and overall objectives of the Ka'iulani Home, stating that it provided "comfortable lodgings for worthy young women" who embraced "pure Christian home life."[17] The journalist gushed over the "natural wood, with culinary, sanitary, and plumbing." Furthermore, "there are hardly any restrictions placed upon the girls beyond such proper and wholesome moral restraint, which is

Kaʻiulani Home for Girls, 1908. *Author's collection.*

deemed necessary and expedient for the welfare of the girls." The article concluded with a specific call for contributions from "our Hawaiian ladies of wealth, as it is for girls of their race this home is primarily established and intended."[18]

By 1907, the new home officially opened with a well-attended reception of dignitaries and locals. Ida, who always preferred to shine the spotlight on others, greeted Governor Carter while taking little credit for her involvement. The governor "expressed himself as more than pleased," and with this endorsement, the home became an established entity in the community.[19]

In 1912, the Kaʻiulani Home for Girls, overflowing with boarders, was chartered and funded by the Kaʻiulani Trust established by Charles Bishop. In the same year, an annex to the home was built in Pālama at the foot of Robello Street. And this time, the *Star Bulletin* drolly noted, it was not funded completely by women, but by the "business men of the city."[20]

The Queen's Girls Again

In a sweetly ironic turn of events, the young women who had gained independence from Kamehameha Schools could now revitalize their monarchy's cultural traditions in a personal way, thanks to Queen Liliʻuokalani. In the fall of 1912,

Lili'uokalani's dog Poni was her constant companion in her late years. *Library of Congress* *3c05894u.*

U.S. secretary of state Philander C. Knox was the guest of honor at a lūʻau held at Lili'uokalani's beautiful mansion. News reports noted it was a "distinctively Hawaiian luau," with "the soft music of Hawaii nei [beloved Hawaii]."[21] At this lūʻau, seventy-four-year-old "Liliuokalani, with grace and handsomely gowned in lavender silk holoku with an overdress of lace,"[22] resurrected a ritual from her royal past by inviting fourteen young women from the Kaʻiulani Home to join her at the banquet. Dressed in pure white, the queen's girls once more, the young women gently waved "white kahilis over the guests."[23]

In March of 1913, yet another branch of the Kaʻiulani Home, christened Hale Lanakila, opened near the pineapple cannery to accommodate forty young women who worked in this factory.[24] To keep the young women safe at night, a shortcut was created to bypass the red-light district of "Iwilei known as a moral cesspool."[25] Hale Lanakila had every modern convenience the young residents could desire. The expansive yard had the most alluring draw, but for the wrong reasons. Misbehaving youngsters were found engaging in mischief on the property in the afternoons, so the female residents turned it around for the betterment of the community. To keep mischievous youth occupied and out of trouble after school ended, a playground was erected on the lawn and opened for children from three until six o'clock, under the watchful eyes of Hale Lanakila's residents.[26] The name "Lanakila" further lived up to its definition, "victorious," when in time it housed government-subsidized female juvenile offenders and successfully rehabilitated them in a structured but homelike atmosphere.

At the grand opening of Hale Lanakila, trustee and treasurer Ida Pope greeted the "more than two hundred people" who attended the reception.[27] None was more important than seventy-five-year-old Queen Liliʻuokalani, who sat on the lānai facing the inner courtyard, where Madame Alapai sang selections of her compositions orchestrated by the Royal Hawaiian Band. Surrounded by Hawaiian girls, this beloved queen, basking in their unconditional love and loyalty, listening to her own compositions, surely must have felt as if the years had melted away. It's also easy to imagine the queen smiling in approval at her old friend Ida, who had faithfully fulfilled and perhaps exceeded her vision for Hawaiʻi's daughters for a quarter of a century.

CHAPTER SIXTEEN

Taking Honolulu by Storm

Honolulu's Summer Institutes

While the motivation for Ida's charity work in Honolulu stemmed from her Christian values, the faculty from the University of Chicago fueled her reformist social agenda. From its inception in 1890, the university was a break-the-mold type of institution. During the summers at the end of the nineteenth century, the Teachers' Association of Hawai'i brought in their faculty to encourage island teachers to take a more progressive stance in their classrooms, exposing Ida to far more liberal ideas than she would have absorbed during her undergraduate years at Oberlin.

Chicago's Progressivists, as they were called, believed that teachers were the means by which society would become more equitable. Dedicated to a mission of social justice, Progressivists posited that public schools should provide individualized instruction, active learning, and a creative curriculum specifically linked to vocations. John Dewey, George Herbert Mead, and Colonel Francis Parker were among those who went to Hawai'i and stimulated Ida to rethink her approach.

Ida found much inspiration in Progressivist methods, even as she sought to strike a balance between this new social agenda and her original roots. The record shows that she had no desire to completely do away with a classical curriculum of great literature, music, art, and poetry—the "food for the soul" approach— but she now felt compelled to expand the school's curriculum even further to be more vocation oriented based on the ever-changing economy.

The University of Chicago

Since the University of Chicago was on the cutting edge of these radical new ideas, Ida wouldn't settle to be an idle participant; she wanted to be an integral part of it, an active leader in the movement for social change in Hawai'i. After conversing with key participants in the Honolulu summer institutes, including visits to

Ida Pope, always looking in another direction: "I am dreaming dreams and seeing visions that may someday be real and vital." *Kamehameha Schools.*

progressive American institutions like the Hull House, Pratt Institute, and more, she became convinced she could learn more only by going back to school herself. Enthusiastic about these new convictions, she was able to persuade the trustees to release her for a few months at a time with teacher Frances Lemmon at the helm. She drew from her savings and took graduate-level classes for three different quarters: autumn 1905, winter 1906, and autumn 1910. By staying with her family in Chicago, she was able to save on housing.

Ida arrived at a stimulating time; in 1904, a Chicago School of Thought had emerged, with an emphasis on seeking solutions to problems of race, crime, and poverty.[1] Called social meliorism, this was a meeting point between science and activism that sought to use scientifically researched methods to bring about social improvement. She would learn that new scientific discoveries in biology and psychology now played a key role in teacher education and child developmental psychology.

Ida's Professors

Once she arrived at Chicago, some charismatically progressive professors in the department of sociology, all of whom addressed questions of social justice even as they were very different characters, influenced Ida.

Dr. Charles Hubbard Judd moved the department away from abstract theory and pushed for the use of scientific methods in education. Dr. Judd motivated his students to study urban social problems within their unique contexts.[2] Ida took four graduate courses under him: Advanced Educational Psychology and Advanced Principles of Education, Industrial Education in Public Schools, and Curriculum. These courses were innovative at this time for using the new and exciting area of applied psychology in the area of education to guide principles of teaching and learning. Ida would have learned how to scientifically study the behavior of her pupils in relation to their educational needs and environment. Dr. Judd was a defense witness at the Scopes Trial whose affidavit stressed that banning evolution from the curricula of public schools would be a mistake.[3]

Ida took three diverse courses under Dr. William Isaac Thomas: Art and the Artist Class, Social Origins, and Mental Development in the Race. Thomas rejected then-current theories of racial inferiority and championed women's social and political rights. His 1907 publication *Sex and Society* speculated that women's intellects might actually be superior to men's—a radical proposition for its moment (women's suffrage was still a decade away). Dr. Thomas had a great gusto for living, enjoying food, drink, cigarettes, and conversation.[4] His flamboyant lifestyle might have seemed exotic to someone like Ida, who worked under ultra-conservative board members in Honolulu.

Dr. Albion Woodbury Small, the dean of the Graduate School of Literature and Arts, personally recommended Ida for the Department of Sociology and taught her in The Conflict of Classes in Modern Society. In Dr. Small's classes, the evils of capitalism were iconoclastically exposed, and he took delight in unmasking time-honored beliefs, prevailing prejudices, and shams in high places. Dr. Small believed that educators like Ida Pope were not "leaders of children," but "makers of society" and that schools should be the key lever for social reform.[5]

Dr. Charles Richmond Henderson, described by one historian as "a rare combination of saint and scholar," held the post of university chaplain and taught courses in ethics and social improvement.[6] Outside the university, he was the international Prison Commissioner for the United States. In the course The Family, Ida was challenged by the man who saw so much suffering in prisons, to face unmet social needs and to alleviate human suffering as her moral obligation.[7]

Each of her professors would have had a distinct appeal to Ida. But rather than making a particular ideological choice between any of their contradictory viewpoints, she appeared to make an agglomeration of all of them as it could relate to her unique educational context in Hawai'i. There is no question that where they all came together was a shared "vision of order and stability in a society that seemed in danger of disintegration."[8]

Many studies conducted by the university contributed to the understanding of urban problems, such as housing, child rearing, and poverty.[9] For Ida, the Chicago faculty offered a new way of addressing social problems, using research and data rather than belief and intuition to design programs. Ida came to understand the importance of helping her Hawaiian pupils discover their aptitudes and interests even as it helped them fit with the needs of their new American community.

For years Ida had been interested in structured vocational training for Hawaiian girls, especially as it related to teaching, nursing, fine sewing, and business skills. But the Chicago experience demonstrated that in order for that training to be effective, she would also have to know the specific business needs of the community and then align the curriculum to those needs. Those needs could then be translated into educational objectives in the Kamehameha curriculum, and help students find niches within Hawaiian society beyond any of their previous alternatives.

The Honolulu Social Survey: Frances Blascoer

In November 1910, Ida attended the very first National Conference on Vocational Guidance in Boston and was stimulated to initiate community changes in Honolulu. Educators, social workers, and corporate figures from forty-five cities met to discuss how to improve the lives of immigrants by making sound vocational choices.[10] Charles William Eliot, president emeritus of Harvard University, told the assembly,

> When Benjamin Franklin's father thought it was time for the boy to choose a trade, he took Benjamin about the town and showed him men at work in all the trades, and it was only after this comparative survey that Benjamin decided to be a printer. A very skillful printer he became by the time he was eighteen years old. American schools should perform this office of all pupils who ask for such guidance.[11]

Ida would have understood this on a very personal level, as two of her students died while training for careers that may not have fitted their temperaments.

One, Grace Beckley, broke down under the stress of passing a teacher's exam and committed suicide at the school. The other, Julie Lazaro, died from a stroke while returning from an unhappy nursing internship in San Francisco. Ida came to understand how important it was to take stock of her girls' interests and aptitudes as they related to their vocation.

Conference presenters and attendees included people like Jane Addams, Homer Folks, G. Stanley Hall, George Mead, Henry Metcalf, and Edward Thorndike.[12] These pioneers in the field of education and sociology joined together for two days of stimulating discourse, and ultimately ignited a national interest in public school career guidance. Outside of schools, the field of social work was undergoing professionalization as governments took more accountability for helping the disadvantaged.

In the first decade of the twentieth century, social work began to provide careers for the growing population of educated women. This conference could very well have been the event where Ida met the feisty Frances Blascoer, a leading figure in the new practice of social surveys, and where the idea to conduct a massive survey in Honolulu originated. Frances, who came from a Sephardic Jewish family, was then acting as the first executive secretary for the NAACP.

Back in Honolulu, Ida had the means to take action because she now held the title of president of the home she founded, now financially solvent. As president of the Board of Trustees of Ka'iulani Home for Girls, Ida officially requested Frances Blascoer to methodically investigate the working conditions among Hawaiian women in the community. Fortunately Frances was available, since she had recently resigned from her job after a public dispute with W.E.B. Du Bois. Ida undoubtedly knew what the outcome would be, but the published results of a scientifically conducted survey would surely bring about necessary changes to alleviate the horrid working conditions she had seen and heard about from her alumnae.

Social surveys were among the tools that developed as part of the study of methods of social improvement at places like the University of Chicago. These were sociological questionnaires assessing the experiences and circumstances of a population. Questions addressed the character of the community, including labor and leisure, local government, industry, heath, sanitation, housing, education, welfare agencies, and crime across the lifespan.[13] Such surveys were promoted as a new, effective diagnostic tool to understand what particular problems ailed a given community. Social surveyors did not just gather facts for facts' sake, but used the gathered facts to stimulate community introspection with the hopes for action.

The Pittsburgh Survey, conducted in 1908 and no doubt the topic of many classroom discussions at the University of Chicago, was the first systematic effort to survey working-class conditions. It painted a dire picture of social conditions and became evidence and propaganda that ultimately inspired broad-based labor reforms.[14] In commissioning a social survey like this one, Ida Pope was suggesting using the latest cutting-edge research methods, for the first time, to measure, both quantitatively and qualitatively, the experience of working women in the Hawaiian Islands.

Getting to Work

Frances Blascoer arrived in June 1912 ready to narrowly scrutinize the islands' working conditions of women. This was a newsworthy event because, in the words of the *Honolulu Star-Bulletin,* it was "a subject in which every woman should be vitally interested."[15] Ida, ready to put her summer vacation to good use, had already recruited Pālama's trained social worker James A. Rath to join her on the Industrial Committee. In the community, she found a cross section of twelve prominent citizens also ready to donate their time and energies to rectify the injustices associated with the exploitation of women in the labor force.

She purposefully recruited three of Honolulu's religious leaders: Father Stephen Peter Alencastre, a Roman Catholic; Bishop Henry Bond Restarick, an Episcopalian; and Dr. Doremus Scudder, a Congregationalist. They may have differed doctrinally, but they all had a deep interest in solving the problems of their community. Under the auspices of conducting a sanctioned survey, each of them was able to look into the dark corners of the Honolulu labor market. No doubt the results would have been rich fodder for Sunday sermons.

The nine others on Ida's committee were people whose names are seen today on buildings and monuments throughout Hawai'i: Mary Dillingham Frear, governor's wife and author; Professor Edgar Wood of Honolulu's Normal School; Arthur Griffiths, president of O'ahu College; Julie Judd Swanzy, leading civic and social figure; Cherilla Lowry, civic activist; Louise Gulick, missionary teacher; May Green Wilcox, Board of Education; alternating Kawaiaha'o teachers Mabel Bosher and Bertha Kemp; and, of course, Nora Sturgeon, always by "Aunt Ida's" side in Ida's causes.

After only a few weeks of initial investigations, it became imperative to conduct a broader survey to assess the entire social condition in Honolulu, much as had been done in Pittsburgh.[16] It seems as if Miss Blascoer could not bypass the horrid circumstances of the plantation workers and those who inhabited the "unornamental tenement blocks."[17] Ida called a meeting to entice volunteers to join one of the five committees on Housing Conditions, Industrial Conditions, Dependent Children, Family Budgets, and the Social Evil (prostitution).[18] These five broad areas of research were subdivided into twelve groups, each of which was assigned a special line of investigation. Ida and Frances led the first two, and James Rath the remaining three.

Dozens of "interested citizens" volunteered to "secure all the data hidden in civil life" particularly as it pertained to the "Social Evil" of prostitution.[19] Riley H. Allen, William H. Baird, George R. Carter, Walter F. Dillingham, John R. Galt, William C. Hobdy, Albert Francis Judd, Roderick O. Matheson, George W. Smith, William L. Whitney, and Garrett Parmele Wilder were the centers of influence in the civil life of Honolulu. Also on the committee was Episcopalian Reverend Leopold Kroll, the center of Queen Liliʻuokalani's spiritual life during this time. Knowing that well-publicized research would galvanize the community, newspaper editors were strategically recruited among committee members. The enlistment of these influential people from diverse vocations was an excellent strategy to open every door in the community to investigation.

The newspapers appeared enthusiastic and optimistic about this massive undertaking: "The coming of Miss FB to conduct a social and economic survey under the auspices of the Board of Directors of Kaiulani Home promises to inaugurate a new era in Island conditions."[20] Frances herself framed the survey's intentions in terms of the cool logic of accounting for the Honolulu community: "A survey is nothing more nor less than a sociological balance sheet or stock taking, whereby is recorded on the one page the city's social problems and on the other is provisions for meeting these problems, the two pages being balanced by recommendations for the establishment of such activities as will fill in the gaps between needs and existing facilities for meeting them."[21]

Rousing the Alumnae with a Feminist Agenda

Despite such neutral rhetoric, Frances Blascoer had a passionately progressive agenda, one that encompassed rights for women to a degree radical for its time. Before the survey even began, Frances held rousing meetings with the young women of Kaʻiulani Home, and the *Hawaiian Gazette* published her "liberal" thoughts.

> I believe that local women should have the privilege of the ballot. They are not disqualified by law as idiots or criminals and as citizens of the United States are forced to abide by the laws. They should have a voice in making them. Women have been educated and have progressed to the point where they are capable of taking a man's place in any profession and of making a success of it. Women today are thinkers, and as such must be recognized

equally. Ultimately the privilege of voting will be granted to the women of Hawaii.[22]

At Kamehameha, Ida was an outward educational reformist, constantly aligning the curriculum to ensure a satisfying career and independence for Hawaiian women. Behind the scenes, she cautiously inculcated her pupils on the importance of women's rights in their merging nation. Her supervisors believed that allowing women to vote could undermine their male authority. Ida's grassroots campaign could remain behind the scenes by using a foot soldier of the feminist movement like Frances Blascoer to stir up and empower Ida's alumnae at the Ka'iulani Home.

Although Frances had a deep knowledge of the social problems facing all women, only Ida knew the unique problems women encountered in Hawai'i. Frances and Ida needed each other to give their passionate convictions the backdrop of careful research. But Frances was not a trusted figure among Hawaiian women, and Ida needed to open doors in the "research field." Soon, it was reported that "Principal Pope" would accompany the research team to the Island of Hawai'i in August to "thoroughly investigate industrial and home conditions on the large Island."[23] *The Friend* opined,

> The results of this survey will place in the possession of all our organizations for social betterment exact data upon which to formulate remedial measures. We must know what we are fighting, where it is entrenched, and hence what tactics are likely to prove successful. The survey will doubtless reveal new possibilities in vocational training for girls and will react healthfully upon educational methods. An intensive study of industrial conditions will be welcomed by the more thotful of our plantation magnates. The Kaiulani Directors deserve the greatest credit and will receive the gratitude of the entire community for their public-spirited wisdom in bringing Miss Blascoer here to captain this campaign.[24]

Over the "better part of the year," working alongside Ida much of the time, Frances Blascoer researched the overall conditions of the community and Hawaiian women in all facets of their lives—at work, at home, and during recreation.[25] This was done by interviews and the examination of responses from questionnaires. It is easy to imagine, since Ida was being pulled in many directions, that she might have been experiencing some severe symptoms of her soon-to-be-diagnosed hypertension. Her siblings collectively expressed a worry about her involvement in these extracurricular activities and pleaded unsuccessfully for her to return home for a recuperative visit.[26]

Ida Publishes Her Hopes for Action

When the survey of the conditions of working women in Honolulu concluded, the results were published in November of 1912, in a one-hundred-page report, *The Industrial Condition of Women and Girls in Honolulu: A Social Study.*[27] Ida wrote the foreword for the publication, boldly stepping out from her role as principal, using at once the tone of an impassioned reformer and that of a pragmatic researcher. Using the survey results as the basis for calls for legislative reforms fulfilled exactly the intent of her Chicago professors by bringing scientific methods to push social change. It's hard not to feel Ida's fury and passion as she put the territorial government on notice that there must be changes in working conditions for Hawaiian women.

> There is a world movement in uplift work for women. Along with the rest of the world, Hawaii is awaking to this call. In all lines of endeavor, there must be a working plan. But first must be facts, writ large and plain. In view of this interest and the desire to do a vital work for the wage earning girls and women of Honolulu, the Trustees of Kaiulani Home secured the services of a trained investigator, Miss Frances Blascoer of New York City to make a study of industrial conditions among the working girls of Honolulu and to present a plan for the organization of a vocational Bureau here in the islands.
>
> With the coming of Miss Blascoer a social survey was attempted, a survey which should be the means of presenting to citizens and social workers the real state of industrial and housing conditions; the character of the amusements offered to our community; facts about dependent children; facts concerning the devastation of the social evil (prostitution). Religious, moral, intellectual, professional and vocational education; community hygiene; sanitary regulations; the beautifying of Honolulu; all these demand the concerted action of women and men.
>
> And then, too, there is the "call of the children" that comes with such strength of appeal from the findings of the Juvenile Court. The dependent child must be considered. The crimes that imperil the virtue of unprotected little girls must not be hidden. The fact must be faced of the incursion of Hawaii by large numbers of unmarried men and the accompanying menace to young women.
>
> Unquestionably, the conditions under which girls and women work should be known by the public. Churches, associations, clubs, individual philanthropists, should have accurate knowledge of social conditions; that pauperizing may be avoided and that the waste of duplication in charita-

ble work may be avoided. Undoubtedly, more light is needed for the conduct of benevolent enterprises, perhaps not more giving but more efficient giving.

Miss Blascoer's report on the industrial conditions of women and girls, it is believed, will prove a basis for the working out of many programs for community betterment. May it prove rich in suggestion to the women of Honolulu. May we all STAND shoulder to shoulder in the task of solving the industrial problem of the girls and women in our midst, and may it give to those who earnestly seek, a mission, a vision of great opportunities. To those who give and to those who receive, may there result a meeting, not at the crossroads of mistrust and suspicion, but on the "main traveled thoroughfare" which leads to mutual helpfulness. Hasten the day of its arriving!

IDA M. POPE
President, Board of Trustees of Kaiulani Home[28]

Results

On August 16, 1912, Frances Blascoer called an urgent media conference to discuss some of the report's preliminary findings. Overall, her judgments would be harsh, and her calls to action urgent. The *Hawaiian Gazette* covered the first-of-its-kind meeting between Blascoer and the city's leaders: "It may well be that the outcome of this meeting will have a political significance in the future which will be for the great betterment of Honolulu. The men were President B. Von Damm and Secretary George G. Guild of the Oahu Central Improvement Association, and Representative Ed Towse as the third member of the municipal research committee of the central association."[29]

The reporter noted Miss Blascoer's self-assurance as she delivered some hard truths skillfully, even cockily, and as she fielded the barrage of questions: "Questions unconfined were showered upon the bright little woman who sat at the head of the table [she] answered each and all with assurance born of knowledge, accompanied with a pleasant smile as much as to say, in modern American style, 'Go [for] it, gentlemen; phase me if you can.'"[30]

She led the discussion on the appalling condition of tenements and wondered why more detached cottages were not built to increase a quality of life for immigrants. Representative Towse justified herding residents into tenement life because of the easy access by the Board of Health, saying, "It would make more work for the health inspectors when the cottage idea is followed." Miss Blascoer put him in his place, to the pleasure of the on-call reporter: "Well, we are not trying to save the board of health from any work, but the lives of the babies."[31] It would appear that she made her point, because in a year's time a publication in Ohio reported, "In Honolulu the housing problem is changing from the tenement form to that of closely packed cottages. It is a decided advance as it holds the family as a unit or tends to do so."[32]

A major item to come under "her scalpel" was plantation labor. Blascoer called for the "work day to be shortened, or at least a rest time in the hottest part of the day" and a plan to train the children of the laborers.[33] Other findings as a result of the survey surrounded garbage collection, infant care, municipal lights, transportation, lack of playgrounds, and a municipal library. But "the grossest shame" of this community, Miss Blascoer stated, was the lack of a public orphanage: "There seems to be no public provision of any kind for these children."[34] When Secretary Guild countered that one was not necessary because "there were not so very many poor people in Honolulu," Miss Blascoer was reported to exclaim, "Oh, you have no idea how many there are. There are many here who die of malnutrition. I think that is one reason why so many Hawaiians die so easily."[35] Miss Blascoer emphatically asked the city's leaders to consider children as "future citizens" over "objects of charity."[36]

Many of the social survey volunteers expressed shock at what they observed among workplaces, and much of the survey results were dedicated to exposing the labor conditions of Hawaiian women to the light—often for the first time. For example, a primary site of labor for women in Hawai'i was the pineapple cannery, but because that work was seasonal, it covered only four months of the year, meaning that despite horrific working conditions, employees were still living in poverty.

The Territory of Hawai'i had no fixed minimum wages or labor laws at the time of the survey, and Blascoer reported that workers' pay and hours were governed by the will of employers. She strongly criticized the cannery owners and cited the Bureau of Labor report: "Cannery work was so much of a strain that workers were unfit to do other work when the cannery season was over."[37] And even after work, when the young women left after up to twelve hours of standing in burning pineapple juice, they had to walk home late at night through the ghetto of Iwilei, where "evil men lurked." Blascoer reported,

> Hawaiian employers, most of whom are kamaainas, sincerely interested in the welfare of the Hawaiian girls and women, have not given adequate thought to the broader social problems of their employees. Kind treatment, good air and light do much to mitigate matters, but no woman or girl can work standing continuously for ten or more hours a day and re-

tain her health. Nor will she in this way become a homemaker, and an intelligent mother and member of this community.[38]

She called for a law to restrict the hours of labor of women and children under the age of sixteen, and to mandate that no female be employed for longer than ten hours a day, and that she not have to work before six in the morning or after six at night. Not long after that, the *Ohio Bulletin of Charities and Correction* reported that a new law in Hawai'i prohibited employers from "employing girls under 16 years before 6 a.m., or after 9 p.m."[39]

The need for the beautifying of Honolulu that Ida referred to in the published foreword began in earnest with a group of women under the leadership of Cherilla Storrs Lowrey, a former Kawaiaha'o teacher.[40] The Outdoor Circle was formed in 1912, in the year Frances Blascoer came to Honolulu. Among its first thirty members were Ida's closest circle, including Ida Sturgeon Waterhouse, Nora Sturgeon Cooke, and Ida's sister Katherine Pope. The ladies were organized into neighborhood circles that addressed the needs of cleaning up and landscaping a particular area. Ida's sister Katherine, now employed at Ida's school as an English teacher, led the Kalihi Circle near Kamehameha Schools. The committees cleaned up vacant lots to create playgrounds for children and cleared open spaces to beautifully landscape public parks. These ladies made history with their antibillboard campaign. Concerned by the unsightly advertisements cropping up all over Honolulu buildings and streets, the Outdoor Circle activists formed a committee to address the "unsightly issue,"[41] which would forever eradicate billboards in Hawai'i and make their state the only one in the nation with antibillboard legislation.[42] Today, the Outdoor Circle's memberships number in the thousands, and the organization is, as it was in 1912, a force to be reckoned with.

Unfinished Business

There were five reports in all for the Russell Sage Foundation: "Industrial Conditions of Women and Girls in Honolulu," "The Social Evil," "Dependent Children," "Housing Conditions," and "Family Budgets."[43] Research reveals that only the first two reports were published and circulated for the public.

When the social survey was over, people were impressed at what was accomplished in such a short time. In October of 1912, board president Pope and her trustees were commended for being an early launching pad for women's involvement in community issues. Ida and her circle of women were contrasted to procrastinating males, who merely "talk" about community problems but provide no solutions. "It remains talk until the Kaiulani Trustees—women—facing the terrible wrong suffered by women and girls at the hands of men in Honolulu gets busy, fetches an expert from New York, organizes the movement, in six months publishes two reports and has good hope of seeing the work completed by a representative committee in record time."[44] In November of 1912, the *Hawaiian Gazette* reminded the community of "the frequent rape of little girls, the wholesale seduction of maidens, the growing insecurity of parks and streets for women at night" and urged social programs to be established as recommended by Ida Pope and her "crusaders."[45]

Without question, Ida Pope was the driving force behind the creation of the first-ever comprehensive survey in the Hawaiian Islands that led to major changes in laws. It was the combination of her knowledge of Hawai'i's unique social problems aligned with Frances Blascoer's commitment to human rights that made the survey happen, but recommendations were not commandments, and many practical suggestions for change would not be fulfilled until years after the report because some would "necessitate legislative action" and "government cooperation."[46]

At the same time, some changes came quickly. Multiple health issues were brought to light and easily remedied in the pineapple cannery that supplied many of Ida's pupils' summer work. As one example of a minor recommendation that did a world of good, the report cited the detrimental effect of pineapple juice on the skin of women cannery workers. Even though they wore rubber gloves, they stood long hours on the floor in acidic juice, which ate away their skin. Frances asked owners not only to regularly flush the floors with water but also to go one step further and elevate workers on protective slats.[47]

Despite her successes, Frances Blascoer may never have forgiven some of the plantation managers for the kinds of abuses she witnessed in the course of the survey. In 1917, Congress passed a new immigration act that included a clause against importing laborers under contract unless they were highly skilled laborers for jobs that could not be filled among America's unemployed.[48] It appears that Frances was still bitter about her encounters with the island's plantation owners, as seen in the following dispatch which she sent to the *New York Times*. Her comments on the labor conditions in Hawai'i were reprinted in what the editor for the *Hawaiian Gazette* termed "one of the weirdest collections of complacently stated perversion of facts yet."[49] Despite his opinion, he published her letter.

> Nearly five years ago, I went to Honolulu to make an investigation into the industrial condition of native girls and women in that city. I found a condition of affairs of which I have never been able to secure an explanation.

The Sugar Planters' Association, employing many thousands of plantation hands, completely evades or is exempted from contract labor laws. Men, women, and children are brought into the islands through the planters' association's station at Honolulu without even passing through the federal immigration station there. The plantations, not equipped with either adequate hospital or even medical attendance, are being infested with all manner of infections. Occasionally a human wreck, blind and decrepit, drifts into Honolulu bearing testimony to this condition of affairs, but the great majority are buried on the plantations. Since I returned to New York the matter has been called to the attention of the department of labor but, although through its children's bureau has undertaken a child welfare survey of Hawaii, nothing has been done in regard to the larger question, so far as I have been able to learn.[50]

In 1917, Hawaiian citizens had more on their mind than Frances Blascoer's frustrations with the loopholes plantation owners found to circumvent laws protecting the human rights of immigrants. Life as they knew it changed when Hawai'i was pressed into service by the United States during World War I.

CHAPTER SEVENTEEN

The Changing Hawaiian Islands

By the time the twentieth century dawned, few places on earth had changed so completely as the Hawaiian Islands. Less than two years after Ida arrived, the troubled and colorful kingdom of Hawai'i was no more. In its place arose the new Republic of Hawai'i, which within five more years was annexed as a territory of the United States. The speedy annexation of Hawai'i in 1898, unquestionably a defense measure taken by the United States in the interest of its own national security, dashed all hopes for Lili'uokalani's restoration to her throne. But, as Ida's sister Katherine wrote in her 1924 published book, *Hawaii, the Rainbow Land*, once a queen, always a queen: "Queen Liliuokalani was never so much the Queen as she showed herself in her later years, in the years when no crown was hers to wear, when she dwelt no longer in a palace, where her hands no longer held the reins of government."[1]

Even as the life of old Hawai'i slipped away and a new one rapidly took its place, the community hoped Lili'uokalani would act and remain as "royal" as she always had been. Katherine Pope observed, "Little by little Washington Place extended its hospitalities, little by little Liliuokalani was persuaded to appear on this and that public occasion."[2] She became the highest-profile personality in Honolulu, and the fact that her entourage treated her with the same deference as when she held the title of queen only enchanted the community more. Reminding them of Hawai'i's departed glories, her presence at high-profile events was eagerly sought.

The Pope sisters along with Lydia Aholo were often invited to gatherings or intimate musical soirees given by Lili'uokalani at Washington Place. In the summer of 1913, they were present when Lillian Nordica, the world-famous opera star, entered Washington Place and bowed low in reverence to Lili'uokalani's royal status. To Ida, who had always treated Lili'uokalani with outward deference, including curtsying and backing out of her presence, such honors were merely a continuation of long-standing practice. But now, making obeisance to the ex-queen became a trend in the first decade of the twentieth century. Both residents and strangers, not with sympathy but with reverence, gave her more respect and ceremonial courtesy than she received as sitting queen. Soon the queen's birthday became a public celebration that continues today.

Even as admiration for Liliʻuokalani signaled nostalgia for the old days, commerce was bringing new businesses—and new visitors. Honolulu, situated in a rich and protected harbor, had become a place of commercial importance. With federal monies, the new territory began to construct wharves, buildings, and utilities on the major islands. A naval base at Pearl Harbor was completed. Transportation between islands had developed. The reef-protected romantic beach of Waikīkī was morphing into a major tourist destination. Postcards, books, magazines, and travel journals promoted the exotic islands as a destination not to be missed. And as the century brought tourists in multitude, new diseases came with them. The magnitude of health epidemics and their grim impact were felt throughout the islands, and they found their way into Miss Pope's school dormitories.

Pleading for a Hospital

As early as 1899, Ida began to alert the trustees that a substantial hospital was needed so that ill girls could be quickly and properly treated. She reasoned that the hired hospital staff could also vocationally train pupils for the nursing profession. Charles Bishop's answer was a strong no: "Any suggestions of new expenses made by Miss Pope under present conditions makes me very impatient. Nurses cannot be *trained* disconnected from a hospital and to *think* of a hospital under care or expense of the estate is absurd and wrong."[3]

In June of 1903, her requests had turned to pleas for a small version of a hospital. By 1904, still having received no approval, she scaled back and asked for a "hospital cottage."[4] By 1905, she pitifully reported that a "teacher's room will be devoted to hospital use."[5]

Even as this series of denials reduced the scale of her ambition, she began teaching the girls, over Mr. Bishop's objections, the essentials of nursing, including "anatomy, physiology, hygiene, dietetics and the elements of bacteriology and medial chemistry" in the hopes that Mr. Bishop would come to his senses and see how great the need was.[6] Besides training nurses for the community, where women and children had the greatest medical needs, her goal was "to treat the sick in her own school."[7] In one month alone, she reported "fifty cases of the La Grippe and three operations for diseased glands."[8]

Kamehameha girls were assigned pen pals at the George William Curtis School in Chicago, and Helen had written to hers,

We are now studying about the southern states. In arithmetic, decimals. Our lessons are manual training, nature study, Hawaiian History, sewing and grammar. In the evening while we are studying our lessons the mosquitoes are biting us. Will you please tell me what kinds of flower do you have at your home?

I remain, your unacquainted friend.

Helen Nahielua[9]

Sadly, Helen Nahielua became ill in 1904 and did not live to receive a reply to her question about the flora of the Midwest. She died soon after returning to the school from an operation for a "diseased gland."[10] Ida poignantly requisitioned a large memorial picture of Helen to hang in the school, ever to wonder if she might have lived had a hospital been available on campus.

Forging Ahead

Ida forged ahead with persistence in training her pupils to be nurses. Even though she did not have a hospital, she assembled the materials to train her students for the profession and to persuade the public that they were credible in that role. At the commencement ceremony of 1905, she showcased her "hospital department,"

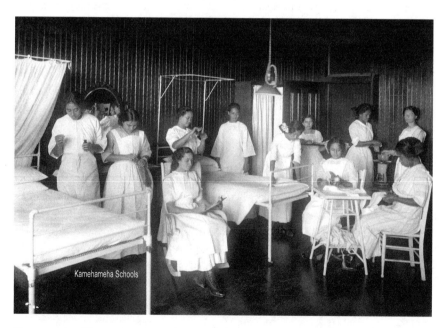

The nursing and hospital equipment was modern for its times. *Kamehameha Schools.*

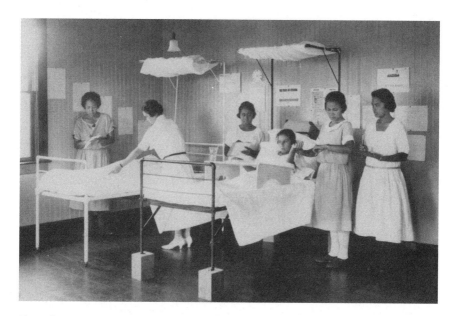

The girls experimented in nursing methods on each other. *Kamehameha Schools.*

displaying a prototype of a complete ward for patients described by the press as follows: "Eatables [were] prepared in a manner to tempt the most feeble patient. There was a table devoted to bandages, another to instruments used by trained nurses in the care of patients. There were medicine chests, a patient's cot, temperature records, etc. Pupils attired as nurses were present."[11]

In her trustee report, Ida matter-of-factly stated, "Instruction has been given in all that pertains to the profession of nursing, including anatomy, physiology, hygiene, dietetics and the elements of bacteriology and medical chemistry. Practical instruction [has been provided], whenever an opportunity afforded, in caring for the sick, doing surgical dressing, and preparing all the dressings, solutions and ointments used in the school."[12]

Ida was undaunted by the struggle to realize her vision. In 1907 she continued to urge the trustees in language that she felt would certainly appeal to their sense of human empathy: "There is much talk among thoughtful people in Honolulu concerning a hospital for women and children. It would be one more avenue of help for Hawaiian girls and the staying of the rapid decline of the race. By teaching the present generation to care for physical well-being the alarming death rate among Hawaiians would be stayed and mothers and young girls would be taught the proper care and nurture of children."[13]

The hospital would be a place, in her mind, that could train her pupils to help take care of the next generation, thereby ensuring a reversal in the "alarming" decline of the Hawaiian population.

Funding Mainland Nursing Training

With no other local option, Ida arranged for a few promising graduates to get skilled nursing training at Children's Hospital in San Francisco. A fund created by the alumnae funded the opportunity for select "Kamehameha sisters."[14]

But one "sister" did not make it back from her nursing preparation in California. It was a forlorn day on November 26, 1909, when Ida ceremoniously received the embalmed remains of twenty-two-year-old Julia Lazaro at the Honolulu wharf. Julia died from apoplexy, or a stroke, just two hours into her return voyage home to Hawai'i from San Francisco.

The newspapers reported an interview with Ida, who conveyed the fact that Julia was returning because neither nursing nor San Francisco was what she ex-

Class of 1908. *Front row:* Lillian Broad, Emilie Dunn, Hannah Aiau, Amoe Akui, Lucille Kamakawiwoʻole. *Middle row:* Esther Purdy and Emma Keau. *Standing in back:* Adeline Hose, Elizabeth Macy, Miriam Mundon, Mary Gohier, Wilhelmina Weight, and Julia Lazaro smiling brightly. *Kamehameha Schools.*

pected. Instead, Julia had excitedly written Miss Pope that she was returning on the *Alameda* to begin training for a career in teaching.[15]

The multitalented Julia who had been endowed with a beautiful voice, was a whiz at archery and became a gifted writer, was now gone just as she finally realized her calling. In a sad irony, a poem on ancient Hawaii she wrote in class was published in the *Evening Bulletin* not long before she died, seeming to foreshadow her own sad last journey.

Alas, alas, dead is my chief;
Dead is my lord and my friend—
My friend in the storm,
My friend in the eight seas,—
Alas, alas, gone is my friend,
And no more will return.[16]

Whether Julia would have died had she stayed in Hawai'i can, of course, not be known. But Kamehameha's graduates who believed they wanted careers in nursing had no choice but to leave the islands and the safety of community, to seek out training that was not available at home. This personal tragedy might have fueled Ida's desire to get nursing training at home, because records indicate that she and her graduates raised a significant amount of money for the proposed Kauikeōlani Children's Hospital in Honolulu. Former Kawaiaha'o Seminary pupil Emma Kauikeōlani Napoleon Mahelona Wilcox and her husband, Albert Spencer Wilcox, heavily endowed this new venture. Emma was doing all she could to protect her heritage in founding this hospital in 1909, and newspapers of the time put Miss Pope right by her side.

When the highly contagious typhoid fever spread throughout the student population in the first months of 1910, Ida might have held out some hope that this event alone would be the catalyst that would help Charles Bishop understand the critical need for isolated quarters. But it was never to be. Ida never got her hospital. It was the one item on which Mr. Bishop would never be swayed. He was afraid that a hospital would tie up time, money, and personnel and most egregiously interfere with the Bishop Estate's basic educational objectives. He did finally authorize a nurse to relieve Miss Pope, but the nurse didn't last.

Keeping House

When Ida returned from her last semester of graduate courses at the University of Chicago in January of 1911, she decided to resurrect a proposal that had been

"A place where, it is hoped, gentle speech and manners will prevail." Senior Hall, 1912. *Kamehameha Schools.*

"A place in which girls are to learn by doing." Private room in Senior Hall, 1912. *Kamehameha Schools.*

ignored by the trustees in 1909. The Kaʻiulani Home afforded her the opportunity to see how her graduates were prepared to live on their own. She discovered that some of them, so focused on careers while her pupils, were floundering in the areas of independent living. She felt remiss that her graduates were too dependent on the boarding school structure. Because every decision about their lifestyle had been made for them since their entry into the school, Ida realized that she might have unwittingly been the one who created this dependence. To aid their transition, Ida had petitioned to construct a home expressly for the seniors in their last year of school, where they could learn to live independently prior to graduation day.

On behalf of her young women, she argued for two things that could be viewed as contradictory: a woman's need to work hard in traditional household duties, and a woman's need to compete in the professional world of men. She unapologetically linked these demands, seamlessly blending the sight of a pragmatist with that of a visionary.

> The modern girl must be prepared to be a homemaker in the old sense of the term, and also an industrial worker; she must be fitted for the traditional sphere of woman with its multiplicity of duties, and also for earning a livelihood in competition with men in the industrial, commercial and professional world. A woman ought to know how to cook and to sew, she should understand the relative nutritive values of different foods and be familiar with the principles of household sanitation and home decoration, and she ought to be able to properly care for children. *On the other hand,* a woman should be able to support herself outside the home, if occasion demand it.[17]

The timing appeared to be right this time around, and the separate home on the campus was dedicated on December 19, 1912, as "Senior Hall," and Miss Pope told the assembled stakeholders,

> Any scheme of education which does not train young women for home life is deficient. Senior Hall is to be a home where the class to be graduated is to have the privilege of personally conducting a house wherein each member shall some time during the year, buy, order, cook and serve the food; become acquainted with food values, and plan menus simple, wholesome and nourishing; launder the table linen; do the general house work. A place in which girls are to learn by doing. A model for the makers of homes in the future. A place where, it is hoped, gentle speech and manners will prevail, and respect for property and the rights of others be observed. A

constant striving for ideals in all that relates to a home, is our hope. In turning the keys to open another door of opportunity to Hawaiian girls, it is with the faith that Bernice Pauahi Bishop, adds her blessing to this new enterprise, and we pray that we may deal aright by all girls who dwell under the sheltering roof of Senior Hall.[18]

Later, the alumnae would rename the home "Pope Hall" over Charles Bishop's strong objections. He felt it unwise to "establish precedents" in naming buildings after educators.[19] This is one instance where the trustees overruled him. The concept of a home management cottage, including the care of live babies, continued when the school relocated to Kapālama Heights in 1931. While the model carried over, the name Pope Hall was dropped in the relocation.

The Alumnae Association: "Progressive Club Women"

To keep close tabs on her graduates, Ida developed an alumnae association and enrolled every one of them as a charter member. Mr. Bishop held out little hope that her "club of graduates" would be sustained due to the character of their race and warned Miss Pope that it would fall short of her "anticipations and hopes."[20] Yet it did take off, and alumnae supported and nurtured one another through the trials and tribulations of life, thereby setting the example for each succeeding wave of girls. From the moment of graduation, it was a given that each one would remain part of the family forever, sharing their burdens and standing guardian over the younger graduates.

The first official meeting was held at the school on June 23, 1899, and Miss Pope proposed a motto of sorts. For Hawaiians who experienced inexplicable pain in the overthrow of their monarchy, it would be important to follow the biblical mandate to not dwell on the past but to consciously choose, each and every day, to count one's blessings. To the alumnae association, Ida offered her favorite inspirational verse from Philippians as their lifelong maxim: "Finally, brethren, whatsoever things are true, whatsoever things are honest, whatsoever things are just, whatsoever things are pure, whatsoever things are lovely, whatsoever things are of good report; if there be any virtue, and if there be any praise, think on these things."[21]

With the spiritual direction clear in their collective minds, Ida labored intensely over the constitution for the new association. She decided to constitutionally align the association with the General Federation of Women's Clubs (GFWC). Founded in 1890, the nonpartisan, nondenominational organization was dedicated to empowering women. The precursor to the GFWC was Sorosis,

Philippians 4:8 was Ida's lifelong mission statement. *Kamehameha Schools.*

established in 1868. It was the first professional club for women in the United States. At its twenty-five-year anniversary gala in March of 1893, Hawaiʻi's beloved Princess Victoria Kaʻiulani, in New York to directly protest the overthrow of her kingdom, was a celebrated guest.[22]

The Kamehameha Alumnae Association subscribed to *The Club Woman,* a monthly magazine for "progressive club women" affiliated with the GFWC.[23] Articles provided guidance and motivational stories to clubs seeking ways to expand their influence. The GFWC developed an extensive hierarchy at the local, state, and national levels and hosted state, regional, and national conventions. Club women advocated woman suffrage as essential to reforming child labor, improving health care and safety, and increasing educational opportunities. The record shows that Ida and her girls did all that and more in their island communities.

It's not clear how a fledgling Hawaiian "band of sisters" became known, but Emma Shaw Colcleugh, a widely traveled feminist and syndicated journalist, solicited from the Kamehameha Alumnae Association a letter outlining their structure. Miriam Hale-Auld, from Ida's first graduating class, wrote the letter, stressing their intellectual pursuits. It was quickly printed in the *Boston Evening*

Transcript under "The State Federation Meeting—Good Club News from Honolulu—Local Notes and Happenings."

Honolulu, Jan. 21, 1901

Dear Mrs. Colcleugh—We are very glad to learn that we have friends far away who are interested in the work of a band of sisters in this small community. You asked for some information concerning our club which I am very glad to give you. We are doing very well, of course, working on slowly; but we hope to do better and better every time. We have no club house, but we meet at the home of any member who volunteers to have the meeting held at her house. We meet on the second and fourth Tuesdays of every month. Our course of study for the past four months has been on the "Transvaal War." At each meeting two or three members are appointed to either read from published articles or to write on a certain topic for the next meeting, of course each member being able to tell something of interest before the club. We have not gone into the reading deeply, but have been interested and glad to learn something from it. We now have taken up the subject of China. Once in a while we have the opportunity of hearing speakers from abroad, women who work in other clubs. We subscribe for the Club Woman. As probably you know, most of us are native Hawaiians, and a few are Chinese, and we use English entirely in our club, although some of our songs are in Hawaiian. Last year an Industrial Class was formed, but we have dropped it for the present, and hope to take it up again. At present we have two branches started up on other islands, one at Waimea, Kauai and the other at Hilo, Hawaii—the latter doing especially well, and we hope to have others started. We have seven different officers— president, vice president, recording secretary, corresponding secretary, treasurer, librarian and marshal. At each meeting the librarian sees that each member takes out a book to read. As I think I have told you all that I think is of importance, I will now close hoping to hear from you again.

Yours truly, Miriam Auld, (Mrs. Harry J. Auld)[24]

In between the regular meetings and socials, Miss Pope stepped in as mother for many alumnae, hosting dozens of "pretty weddings" throughout the years at the school.[25] When her graduates became mothers themselves, she invited professionals from every field to talk to them about raising children, caring for family and home, understanding nutrition, and other practical life skills. In December of 1909, so many had children of their own that Ida, in a grandmother's role, threw a Christmas "Children's Party" for fifty mothers and their children.[26] At

this point, there were 136 Kamehameha Schools alumnae on the association's ros-
ters, and she kept in contact with every one as she reported to the trustees, "[I
visited] all the members of the Kamehameha Alumnae association in Honolulu,
and have written at least once to every member, in all the Islands. These calls have
been made for the purpose of showing an interest in former pupils and of knowing the real condition of the home life and of the ones who are working for a
livelihood."[27]

To her pleasure, these visits showed her graduates were generally prosperous
and healthy and had taken her religious precepts to heart. "Home conditions are
certainly improving. A larger number are owning their own homes and improving them. Care and taste are shown in the houses and grounds. Children are more
carefully nurtured. Many who live in Honolulu use gas stoves in their kitchens.
A number are raising chickens to increase the family income. The majority are
church members, a goodly number are actively engaged in Sunday school work
and belong to Christian societies."[28]

In her fifteenth year as head of the school, Miss Pope told the graduating
class, "A woman without religion is like a flower without perfume."[29] In the same
address, she warned her girls against having elitist attitudes because of their education, and emphasized their duty to continue to serve in the community and to
lead by example: "These islands expect much from Kamehameha and it is proper
that they should. 'What do they expect from us?' you ask. Something of a finer
and better quality than is found in the lives of those who have not had your opportunities. You are not to despise such but to be an inspiration to them. Look on
what you have received as a sacred trust and do not use it for selfish ends. Set an
example in courtesy, cleanliness, purity, and industry, wherever you go."[30]

And set an example they did. One of many illustrations of how the enthusiastic alumnae served their community involves Julia Lovell Bowers. She was in the
first graduating class and also served six terms as president of the alumnae association. When horrific stories of sexual attacks on women at night around the
docks became known, she went into action. The Inter-Island steamers docked at
Honolulu after midnight, leaving "innocent or ignorant" young women far from
safety.[31]

Julia personally stood on the dock in the middle of the night to meet every
boat and thereby ensure the safety of women. A news reporter, describing "her
motherly presence at the wharf at night," asked the public to speculate on what it
"may mean to unaccompanied women travelers" and wrote that the value "would
be very hard to estimate. She meets every Inter-Island boat."[32] In one month alone,
her personal reports revealed that she met 362 women. Notes scrawled in her led-
ger made statements such as, "S.S. *Maui*, 4:20 a.m. Hawaiian girl had expected

her friends to meet her but they failed to show up. I took her home. Friends very grateful. The girl was 15 years old."[33] Another, "*S.S. Kinau*, 2:30 a.m. Took Chinese woman to her friends in the River Street section. She was quite helpless and had two small children with her."[34]

During World War I, the alumnae raised funds for the war relief effort by holding concerts and dances. Somehow, they "adopted" a young French boy whose family was in a desperate condition. Young Andre Couillarde's father had been shot in the head during the Battle of Marne. Ida's graduates wrote letters of encouragement and financially supported little Andre. In return, he wrote many grateful letters to his "dear and kind godmothers"[35] over the years.

Stories like these helped the alumnae to lift each other up, and their reunions were festive affairs worth covering in the press. In 1902, *The Friend* observed the mature alumnae and noted their "noticeable bond and sisterhood" and compared them to "laughing schoolgirls."[36] On December 17, 1904, the alumnae association gave Ida a surprise reception to honor her ten years of service to them, which the press noted: "Seldom has an instructor so endeared herself to her many pupils and the girls of Kamehameha will always remember her earnest efforts on their behalf and her untiring zeal for their general welfare."[37]

Ida, *Hānai* Mother

The biggest surprise of all occurred in Ida's forty-eighth year of life when a graduate gave her the ultimate gift: a child to raise as her own. In 1910, Esther Staines-Kanuha, dear to Ida since the days of Kawaiahaʻo Seminary, offered her fifth child, her four-year-old daughter, Gladys, to Ida as Ida's *hānai* daughter. Esther's husband and Gladys' father, David Kanuha,[38] a member of the counterrevolution of 1895, had been the tailoring teacher at the Kamehameha School for Boys when Ida played matchmaker and arranged their marriage.

Too young for Mother Pope's school, Gladys attended classes with the small boys in the Preparatory Academy. Reflecting on these years, Gladys recalled that Ida uncharacteristically indulged her and she became "very spoiled" and "not the most well-behaved creature on earth." She remembered "Mama Pope" asking at the end of each school day, "How was your day, Gladys?" and that she herself would reply, "Very good, I only had to stand back of the piano twice today."[39]

Ida would not live long enough to raise Gladys to womanhood, but perhaps her imprint was on her, because Gladys was known as a firebrand for civic causes and specifically compared later in life to Ida Pope with the adjectives "strict, hardheaded, and strong-willed."[40] Gladys Kamakakūokalani ʻAinoa Brandt later stepped into the same role as Ida Pope and carries the distinction of being the

Miss Pope declared, "There must be a place for the Hawaiian girl. She has it by right of Inheritance and the bequest of Bernice Pauahi Bishop." Ca. 1911. Small girl in front, likely little Gladys. *Kamehameha Schools.*

Gladys Kamakakuokalani Ainoa Brandt (1906–2003). *Kamehameha Schools.*

very first appointed native Hawaiian principal at the Kamehameha School for Girls in 1963. She was given many awards and recognitions throughout her life for being a "champion of Native Hawaiian culture."[41]

No greater example illustrates how Ida successfully straddled the line between the two cultures. A *hānai* adoption was non–legally binding and a widespread practice throughout the history of Hawai'i, but it would have been rare to place a child outside his or her native culture. If Gladys' parents were concerned at all regarding an imbalance of attachment to the American way of life, they must have felt similar to Queen Lili'uokalani: an education under Miss Pope would give Hawaiian girls a full advantage in the new unfolding economy in a way that they could not.[42]

Funding the Alumnae

Whereas typical alumnae organizations provide funds for their alma mater, Miss Pope's alumnae association became a support network where alumnae raised money for each other, to strengthen one another's well-being. To aid the alumnae, Ida, with the help of Professor Edgar Wood of the Honolulu Normal School in 1902, devised a unique plan, establishing the "Honor and Trust Fund." Deserving students who desired teacher training but had insufficient means could now get loans to cover their education and pay back the money once they were working. Under the auspices of the Honor Loan and Trust Association, influential people like the Athertons and Cookes, as well as Charles Bishop, contributed to the fund. The *Hawaiian Star* in 1908 pronounced the effort a success and reported that a number of graduates had teaching positions and "met their obligations with great fidelity."[43]

Not all her graduates wanted to be teachers, so in 1909, Ida designed the Kamehameha Alumnae Loan Fund. She had high hopes for the project, telling the trustees, "If it works as successfully as the Honor and Trust Fund, it will be a valuable project for the alumnae to be engaged in."[44] She held many elaborate fundraising benefits on the campus in order to "loan money to deserving members of the association who desire to go to the mainland to study."[45] She successfully operated it under the same businesslike terms as the Honor and Trust Fund.

Financial support was not limited to continuing education. In 1910–1911, Ida began fund-raising all over again, this time to start a relief fund to help her graduates in need of emergency financial assistance. She urged the alumnae association members to raise a full $5,000 to act as the principal for this fund, as only the interest would be loaned out, and she asked that they not go outside the association to do so. In her view, family should help family. The alumnae responded, making regular donations and contributing receipts from fund-raising events such as bake sales, lūʻaus, dances, concerts, and pageants. Miss Pope served as treasurer of this impromptu bank for many years. Records reveal scrupulous attention to detail, down to the ten-cent tissue used for table decorations.[46]

A Rest House: "The Need Is Great, Almost a Crying One"

As the opening of the Panama Canal was about to occur, the Hawaiʻi Promotion Committee seized an opportunity to coincide with this event. With the certainty of reduced transit time for ships going between ports in the Atlantic and Pacific Oceans, the primary motive was for Hawaiʻi to "be seen" in order to produce a revenue stream for Hawaiian businesses. The Mid-Pacific Carnival with all the charms of the islands was heavily promoted in the United States, and soon tourist-packed steamers began arriving for the weeklong festivities in February of 1914.

Kamehameha Schools had been entreated to provide a main cultural event for the throngs. Ida began preparing the girls to perform alongside the boys in a "living motion picture" of an ancient Hawaiian legend on the beach at Waikīkī.[47] "The Wooing of Umi and Piikea" [A pageantry illustrating early Hawaiian court pomp] required grueling preparation, and the *Star Bulletin* had nothing but praise for the pageant and reported Miss Pope "had the principal work of drilling the company in the old meles [chants, songs, or poems], through which the story is told."[48]

During the production, a reporter from the *Advertiser* scanning the crowd noted astonishment and wonderment when his "eye caught Queen Liliuokalani, the last native ruler of the islands, sitting side by side with S. B. Dole, the first president after the overthrow of the monarchy." He could not help "reflecting at the changes which have taken place in the government and peoples of the Islands in the last twenty years."[49] This moment in time that brought former enemies, now in their twilight years, to sit shoulder-to-shoulder in the grandstands was probably not lost on Ida either. She had sought the queen's favor for over two decades, and likely hoped for her approval of the historically accurate pageant demonstrating cultural practices long forbidden Hawaii's daughters.

However wonderful it was, once the event was over, her report to the trustees cited a personal "strain" due to "Umi and Piikea."[50] Productions like this, on top of her school and alumnae obligations, together with the multitude of causes she constantly championed, seemed to have completely frayed her nerves. The tension following the Mid-Pacific Carnival is seen in several school reports that testily reminded the trustees that many necessary matters had been ignored by her written "suggestions."

A few months prior to the carnival, Ida sent the trustees two emotionally charged requests for a "Rest House" for herself and her teachers. The male staff lived in detached quarters at the boys' school, so her specifications of one large sitting room, two bedrooms, and a bathroom were not excessive. She reminded the trustees that there was not one single place to retreat from the deafening noise from "100 healthy young spirits and the practicing of twenty pianos!"[51]

> I wonder sometimes what is *not* expected of teachers. Poise, control, adaptability, a calm outlook are the requisites of Christian workers in any sphere. But these virtues flourish in places that conduce to meditative reflection, in times of quiet and repose. A woman is a highly organized nervous creature and if she is fine and sensitive she requires soil for ample growth. A little leaven of quiet and time for diversion should help give the buoyancy and life and add its flavor to the whole atmosphere of the place.

Ida lived in one of the most vibrant and beautiful places in the world, yet told the trustees that her and the teachers' "social life" was "deadly dull."[52] She expressed a mediocrity from living solely with females.

> Constant school routine where the teacher must be the mental stimulus for her classes, leads to much weariness and fatigue and not much energy left at the close of the day. Living under the roof with over a hundred people, with only the feminine element meeting three times daily round the table there is brought about an unnatural way of living and it is not always enlivening; students do not bring the kind of social touch that educated women have a right to expect. Along with work should come the joy of living, a play time that appeals to varied tastes. We live too much to ourselves which tends to emphasize trifles and make them loom large on the daily horizon.

Since home and work were one and the same, there was no escape from the around-the-clock duties, "urgent" needs, and problems to be solved from an endless rotation of trustees, teachers, pupils, and alumnae. Add her worthy but grueling community campaigns into the mix, and it's clear that her lifestyle wasn't sustainable. Focusing on the needs of everyone at the expense of her own was a disservice to herself because symptoms of hypertension worried her enough to ask for a summer off. As she prepared to leave for Chicago in the summer of 1914, she pleaded with the trustees to erect the "Rest House" in her absence. Ida's last words abstractly stated her reality: "Overstrain is liable to produce nervous disorders" and "The need is great, almost a crying one!"

Miss Pope's Last Reunion

A tiny and yellowed newspaper clipping is glued on a page in Ida's scrapbook, the date May 16, 1914, written upon it in her distinctive backhand slant. The article, titled "Reunion of Alumnae Is Largely Attended," reported, "Five hundred persons attended the Kamehameha alumnae reunion at the school. A splendid program was given, following several hours taken up with dancing. The treasurer's report, presented by Miss Pope, was an encouraging one and showed the association to be on a secure financial footing."[53]

No doubt, every alumna in attendance would have noticed that Miss Pope was not in the best of health. Privately, teacher Frances Lemmon was "afraid" that Ida was approaching "nervous prostration," a mental breakdown, due to the strain of meeting everyone's needs, including hers.[54] But with her usual cheery "Don't-worry-about-me" attitude, Ida assured everyone that a summer with her family would restore her strength. Nobody could have imagined that this would be her last reunion.

CHAPTER EIGHTEEN

Last Aloha to Mother Pope, 1914

ALOHA is a priceless lei, an endless chain
Of friendship, love, remembrance—all in sweet refrain.
—Margaret K. Morgan, Legends and Lyrics of Hawaii

Arriving Rundown in Chicago

In the latter part of June of 1914, Ida arrived in Chicago in a noticeably "rundown condition."[1] Ida confessed to her sister Anne, whom she had not seen in four years, that she "had not been well" for some time.[2] But, with her characteristically indomitable attitude, Ida told her sister she thought she would be just fine "after a rest."[3] With their sister Lois Prosser and brother Henry Pope at their respective summer homes in Wisconsin, Anne and Ida stayed in the Prosser apartment on a street that faced the beautiful tree-lined vista of the famed Midway Park.

Despite Ida's obvious fatigue, education was on her mind and she "gathered books for future study, read an excellent report of the schools of Scotland [and] sent to Washington for bulletins on vocational education in the Philippines."[4] Ida, who always took great pleasure in shopping, did, however, make multiple trips to Chicago's elegant retail center, State Street. She knew she would never see such sophistication in Hawai'i's shops, so to her own delight she shopped in the most prestigious department stores, including Marshall Field, Carson Pirie & Scott, and Charles A. Stevens. But Kamehameha was never far from Ida's mind, and while shopping in Field's department store, she gathered information on home furnishings in order to tastefully upgrade the common rooms at Kamehameha and had "long conferences at McClurg's book store"[5] regarding fresh reading material for the school.

Ida, who had already prearranged the meeting, would not miss formally welcoming the newly recruited principal of the Kamehameha School for Boys, Ernest C. Webster, and his family, who were departing from Chicago to Honolulu. Despite the fact that she was in poor health, she felt it important to welcome

"She was a teacher, a principal, and above all, a mother." *Kamehameha Schools.*

Mr. Webster and his family, give them a tour of Lincoln Park on July 5, and share a cup of tea. Ida wrote to Lois that she was "pleasantly impressed with Mr. and Mrs. W—and the two little Websters."[6]

Anne saw that all this activity took its toll and became concerned enough to make an appointment with Dr. Lewis, their family doctor, to examine her sister. The doctor's findings revealed that Ida was suffering from exhaustion, heart problems, and dangerously high blood pressure. He soon urged an operation, a type that was never identified in any correspondence.

Anne scheduled a medical treatment for herself on the same date in the same hospital, so they could convalesce together. Throughout her life, Anne had

Chicago's State Street was a shopping mecca during the 1900s. *Library of Congress 4a25229a.*

suffered from a chronic condition due to her crooked spine, and was periodically put in spinal plaster casts to correct the problem. Anne believed there was no better way to endure her own pain and recovery than with her beloved older sister beside her. The plan was for the sisters to have their medical procedures simultaneously and then travel to their siblings' lake homes in Wisconsin for rest and recuperation among the extended family.

Ida Enters the Hospital

Ida's three weeks in Chicago were filled with an astonishing level of activity, considering her weakened physical condition. But her freedom to roam in the city soon came to an end when she was admitted to St. Luke's Hospital for her procedure. Not surprisingly, once there, she found it difficult to follow the doctor's order for complete rest, and the annoyance with her condition is obvious in her unguarded words to her older sister.

St. Luke's Hospital
Chicago, July 9, 1914

My dear Lois—

Anne had her cast put on this morning and is on her back until it gets dry. When it is set she is coming over to my room to stay. Dr. Lewis is having all of my fluids tested. I thought he would be in this morning to report on the urine test but he has not come in yet this a.m. I shall not stay here many days longer. I am thinking of asking the trustees to stay on this side of the Pacific through September and then I shall not need to rush so—

I have done an impertinent thing. I have had some things charged on Fields and Carson Pirie on your account. I have all of the checks and shall have a check sent to you in a day or so. I returned a dressing sacque (7.50) which will not appear until the July bill comes. It may be better to wait until I know what the cost of the dress was on the Carson Pirie bill. The check did not come with the dress and then I had a waist charged at Stevens. I was afraid there might be a mix up, if I had them charged to my Honolulu account.

We have both enjoyed the letters from Ruth and Katherine. Joe and Henry have been to see us and Joe says the Onekama place has greatly improved. I am wild to see it, but in the meantime do not paint everything in sight. I am wild to see it all and shall as soon as possible.

Anne and I did so enjoy the freedom of such a big apartment and I just spread myself when I came from Dr. Lewis's or from down town. I greatly appreciate your letting me stay there. We left everything in good order. I covered the couch cushions and put moth powder about. I hated to come away for I enjoyed it so much. I am trying to answer lots of letters but do not progress very well flat on my back. I shall be glad to get away from the hospital although everybody is so nice and kind, I am just vegetating like a cabbage.

Love to the girls

Lovingly,
Ida M. Pope[7]

The Stroke

After her hospital release, Ida was ordered to stay in the city and rest in bed with no visitors or risk serious repercussions. Dr. Lewis told her that because of her hypertension, "there was danger for her at any time, though she might have no trouble for years."[8] Back at the apartment, Anne said they purposefully "never spoke of the danger," but "lived in the present."[9] Ida's last letter, written the day before she died, revealed that her blood pressure was perilously high and she was resolved to obey doctor's orders, because she was eager to return to Hawai'i with health restored. Even though she told Anne "I listen to the quiet. It rests me," her last letter revealed her increasing impatience with being flat on her back.

Chicago, July 13, 1914

My dear Lois—

Dr. Lewis says, "flat on your back and absolute quiet and no visiting" until further orders. The high blood pressure means ragged nerves and if I do not get better hold of myself, I shall be unfit for my job and so I am going to be tractable and obedient and return to Kamehameha vigorous and ready for the fray.

Joe has told me about the house and grounds and when I lie here flat on my back, I picture how it all looks. I feel like cutting and running this morning, it is so sizzling hot in Chicago—but before long I shall make my exit by the doctor's leave.

When I hear from you about the Carson Pirie bill I will forward a check at once. The papers are full of bargains in the stores and I am tempted to go down town, but of course I shall refrain.

Love to the girls—Anne sends love

Lovingly,
Ida M. Pope[10]

The letter was never mailed, because the very next day, July 14, three weeks after her arrival, Ida, only fifty-two, perished. She would never make it out of the "sizzling" heat of Chicago, to her siblings' homes by the lake, or back home to Hawai'i and the girls she loved. Her desolate brother Henry informed a news reporter that soon after a "hearty meal and in her customary good spirits," she was suddenly "stricken by death at 8:40 p.m."[11]

"To the Children of Miss Ida M. Pope"

Three days after Ida passed away, Anne personally delivered the devastating news to her sister's "children." Because their "hearts and minds swung together in perfect harmony," she felt that only *she* could reiterate her sister's hopes and dreams for their collective lives.[12] "To the Children of Miss Ida M. Pope" was published in *The Friend*. Because it was circulated to every island, it reached nearly all of Ida's alumnae in one fell swoop. Anne shared their first meeting.

> As I waited in the morning with my face to the east, the world seemed full of hope and promise. As I saw her walking strongly and surely toward me, my crutches seemed to fly and carry me to her. My meeting with her on the beautiful Midway compensated for my wait of four years. Almost as soon as we went into the house, she wanted to open her trunk, as she had gifts for all. Like a true Hawaiian, she showered us with her choicest treasures. Many had been gifts from you. Our house was filled with your aloha and we felt it.

She described their quiet filled days of convalescence, where they would sit outside in the evenings, discussing Ida's hopes and dreams for her Hawaiian "daughters."

> We had many beautiful days together—days full of rest and peace and quiet. She sometimes said: "I listen to the quiet. It rests me." Often in the evening we sat on the Midway to watch the sunset. Many times as we sat there she talked of you and of her plans for you. She had great aloha and was a friend to you. She wanted to study and make her school better for you. She was willing to spend all her strength and money for you, her children. She gave to you as a true Hawaiian gives. She wanted her school to give you such a practical, efficient training, that there would be no break between school and later life. She wanted you to be independent, self-supporting women. Also, she wanted to give you an appreciation of the most beautiful things of life and to fit you to take your place with dignity among any people of the world.

Anne shared the heartbreaking moment on the Midway when she watched her sister's body taken away: "As I stood on the Midway and watched her disappear into the sunset, I thought of you with deep aloha and knew that a great sun had set in our lives forever, but I knew that because of her wonderful influence you and I could go on as she would have us, even in the dark."[13]

The Shock in Hawai'i

Headlines proclaiming the death of "Mother Pope" caused a wail from island to island. The grief expressed spanned class and culture, from the distinguished senator Alfred F. Judd, who proclaimed, "The death of Miss Pope is an irretrievable loss to the Kamehameha Schools and to the Hawaiian race,"[14] to the humblest "words and sobs" from scores of "her children" across the islands.[15]

Reverend Dr. Doremus Scudder, Ida's pastor who helped her with Honolulu's social survey, in his role as the editor-in-chief of *The Friend*, wrote a front-page tribute that captured the essence of her like no other, according to her family.

> She had both woman's intuition and man's power of cool judgment, a very rare combination. She was also an executive of unusual ability, possessed a fine business head and was a master of detail. She had tact and knew how to bide her time. Furthermore she was genuine enough never to push herself forward, and was content to do the work and let others seem to lead. Her intellectual power was matched by her largeness of heart. She had the divine quality of loving persons irrespective of their seeming loveliness or unloveliness. She gave herself to the cause of mothering Hawaiian girls, so many of whom have no real mother. In this service she never spared herself and to it she sacrificed her life.[16]

Anne Sets the Record Straight with the Trustees

Two weeks after Ida's death, Anne wrote a letter to Kamehameha School Trustees, making sure they understood her sister's motivations and educational objectives. It could be she needed to cathartically express and summarize Ida's ambitions for the record, in order to ease her pain and remind them of her sister's ultimate sacrifice for Hawaiian women.

> July 27, 1914
>
> Gentlemen:
>
> I am taking the liberty of writing to you because I believe that you, too, have a sorrow in the death of my dear sister, Ida Pope. I had three wonderful weeks with her, during which I gathered some of her thoughts about Kamehameha. I know, as my sister knew, the great press of your affairs, yet I must send this letter, telling of her ideas, for I cannot help believing that a fuller knowledge of them will be of value to the schools, and thus to the Hawaiian People.
>
> Ida was a well equipped modern educator, whose training was always being added to, but was never completed. She studied educational literature, making a special point of psychology and pedagogy. She believed

that every teacher should have a thorough knowledge of the best methods of social service work. When in the States, a large part of her vacations were spent in study, in conference with eminent educators, and in visiting notable schools—Hampton Institute, Lewis Institute, Pratt Institute, Dr. Dewey's famous school, Colonel Parker's School, the Boston Trade Schools, the School of Education at the University of Chicago. At the university, she studied sociology and vocational guidance, making the study of the Hawaiian race her special interest. She learned to look at the Hawaiians in relation to other races, and to understand better their place in the great march of life, thus getting a broader view of their problems and their position in the world. Miss Pope understood that she was working for a young race that was being forced into quick development, and she fitted her methods to this situation.

She was an organizer who saw the end to be accomplished, but was interested in the minutest details necessary to its accomplishment. She was a keen and true observer, with an open and receptive mind. She had natural and quick insight into situations and people, and she never settled problems in a personal way. She was patient. She could wait for a race, a society or a point of view to develop if it moved ever so slowly. She had a broad sympathy that embraced the smallest needs of a pupil or the greatest needs of the community.

She knew that her high aims for the Hawaiian girls could be realized only through competent teachers. She knew the tremendous drain on their strength and time, and of their loneliness so far from home. For these reasons she believed in making their life at the school as home-like, pleasant and comfortable as possible. She believed in any luxury, serving in any way to lessen the strain of their work, thinking that conservation of the teachers was not only just to them, but important to the welfare of the school, and she, therefore, took much satisfaction in the Teacher's Rest House.[17]

She had faith in the Hawaiian girls and had a high ideal for them. She wanted the Hawaiian girls to be useful members of the neighborhoods in which they lived, not only through their standards of living and self-support in valuable vocations, but through common service. In addition she wished the Hawaiian girls to be happy and joyous, as is their birthright.

The opportunities that were given to Miss Pope were appreciated, but she saw far ahead and was ready for more. She hoped that a small hospital would soon be built and the last week of her life, while at St. Luke's Hospital, she studied its good and bad features for future use. Any training the girls would receive in a hospital would be of great value to them, their families and their neighbors. Ida Pope's whole idea of education could find complete expression through this hospital.

She hoped to see the girls' school grow into a Technical High School, including continuation work, closely connected with the economic life of the Hawaiian Islands. Modern life is crowding the Hawaiians so fast, that a great leap in manner of living and thinking, had to be made. She saw that, as time goes by, education will be less institutional, that the pupils will live more at home, and thus have a more normal family life, and that they will come to the school for education and guidance all of their lives. In a generation or two there will be no break between the home, the school and later life. Ida Pope saw that schools alone could not educate the children in any country, but that the whole community must cooperate with the homes and schools. She had felt this for years and all of her observations and study strengthened this idea. She saw that all life is a unit.

Ida Pope was not an educator, or a rare woman, she was a mother, a great mother, who understood, loved, pitied, had faith in and was ambitious for her children, theirs to be called on at all times, a mother who could forgive all failures, a mother who desired all good things for her children. For their sake this letter is written to you, for I feel the loss of an enlightened educator, the devotion of a strong woman, and the love of a mother to Kamehameha and to the Hawaiian people.

Anne Pope
Chicago[18]

Memorializing Miss Pope

While the Popes were back in Bucyrus preparing to quietly bury their sister alongside their parents, there was a flurry of activity in Hawai'i. In the weeks following her death, several memorial services were held throughout the islands. The first song-filled service was held in the Wailuku Union Church, on September 18, organized by the alumnae who lived in Maui. They decorated the church with fragrant boughs of "golden shower," whose showy yellow blooms they knew Ida loved. They also sang "one of Miss Pope's favorite hymns, Queen Liliuokalani's Prayer."[19] The queen composed this piece under the politically charged circumstance of being imprisoned, and this song, roundly recognized as one of religious devotion and forgiveness, obviously spoke to Ida's heart. One graduate told the assemblage of mourners,

She gave the best part of her young life to develop in the Hawaiian girls a character of true womanhood. She was a woman of dignified, business-like personality; firm yet kind, leading a life of true self-denial, sincerity, and all that makes a life of noble Christianity. She was a teacher, a principal, and above all, a mother and there is in the heart of every true Kamehameha girl a great "ALOHA" for her.[20]

The following day, September 19, the pews were full at Kawaiaha'o Church across from the palace. It seemed the entire community showed up to hear eighty-year-old Reverend Henry Hodges Parker eulogize Ida Pope. Fully fluent in Hawaiian, he had ministered to the royal family in both life and death in his fifty-four years as pastor.[21] Ida, who was present when he memorialized Princess Ka'iulani, had a deep respect for Reverend Parker, whom she thought was eloquent and sincere. Ida Pope and then Lili'uokalani in 1917 would be among his last memorials.[22]

At the school memorial service, which was held at twilight, September 20, 1914, at the Bishop Memorial Church on the campus of Kamehameha Schools, Uldrick Thompson, now vice president of the boys school, looked deeply into the tear-stained faces of the grief-stricken young women, and told them that while they would "go to her no more," they should be encouraged because they carried her spirit within them.[23]

Mr. Thompson ended the music-filled service by reminding all in attendance that among her favorite hymns was "Under His Wing." This hymn assured shelter and safety under God's protective power, much like the sheltering wing Ida provided girls during an unprecedented era in their history. When World War I began two weeks after her death, their world would once again be shaken. But Mr. Thompson needn't have worried; Kamehameha graduates proved they were strong, resilient, and adaptive women. As hard as Miss Pope tried, she could not prepare the world for her alumnae, but she successfully prepared her alumnae for the world.

In the darkest period of Hawaiian history, the queen gave her people a garden as a sanctuary, a safe gathering place, when it was illegal for them to gather in public. This event coincided with the opening of the Kamehameha School for Girls. The garden's name, Uluhaimalama, translates "As the plants grow out of the dark into the light so shall light come to the nation."[24] For many Hawaiian girls, the school was their Uluhaimalama, and Ida Pope was a bright, shining light in that garden.

While the memorial services were a fine tribute, the more lasting memorial to Ida came in the form of a charitable fund for Hawaiian girls. Her alumnae jumped into action and responded to her passing in practical ways that Ida herself would have wanted. Their plan was to fulfill one of Ida's unmet dreams and build yet another Ida Pope–inspired boarding house specifically to house girls from neighboring islands in a homelike environment so they could attend high school in Honolulu.[25]

The Ida M. Pope Memorial Fund Association began fund-raising weeks after her death on virtually every island and earnestly in 1919. Through food sales, fairs, dances, concerts, lūʻau, and donations for four years, their labor of love yielded $45,000. When the territorial government finally established high schools on the other islands, the Ida M. Pope home was no longer a dire need. The funds were then diverted to a scholarship plan[26] and turned over to the Hawaiian Trust Company for this purpose.[27]

Her name and legacy live on in the Ida M. Pope Memorial Scholarship fund. To date, thousands upon thousands of Hawaiian women have acquired a college education through this fund. Ida would be well pleased by the number of recipients because she believed that the benefits of a well-educated society of women extended beyond economics.

Remembering Lydia in Her Will

Ida never left anything to chance. While she could not imagine that she would die so young, she was practical by nature. On April 18, 1914, a short while before leaving Hawaiʻi, Ida, expecting the best but preparing for the worst, privately had a will drawn. Although Ida had two single sisters who could have put that money to good use, the bulk of her savings account was bestowed upon Lydia Aholo, whom she loved like a daughter. She apparently wanted to ensure that Lydia, who had been by her side from age twelve to thirty-eight, could live independently. While the sum may seem small in modern terms ($500), it was a significant amount for Ida, and for Lydia. To many other alumnae, Ida left a variety of personal belongings that were distributed throughout the islands upon her death. To her sister Katherine, who stayed behind in Honolulu, she left a handwritten note on school letterhead stating that her practical items, including a sewing machine and a typewriter, were to be sold to "defray funeral expenses." She undoubtedly did not want any money from the alumnae funds to be spent on her death.

Heartbroken Lydia, who had sat behind Miss Pope's desk for almost two decades, was now needed to clarify the school's policies and procedures. When Charles Bishop died a year after Ida, it was Lydia who organized and rallied the alumnae to participate in his memorial. Now in middle age, she would need to rely on her own judgment for perhaps the first time in her life. It was clearly more than she could bear and it culminated in an emotional breakdown.[28] When exhaustion, depression, and sickness descended upon her, she left her job at Kamehameha and sought solace not with the queen but with Ida's sisters, Lois, Katherine, and Anne, in Chicago, as she recounted at age ninety-two:

> Oh, I took sick. I had to go to the mainland for rest. That was in 1917. I went to say goodbye to the queen, and she was so feeble, you know. And before I left, she said "In my room there's a lei with Lehua [blossoms from the Ohia tree] You know, in Hilo you see those trees with those yellow blossoms? You go in my room and get that lei and put it on and wear it down to the boat." Oh, beautiful. "You go in my room and get that lei and put it on and wear it down to the boat. Remember me." So, I kissed her goodbye.[29]

In ancient times, Lehua was a symbol of strength,[30] and the queen may have intuitively known Lydia would need all that it symbolized in the days to come. Her grief and guilt at not being present with the queen when she died in November of 1917 are painfully evident in her tone: "I didn't know what to do. Wished I could come home, but I couldn't, so I just stayed. Oh, I tell you. All the things that I've gone through, I wonder how I ever lived. Oh, sad things, you know."[31]

The deaths of her two mother figures ultimately forced Lydia to make sense of who she was, where she was headed, and what acquired skills would take her there. Now middle aged and single, she was pushed into the world of adult choices. Her first choice was to return to Kamehameha Schools, to the familiar environment of structure and routine. The bookkeeping, accounting, and stenography skills she learned sitting beside Miss Pope's desk kept her securely employed for many years. The music skills she learned through life with the queen provided comfort and ministry opportunities throughout her life. As time went by, the resilient Lydia emerged from her shell. In 1923, Lydia was hired as Kamehameha's first formal Hawaiian language teacher.

"Haole Mother's" Lasting Legacy

Throughout the years, the alumnae, through their official association, formed deep bonds of friendship. History reveals that filial duty was a strong theme in the lives of Miss Pope's graduates. They worked for the welfare of each other rather than for individual advancement. Lydia Aholo, who lived to be 101, would be the longest-living survivor of this first close-knit group. As the alumnae aged, they directly carried Ida's legacy and memory well into the second half of the twentieth century.

McGregor and Lydia Aholo, longest living survivors from the class of 1897 in 1969. *Kamehameha Schools.*

When women finally did get voting rights on August 26, 1920, Kamehameha graduates across the islands made the news when they competed with each other to earn the distinction as "first in line" to register. Alice Stone Blackwell reported to the American press that Hawaiian women, who had been disenfranchised by the United States, were taking back the positions they held in "the days of the monarchy."[32] It's not surprising that when the process began in the islands, native Hawaiian women accounted for more registrations than any other races, including haoles.[33]

In the spring of 1954, a group of students at the Kamehameha School for Girls were given a senior English "cooperative project."[34] The assignment was to canvass the islands to interview any surviving alumnae from Miss Pope's era. The stories of those *kūpuna,* or honored elders, were compiled and jointly edited as "Haole Mother in Hawaii," a story published in *Makers of Destiny, Hawaiian Style.*[35] As a "finale to their research," the girls hosted a tea party to bring together twenty-five alumnae, now senior citizens, to reminisce about the unforgettable Miss Pope.[36]

The *kūpuna* described Miss Pope as a mother—for some, the only mother they had ever had. And she had been so much more: principal, teacher, nurse, bookkeeper, maintenance worker, spiritual mentor, and grandmother to their children. "Miss Pope expected us to put into practice what we had learned, and often made follow-up calls on her girls after they had graduated. She visited our homes and gave us bits of advice and commended us on the work we were doing. Her never-failing efforts left a strong and lasting impression."[37]

The elders remembered that every morning at precisely eight-thirty, the whole school would assemble for a devotional session with Miss Pope. Even though "her prayers were short and simple," they were "filled with pure, deep thoughts." As one grandmother stated, "I will never forget those prayers."[38] Following Miss Pope's spiritual devotions, they remembered being empowered by her mini-lectures on current topics as well as the never-ending importance of manners and etiquette.

The twenty-five elders worked on a group poem with the high school students, beaming in their recollections of a small and plump "mother-away-from-home," who every evening "stepped quickly through the dark halls of the dormitory. Her tiny blue eyes squinting into each quiet room"—and then, "after smiling and sighing quietly, walking down the hall, her footsteps softly receding."[39]

To Miss Ida M. Pope:
You came to our Islands at a time
When we needed you the most—
When women were thought to be
Some lesser creature.

You raised us out of ignorance and superstition
Into our rightful places in the sun.
You were our teacher, counsellor, doctor,

Confidante, friend, and
A Mother-away-from-home.

You taught us a lesson
We'll never forget:
To think on things that are true and honest,
Just and pure,
And of good report.

You taught us always to uphold
The principles of Womanhood.
You taught us to love and befriend,
To clean, to feed, to help.
You made us Women.[40]
—Kamehameha Girls' Alumnae group poem generated at the 1954
   springtime tea

Notes on Sources and Research

The bulk of Ida May Pope's papers are housed at two main institutions. Her personal correspondence is held at the Huntington Library in Pasadena and her professional correspondence including twenty-five years of school reports are held at Kamehameha Schools Archives in Honolulu. The late Mrs. Mary Lois Ivey and other members of Ida's family, notably great-grandnieces Joanne Calendar and Lois Taylor, freely shared their personal documents from family Bibles, genealogies, marriage and death certificates, diaries, and treasured photographs with histories to match.

This book also weaves in the voices of Ida Pope's teaching contemporaries, including unpublished letters from Lilla E. Appleton (Oberlin College Archives), Iretta Hight-Retan (Kamehameha Schools Archives and the Schlesinger Library), Carolyn Babb (the Bancroft Library) at University of California, Berkeley, and Helen Norton (Hawaiian Mission Children's Society) and great-nephew James Benjamin. Prominent among these are the letters of Carrie P. Winter-Kofoid, who traveled and worked with Ida Pope. These letters, along with a few from Ida Pope herself, were part of the Charles A. Kofoid bequest to the Scripps Institution of Oceanography, now housed at the UCSD Libraries (University of California, San Diego). Winter's letters were transcribed, edited, and researched by myself and Deborah Day, resulting in the 2013 publication of *An American Girl in the Hawaiian Islands: The Letters of Carrie Prudence Winter (1890–1893)* (University of Hawai'i Press).

Lydia Kaonohiponiponiokalani Aholo, at ninety-two years of age, consented to a recorded interview oral history by Helena Allen in 1969. This two-sided reel-to-reel magnetic tape is now housed at Kamehameha Schools Archives. Allen purportedly used the taped stories as a foundation for *The Betrayal of Liliuokalani: Last Queen of Hawaii 1838–1917* to vividly describe the queen's life through the eyes of her *hānai* (adopted) daughter, Lydia. It seemed logical for me to hunt for the recording, as the next step in learning more about the Hawaiian woman Ida Pope generously remembered in her will. I eventually discovered the master tape, which was long presumed destroyed, in California in the possession of the executor of Allen's estate. The story of my hunt and retrieval of the tape were recounted in the December 2011 article "Lydia's Voice" by Mike Gordon of the *Honolulu Star-Advertiser*. During transcription, I discovered, as others had suspected, that much of Allen's book fraudulently quoted Lydia's remembrances of the queen. In an effort to right a wrong, I coauthored "Lydia K. Aholo—Her Story Recovering the Lost Voice," published in *The Hawaiian Journal of History* (47 [2013]: 103–145). Lydia's voice lends authentic and poignant data to this book.

Of special note are the Lilla Estelle Appleton Papers housed in the Oberlin College Archives, which include a lifetime of correspondence and diaries, as well as a transcribed diary, titled "Revolutionary," that gives a day-by-day account of the days leading up to and immediately following the 1893 overthrow. Lilla Estelle Appleton was an accomplished and prolific amateur photographer and took and/or developed many photographs around the Hawaiian Islands including Kawaiahaʻo Seminary and its students. Appleton's great-grandniece, the late Susan Elizabeth "Betsy" Lang, generously offered Estelle's entire selection of photos for my research purposes. Charlotte Mitchell also graciously shared photos and diaries from her private collection. Research archives across Hawaiʻi hold Appleton's photos unaware of the provenance.

When primary source material was quoted, every effort was made to accurately and faithfully represent any original letter or report cited in transcription. To this end, errors in grammar or spelling were left uncorrected, with the exception of names of well-known people (e.g., "Cooke" for "Cook") and a few historical places. Some sentences were shortened and paragraph breaks inserted in the interest of clarity without disrupting the sequence of the original letter. In a few instances, a bracketed word was inserted for clarity and/or readability. In order to avoid distraction for the reader, hyphens and ellipses were not used when words were removed from a single sentence.

"The List of Individuals Mentioned in Letters and Reports," identifying key individuals, was a daunting undertaking. A master list was created and classified into three broad groups: the white *kamaʻaina*, or native-born in Hawaiʻi, the American educators, and the Hawaiian pupils of Ida Pope. From that master list, the "List" for this book was culled.

Of the three, the easiest group to accurately identify was the white *kamaʻaina* that dominated the Hawaiian economy in the late nineteenth to twentieth century. Much has been published about this influential group; the main challenge to accurate identification was that frequent intermarriage among a relatively small group of families made it difficult to determine exactly which Mrs. Cooke or

Mr. Castle was being discussed. This necessitated looking at people in context and checking against other sources.

The second group consists of Ida's American teaching colleagues. Following nineteenth-century protocol, correspondence and reports usually referred to adults in this group by last name only (Miss Harris, Miss Brewer). Steamship passenger lists published in newspapers provided first names or initials of the teachers arriving and leaving Honolulu, which aided identification. While many of these teachers changed their names upon marriage, college biographical directories and alumnae reports were extremely useful. Archives at Mount Holyoke College, South Hadley, Massachusetts, and Oberlin College yielded class files, photographs, alumnae reports, newspaper articles, and letters, and these materials contained abundant information.

The third group consisted of students. This was the most complicated group to research for a number of reasons, including the fragmentary nature of record keeping. School records for the first Kawaiahaʻo Seminary no longer exist. Even though teachers diligently recorded pupils' names, the spellings of the names were suspect due to multiple versions; thus, conclusively identifying students from the seminary was challenging, as it required three or more facts collected from credible sources. The Ulukau Hawaiian Electronic Library indexes genealogical records kept in the Hawaiʻi State Archives as well as Hawaiian genealogies, books, and newspapers, and this site was an invaluable research tool for this project, as was Ancestry.com.

For this book, the archives at Kamehameha Schools were the most important resource. Some, but not all, records survive from the Kamehameha School for Girls' early years. Ida May Pope's detailed notes in volume A–K of the school's early admissions records have been preserved in the school archives. (Volume L–Z has unfortunately been lost.) These records also provide names of parents, guardians, and tuition sponsors; age at entrance; nationality/heritage; island home; and date of graduation.

Alumnae records yielded rich information such as married names and occupations. The school newspaper, *Handicraft,* and Ida Pope's "Memory Book" were a treasure trove of anecdotal information. The names of Ida's alumnae and activities were often reported in the periodicals of the time; thus, the Library of Congress' website *Chronicling America* was an invaluable research source for Honolulu newspaper articles highlighting the activities of the Kamehameha School for Girls Alumnae Association and its members, both individually and corporately.

Ultimately, identifying each woman whose life Ida May Pope personally touched would require a book of its own. Because many of her students went on to become teachers and principals themselves, her influence went on to affect many further generations. Her own meticulous records, as well as reports in the Hawai'i State Archives from education officers and authorities during the monarchy, provisional government, and territorial government, could provide an invaluable first step towards uncovering these many histories and the remarkable woman who influenced them all.

Individuals Mentioned in Letters and Reports

Ahia, Mary (1877–1947). Born in Wailuku, Maui, one of six children of Abraham Fred Beckley Kekapala Kepoomahoe Ahia and Milaina Kale. Her mother was a retainer in the household of Queen Liliʻuokalani and mentioned in the queen's autobiography. Mary boarded at Kawaiahaʻo Seminary beginning in 1892 along with her sister Nancy. Her brother William Mililani Ahia was a graduate of the Kamehameha School for Boys and later served as a senator in the Territorial Senate. Married (1905) Charles Burnette Wilson and became stepmother of Honolulu mayor John H. Wilson.

Ahia, Nancy (1876–1918). Born in Wailuku, Maui, one of six children of Abraham Fred Beckley Kekapala Kepoomahoe Ahia and Milaina Kale. Her mother was a retainer in the household of Queen Liliʻuokalani and mentioned in the queen's autobiography. Nancy boarded at Kawaiahaʻo Seminary beginning in 1892 along with her sister Mary. Her brother William Mililani Ahia was a graduate of the Kamehameha School for Boys and later served as a senator in the Territorial Senate. Married (1895) Solomon Mahelona. Was a teacher and is mentioned in Ida May Pope's Memory Book. Was also matron of the Kalihi Boys Home (1918–1921).

Aholo, Lydia Kaonohiponiponiokalani (1878–1979). Born in Lahaina, Maui, to Luther Aholo, lieutenant governor and minister of the interior during the reign of King Kalākaua. Her mother, Keahi, died shortly after her birth. Lydia was adopted by Queen Liliʻuokalani and given the queen's own English birth name. Sent to Kawaiahaʻo Seminary at the age of five by Liliʻuokalani, and in 1894, followed Ida Pope to the Kamehameha School for Girls, fully sponsored by Liliʻuokalani. Graduated with the first class of the Kamehameha School for Girls (1897) and remained behind to be Ida Pope's office assistant and the bookkeeper for the school. Holds the distinction as Kamehameha's first teacher of the Hawaiian language. School records indicate she "retired" in 1928 after three decades of association with the school. In 1962, was honored for her lifetime contributions to Kamehameha Schools with the distinguished Ke Aliʻi Pauahi award. After she left Kamehameha, worked as a bookkeeper at the Teacher's College of Hawai'i and for the Hawaiian Homes Commission on Moloka'i. Never married and was very active in the Mormon Church and in the life of her famous musician great-nephew, Alfred Apaka. Died July 7, 1979, at age 101.

Appleton, Lilla Estelle (1858–1937). Born in Victory, Vermont, to George Ashley Appleton and Fanny Reed Wooster. Was educated at the State Normal School in Randolph, Vermont (1880); Oberlin College (1886 and 1890); State Normal School, Oswego (1897); ultimately received a PhD from the University of Chicago in 1909. Professional experience included Vermont Public Schools (1875–1881); Lake Henry, South Dakota (1888–1889); Santee Indian Training School in Santee Agency, Nebraska (1889); Kawaiaha'o Seminary (1886–1888, 1891–1893); Kamehameha Preparatory (1893–1894); teacher and lecturer, South Dakota, Minnesota, and Washington; head teacher, Training Program, Upper Iowa University, Marshall College (1907–1916); head, Department of Psychology and Education at Oxford College for Women in Oxford, Ohio (1919–1928); researcher, University of Chicago (1928–1937); author of many published articles in education, ethnology, and sociology. Prepared a stereopticon lecture titled *The Geographical Features and Social Conditions on the Hawaiian Islands* and toured with it in 1897. Died of abdominal cancer in Chicago; buried in Granby, Vermont. Her papers are in the Oberlin College Archives and with the Vermont Historical Society.

Babb, Caroline May Holden (1866–1924). Born in Casco, Maine, to Jesse Francis Holden and Sarah Books Sawyer. Graduated from North Bridgton Academy. Married George Herbert Babb in South Windham, Maine in 1891 and had four children. Arrived in Hawai'i aboard steamer *Australia* (September 1891) with her husband, who had been recruited to teach at the Kamehameha School for Boys. Died in Sebago, Maine. The Caroline and George Babb Collection is housed at the Bancroft Library, UC Berkeley.

Babb, George Herbert (1864–1950). Born in Sebago, Maine, to John Calvin Babb and Annette Douglass. Graduated from Orono State College in Maine (1890). Married (1891) Caroline M. Holden in South Windham, Maine, and had four children. Was the manual arts teacher for the Kamehameha School for Boys (1891–1894). Then became principal, Manual Training School, Portland, Maine (1895–1917). Rose to prominence in the Maine legislature, serving in both the House of Representatives (1917–1918) and the Senate (1919–1922). Died in Augusta, Maine. The Caroline and George Babb Collection is housed at the Bancroft Library, UC Berkeley.

Bingham, Elizabeth "Lizzie" Ka'ahumanu (1829–1899). One of seven children (five survived infancy) born in Hawai'i to Reverend Hiram Bingham, the recognized leader of the early mission days, and Sybil Moseley. "Lizzie" received her middle name from Queen Ka'ahumanu. Reverend Bingham and Sybil's two older daughters, Sophia and Lucy, were sent back to the United States when they reached the age of seven. They married and raised families in Michigan and Florida. When Reverend Bingham returned to New England in 1840 with his very ill wife, the three younger children, Lizzie, Hiram, and Lydia, accompanied them home. Lizzie took classes at Mount Holyoke Seminary until 1851. Taught at several private schools. Returned to Honolulu to assist her sister Lydia and then took over the principalship of Kawaiaha'o Seminary from 1873 to 1881 after her sister left to marry missionary Titus Coan. Died after a long period of invalidism in 1899. Her last residence was with her brother Hiram, sister-in-law Clara, and sister Lydia at the Honolulu family home, dubbed Gilbertinia. Her papers and detailed deathbed scene written by her sister-in-law, Clara Bingham, are at Mount Holyoke Seminary Archives, Massachusetts.

Bingham-Coan, Lydia Denton (1834–1915). One of seven children (five survived infancy) born in Hawai'i to Reverend Hiram Bingham, the recognized leader of the early mission days, and Sybil Moseley. Their two older daughters, Sophia and Lucy, were sent back to the United States when they reached the age of seven. They married and raised families in Michigan and Florida. When Reverend Bingham returned to New England in 1840 with his very ill wife, the three younger children, Elizabeth, Hiram, and Lydia, accompanied them home. Lydia was educated at York Square Seminary in New Haven, Connecticut. Was principal of Ohio College for two years until she was persuaded to return to the land of her birth in 1867 to establish the Kawaiaha'o Seminary. Was principal for six years before her marriage (1873) to Reverend Titus Coan. She is well known for her books on early mission life in Hawai'i. After her husband's death in 1882, moved from Hilo back to Honolulu, where she spent the rest of her life with her brother Hiram, sister-in-law Clara, and sister Lizzie at the Honolulu family home, dubbed Gilbertinia. Was the last surviving member of Hiram Bingham's family.

Bishop, Bernice Pauahi (1831–1884). Born in Honolulu to High Chief Abner Pākī and High Chiefess Kōnia. Was the great-granddaughter of Kamehameha I, who united all the islands of Hawai'i under his rule in 1810. At age eight, was boarded at the Chiefs' Children's School, directed by Amos and Juliette Cooke. Lili'uokalani was her foster sister. Bernice broke tradition and married (1850) New Yorker Charles Reed Bishop in the school parlor. This union produced no children.

She refused the offer to be queen of Hawai'i (1872). Died of breast cancer and is buried in the Royal Mausoleum. Her legacy, Kamehameha Schools, is the primary beneficiary of her trust. The Bernice Pauahi Bishop Museum, built by Charles Bishop in honor of his wife, is world famous and houses priceless artifacts from the Kamehameha dynasty. During her lifetime, she gave to many causes, and her beneficence is seen today on many institutions.

Bishop, Charles Reed (1822–1915). Born in Glens Falls, New York, to Samuel Bishop and Maria Reed. Arrived in Honolulu in 1846 and by 1849, rose to collector general of customs. Married Bernice Pauahi (1850) and was made a lifetime member of the House of Nobles. Joined the Privy Council; helped organize the Royal Hawaiian Agricultural Society; opened Bishop and Company (predecessor of First Hawaiian Bank); served several Hawaiian monarchs in a variety of positions, such as foreign minister, president of the board of education, and chairman of the legislative finance committee; sat on the boards of many charities; and donated generously to Hawai'i schools, hospitals, churches, and social-welfare organizations. His wife died in 1884. As one of five trustees, she had selected to manage her estate, and as the coexecutor of her will, he set in motion the process that resulted in the establishment of Kamehameha Schools in 1887. In 1889, he established the Bernice Pauahi Bishop Museum to honor his wife. He departed Hawai'i in 1894 and died in Oakland, California. His ashes were transported back to Hawai'i to be reunited with wife at Mauna'ala, the final resting place for Hawai'i's royalty, in the vault of the Kamehamehas. In 1916, a stone monument was erected adjacent to the tomb to honor him. Today, he is considered one of Hawai'i's greatest benefactors.

Bishop, Cornelia Ann Sessions (1826–1920). Born in New York to John and Eliza (Winne) Sessions. Lived and taught in Albany, New York, until she married (1852) Sereno Bishop. They had five children. The Sereno Edwards Bishop Collection is housed at the Huntington Library.

Bishop, Sereno Edwards (1827–1910). Born in Kailua, Hawai'i, to missionaries Artemas Bishop and Elizabeth Edwards. Graduated from Amherst College (1846) and Auburn Theological Seminary (1851). Married (1852) Cornelia Ann Sessions and had five children. Returned to Hawai'i (1853) to become seaman's chaplain in Lahaina, Maui. Served various churches and was principal, Lahainaluna Seminary (1856–1877); member, Board of Trustees of Kawaiaha'o Seminary until 1887; member, Hawaiian Government Survey Department (1877–1881); editor, *The Friend* (1887–1902); author of *Reminiscences of Old Hawaii*. The Sereno Edwards Bishop Collection is housed at the Huntington Library.

Blascoer, Frances Helen (1873–1938). Born to Samuel and Julia Blascoer in Marshall, Wisconsin. Was one of five daughters. Was the NAACP's first executive secretary, serving 1910–1911. Recruited by Ida Pope to be a special investigator for the Board of Trustees of the Kaʻiulani Home and conducted a massive social survey in 1912. In 1915, was a special investigator for the Committee on Hygiene of School Children of the Public Education Association of the City of New York. Author, *The Industrial Condition of Women and Girls in Honolulu: A Social Study* (Honolulu, 1912) and *Colored School Children in New York* (New York, 1915). Lived in China from 1917 to 1922, serving in a variety of occupations. In her later years, became an antiques dealer in New York. Spent her last years in the Creedmoor Division of the Brooklyn State Hospital.

Brandt, Gladys Kamakakūokalani ʻAinoa (1906–2003). Born in Hawaiʻi to David and Esther Staine-Kanuha. Later in life, her parents (Kanuhas) changed their last name to ʻAinoa. Gladys was given in the *hānai* tradition to Ida May Pope at age four. Married Isaac Brandt. Made history in Kauaʻi as the first woman high school principal in Hawaiʻi. Rose to district superintendent of public schools on Kauaʻi and later principal of the Kamehameha School for Girls. Later was trustee for Kamehameha Schools and Office of Hawaiian Affairs. Throughout her life, was a fierce defender of Hawaiian traditions. Collaborated on *Broken Trust*, published in 1997, a book that criticized the financial mismanagement of Kamehameha Schools. The Historic Hawaiʻi Foundation recognized her as a "living treasure."

Brewer-Fowler, Margaret Abernethy (1863–1931). Born in San Francisco to John Hiram Brewer and Margaret Abernethy. After graduating from Oakland High School, taught at the Anna Head School for Girls in Berkeley. Teacher, Kawaiahaʻo Seminary (1883–1891); Punahou Preparatory School, where she taught for a decade; principal, first and second grades, Punahou Preparatory School (1890). The *Honolulu Gazette* announced her engagement (1896) to Dr. Jared Smith, a government physician at Koloā; he was murdered the following year to prevent him from signing an order for the removal of a Hawaiian girl suspected of having leprosy. She received an MA, New York University (1899). Married (1903) businessman millionaire Eldridge M. Fowler, a widower, and settled in Pasadena, California. She founded Boys Republic (1907), a youth facility and school for troubled boys, and settled in Casa Colina, near the school. There met Ellen Browning Scripps and the early faculty of Scripps College and served as a founding member of its board of trustees. On February 6, 1945, fourteen-year-old future actor Steve McQueen credited the school for saving his life. Mrs. Fowler's extensive, beautiful, and rare textile collection was donated after her death in 1931 to the Honolulu Academy of Arts.

Bridges-Kaʻai, Ella Kamakea Pahu (1877–1956). One of four children born in Honolulu to Captain George Allen Bridges and Maria Kaʻainahuna Kaleimakaliʻi, his second wife. Captain George Allen Bridges was previously married to Keliʻihoani, the older sister of Kaʻainahuna and they had one daughter. Ella was a descendant of the Ruling Chief Kekaulike of Maui on the side of her grandfather, Kaleimakaliʻi. On the side of her grandmother, Kamakea, she was a descendant of the Ruling Chief Keawe of Hawaiʻi. At age twelve, Ella was incorrectly diagnosed and sent to Kalaupapa as a leper from Kawaiahaʻo Seminary. After ten years of quarantine, she was released in 1900. Married James Keawelau Pahu (1876–1903) in 1901. They had four children, two of whom died young, and two, Adelaide Keliʻihoalani and James Keawelau, who survived to adulthood. She then married David Kukapu Kaʻai Jr. (1883–1953) in 1907. They would have seven children, six natural (Lihue, Samuel, Margaret, Ella, Matilda, and Pearl) and one adopted (Richard). Ella Kamakea Bridges was the younger sister of Mary Ellen Bridges.

Bridges-Pahau, Mary Ellen Hanau-umi-a-Kanoena (1872–1919). One of four children born in Honolulu to Captain George Allen Bridges and Maria Kaʻainahuna Kaleimakaliʻi, his second wife. Captain George Allen Bridges was previously married to Keliʻihoalani, the older sister of Maria Kaʻainahuna, and they had one daughter. Mary Ellen was a descendant of the Ruling Chief Kekaulike of Maui on the side of her grandfather, Kaleimakaliʻi. On the side of her grandmother, Kamakea, she was a descendant of the Ruling Chief Keawe of Hawaiʻi. Mary Ellen was educated at Kawaiahaʻo Seminary. Married (1894) Robert Kolomoku Pahau (1872–1913), and they had two children, Robert Kolomoku Pahau Jr. and Lydia Kalohialiʻiokawai Pahau. Mary Ellen was the older sister of Ella Kamakea Bridges.

Carpenter, Helen E. (1830–1914). Born to Ira Carpenter and Elizabeth Abell in Sturbridge, Massachusetts. Graduated from Mount Holyoke Seminary in 1855 and taught at Rockford Seminary. Was hired by the American Board and went to Hawaiʻi in 1871 to teach at the Maunaʻolu Seminary in Maui. In 1891, returned to Honolulu to help out missionary teachers but returned to New England in 1892. Was one of the pioneers in female education in the islands. As an appreciation for her work for Hawaiian girls, received from King Kalākaua the Royal Order of Kapiʻolani. Became blind in 1913. Died in Woodstock, Connecticut.

Carter, Joseph Oliver (1835–1909). Born in Honolulu to Joseph Oliver Carter and Hanna Trufant Lord. Attended school in Boston at an early age and returned to Hawai'i in 1847. Worked for the *Pacific Commercial Advertiser* until 1872, when he was elected to the Hawai'i legislature. Was appointed registrar of public accounts in 1874, after having been financier to prominent families in Hawai'i. In 1891, became president of C. Brewer and Company. Throughout his life, played an important role with Hawaiian royalty and was the privy councilor to Queen Lili'uokalani. During the 1893 revolution, stood by the queen's side. After the overthrow, resigned his position at C. Brewer and Company due to political differences and opened his own business. Continued to be in charge of the business affairs of the former queen, as well as trustee for the B. P. Bishop Estate, Kamehameha Schools, and various private accounts and estates. Held various other positions including at the Board of Health of the Republic of Hawai'i and as superintendent and teacher at the Bethel Church. Married Mary Elizabeth Ladd (1859), and they had six children. Carter became blind in his last years, but continued his business dealings until his death in Honolulu. The Joseph Oliver Carter papers are housed at the Huntington Library.

Castle, William Richards (1849–1935). Born in Honolulu to missionary banker Samuel Northrup Castle and Mary Ann Tenney. Entered Oberlin College as a prep student (1864) but never graduated due to ill health; LLB, Columbia College (1873); honorary AM, Oberlin College (1885). Married Ida Beatrice Lowrey (1875), and they had three children: William Richards Jr., Alfred Lowery, and Alice Maud. Practiced law in New York City (1873–1876); returned to Honolulu and practiced law there. Attorney general, Kingdom of Hawai'i (1876); member, Hawai'i legislature (1878, 1886–1888); president and attorney, Honolulu Gas Company; trustee and treasurer of Kawaiaha'o Seminary; member, commission sent to Washington, D.C., to initiate annexation (1893). Served in Washington as Hawaiian minister (1895). President, Board of Education, Republic of Hawai'i for three years. With his father, financed the creation of the 'Ewa Plantation Company. One of the founders of the Honolulu Rapid Transit Trust and Land Company; trustee of O'ahu College; member, Hawaiian and American Bar Associations, where he did considerable pro bono work for native Hawaiians. Was a member of the National Municipal League, National Economic League, American Academy of Politics and Social Science, Sons of the Revolution. Was the president of the Samuel N. and Mary Castle Foundation until his death. The foundation is known for its philanthropy creating social equality and improved educational access for Hawai'i's young children.

Chamberlain, Martha Ann (1833–1913). Born in the "Chamberlain House," still standing on King Street, next door to Kawaiahaʻo Church in Honolulu. Was the fourth child of Levi Chamberlain and Maria Patton Chamberlain. Graduated from Mount Holyoke (1853). Taught at Kawaiahaʻo Seminary at intervals from 1869 to 1881. Began a school for missionary children in Hilo (1880–1883). Was a city missionary in Honolulu from 1887 to 1891. Spoke fluent Hawaiian and taught Sunday school throughout her adult life. Was the corresponding secretary for twenty-five years for the Hawaiian Mission Children's Society and Mount Holyoke alumnae meetings. Was stricken with paralysis in October 1904 while residing at a woman's missionary society.

Clark, Ephraim Weston (1799–1878). Born in Haverhill, New Hampshire, to Edward Clark and Elizabeth E. Weston. Graduated from Dartmouth College (1824) and Andover Theological Seminary (1827). In 1827, married Mary Kittredge (1803–1857), and the following year, they went to Hawaiʻi with Third Company. He was stationed in Maui until 1843. They had eight children. He served as pastor of Kawaiahaʻo Church from 1848 to 1863. Second wife was Sarah Helen Richards. In 1864, he resigned from the American Board and was put in charge of the Hawaiian printing at the Tract House in New York. Translated many books in Hawaiian over the years. In 1872, moved to Chicago to be near two of his children. Remained there until his death.

Coleman, Harriet "Hattie" Angeline Castle (1847–1924). Born in Honolulu to Samuel Northrup Castle and Mary Tenney; sister of Caroline "Carrie" Castle. Attended Punahou School and Oberlin Preparatory (1865–1866). Teacher at Punahou (1867–1869). Married (1876) Charles Carson Coleman and had two children. Educated at Froebel Training School for Kindergarteners in Chicago, led by John Dewey. Was a good friend of Jane Addams, a member of the Children's Aid Society; was the founder of the Free Kindergarten Association in Honolulu; served on the Women's Board of the Pacific.

Cooke, Amos Starr (1810–1871). Born in Danbury, Connecticut, to Joseph Platt Cooke Jr. and Annis Starr. Married Juliette Montague (1836). The Cookes arrived in Honolulu in 1837 with the largest assemblage ever sent by the American Board, primarily composed of married teaching teams. The Cookes were assigned to English language private schools, supported by the missionaries. In 1839, the Cookes were offered the momentous responsibility of teaching and sequestered living with the children of Hawaiʻi's highest chiefs. The Cookes served in the Chiefs' Children's School for ten years, educating many notable figures in Hawaiian history. Amos Cooke left behind twelve leather-bound volumes of intensely private diaries, housed at the Hawaiian Mission Children's Society (HMCS), that are full of self-admonition, frustration, and confessions that spanned the decade. The diaries chronicle numerous occurrences of extremely harsh punishments on the young royals. Amos Cooke documented his internal struggle so thoroughly that it is not surprising to learn that he died in 1871 at an "insane asylum," diagnosed with "derangement of the mental faculties," a strong indication that his outbursts with the royal children were precursors to a mental disorder, understood today as Huntington's disease. After leaving the school, he became assistant superintendent of secular affairs for the mission in 1849 and served in that position until 1851, when he entered the mercantile business with Samuel N. Castle, establishing the firm of Castle & Cooke. The children of Amos and Juliet Cooke were Joseph Platt Cooke, Martha Eliza Cooke, Juliette Montague Cooke Atherton, Mary Annis Cooke Turner, Charles Montague Cooke, Amos Frank Cooke, and Clarence Warren Cooke. His papers can be found in the Connecticut Historical Society and the HMCS Library. Today, the Cooke Foundation supports many worthy endeavors in the Hawaiian community.

Cooke, Juliette Montague (1812–1896). Born in Sunderland, Massachusetts, to Caleb Montague and Martha Warner. Was educated at Miss White's School, Amherst, Massachusetts, and attended lectures at Amherst College. Later, enrolled at Ipswich Seminary. Married (1836) Amos Star Cooke in an arrangement facilitated by the American Board. The Cookes arrived in Honolulu in 1837 with the largest assemblage ever sent by the American Board, primarily composed of married teaching teams. The Cookes were assigned to English language private schools, supported by the missionaries. In 1839, the Cookes were offered the momentous responsibility of teaching and sequestered living with the children of Hawai'i's highest chiefs. The children of Amos and Juliette Cooke were Joseph Platt Cooke, Martha Eliza Cooke, Juliette Montague Cooke Atherton, Mary Annis Cooke Turner, Charles Montague Cooke, Amos Frank Cooke, and Clarence Warren Cooke. Juliette Cooke until her death stayed busy in the missionary community, mainly at Kawaiaha'o Seminary, where she lived across the road. "Mother Cooke" was seen as both a kindly grandmother and a teaching adviser to newly recruited teachers. Their papers can be found in the Connecticut Historical Society and the Hawaiian Mission Children's Society (HMCS) Library.

Cope, Mother Marianne (1838–1918). Born to Peter Koob and Barbara Witzenbacher and baptized Barbara Koob in Germany. The family moved to New York in 1839. After her father's death in 1862, she applied for admission to the Sisters of the Third Order of St. Francis; was accepted into the order and sent to Syracuse, New York. In 1883, Mother Marianne and six sisters led the mission to Hawai'i to minister to the lepers. The mission at Kaka'ako in Honolulu was the first Franciscan mission to be established in Hawai'i. Father Damien, who had been on Moloka'i since 1873, pleaded with Mother Marianne to take over the care at Kalaupapa on Moloka'i, and in 1888 she consented to live among the lepers. Even though she worked for thirty-five years with afflicted children, she did not contract Hansen's disease. She is buried at Kalaupapa beneath orange trees she had planted.

Dole, Sanford Ballard (1844–1926). Born in Honolulu to missionaries Daniel Dole and Emily Hoyt Ballard. Married (1873) Anna Prentice Cate. Attended Williams College; studied law in Boston. In 1884 was elected to the House of Representatives, Kingdom of Hawai'i. Associate justice of the Hawaiian Supreme Court (1886). Joined the Hawaiian Patriotic League, which sought to limit the power of King Kalākaua and imposed the Bayonet Constitution. A leader of the coup d'état to overthrow the queen. President of the Provisional Government of Hawai'i (1893–1894) formed immediately after the overthrow of Queen Lili'uokalani. President, Republic of Hawai'i (1894–1900); first governor, Territory of Hawai'i (1900–1903). U.S. district judge until retirement in 1916. Author of *Memoirs of the Hawaiian Revolution* (1936).

Dyke, Charles Bartlett (1870–1945). Born in Ohio. Met and married Stanford classmate Estelle Minnie Darrah (1898). They had no children. Graduated from Stanford University, 1897; Columbia University, 1899; Teacher's College, Columbia, 1900. Arrived in Honolulu in 1901 to administer the schools with the designation "Principal of the Kamehameha Schools." Left in 1904 to administer in the State Preparatory School in Boulder, Colorado, in 1906–1911.

Frear, Mary Emma Dillingham (1870–1951). Born to Benjamin Franklin Dillingham and Emma Louise Smith, in Honolulu. Attended Punahou School and then went to Wellesley College, where she received her BA in 1893. Returned to Hawai'i and married Walter Frances Frear (1893). Queen Lili'uokalani had appointed her husband to the judiciary. He was Hawai'i's third territorial governor (1907–1913). The Frears had two daughters. Mary Frear was the inspiration of the formation of the College Club in 1905. The College Club initiated many social programs that benefitted the community. She was a prolific author of varied published works. A gifted author of prose, particularly on Hawaiian subjects, Mary Frear was awarded an honorary Doctor of Letters degree in 1943 by the University of Hawai'i. Served on the Board of Regents for twenty-three years as regent of the University of Hawaiʻi. Upon her death, the *Honolulu Star-Bulletin* described her as one of "Hawaii's unostentatious benefactress[es] in a thousand good deeds."

Gulick, Louisa Lewis (1830–1894). Born in New York City to Junius Sidney Lewis and Sarah Wardell. Attended Rutgers Seminary for two years and taught for a short while in North Carolina. With her mother, engaged in city missionary work in New York. Married Dr. Luther Halsey Gulick (1851), and they had seven children. Three weeks after the wedding, they sailed from Boston for the Hawaiian Islands and then on to Micronesia as missionaries. There, Louisa became an organist and a schoolteacher while her husband preached and provided health care. Upon their return to Honolulu in 1865, Louisa founded the seeds of Kawaiahaʻo Seminary in her "Family School" for the daughters of missionaries. After her husband's death in 1891, joined her married missionary daughter, Hattie M. Clark, on the island of Kyushu in Japan. In 1891, their son Luther Halsey Gulick designed the YMCA triangular logo and is known today as basketball's "godfather." Luther and his wife, Charlotte Emily Vetter, also founded the Camp Fire Girls. Louisa is buried in Kobe, Japan.

Harris, Eva L. (1868–1952). Born in Huron, Ohio, one of five children of Thomas J. Harris and Susan Jaffrey. Attended Oberlin High School/Academy. Taught at the Ohio State Imbecile Institution. Teacher at the Kawaiahaʻo Seminary (1892–1893). Supported two sisters at Oberlin High School/Academy, Edna Belle and Elma May Harris. Succumbed to "hysteria" in Honolulu and was treated by Dr. C. B. Wood. Ida May Pope accompanied her back to San Francisco for mental treatment. Her Oberlin file notes that she attended the University of California, but other sources say she attended the University of San Francisco. Without a medical degree, practiced as a physician in Oakland, California, and was a member of the homeopathy society. Resided at the Claremont Country Club in Oakland with her sisters until her death.

Hight-Retan, Iretta May (1866–1925). Born in Genoa, Michigan, to Nathan Hight and Elizabeth Bennett. Attended Oberlin College (1887–1889) but was forced to leave in order to support her younger brother and sister Rose. Arrived in Hawaiʻi to teach at Kamehameha Preparatory Department from 1888 to 1889. Moved to the Kamehameha School for Boys from 1890 to 1892. Her brother Edwin died during his sophomore year at Oberlin, while she was in Honolulu. She married (1892) Frederick Smith Retan, a Baptist minister who left the ministry to sell insurance. The family lived in Michigan, New York, and Vermont before moving in 1910 to Boston, where Fred Retan worked for the Home Life Insurance

Company and was later a general insurance broker. The Retans settled in West Newton, Massachusetts, and were generous and hospitable to Hawai'i travelers. They had three daughters, Vera, Lucile, and Emma. Emma developed polio and became acquainted with Franklin D. Roosevelt in the course of her treatment. FDR sent a moving condolence letter to her husband upon her death.

Hoppin-Renton, Helen Frances (1861–1946). Born in South Haven, Michigan, to Thaddeus Hoppin and Catherine Ann Stuart. Received an AB, Oberlin College (1886). Was an early teacher at Kawaiaha'o Seminary. Both of her sisters, Jessie and Ruth, taught in Honolulu. Along with Ida Pope, she accompanied Queen Lili'uokalani to Moloka'i. Married (1894) widowed Union Mill Sugar Plantation manager Henry Herbert Renton in Kōhala, Hawai'i. Died in Saratoga, California.

Hyde, Charles McEwen (1832–1899). Born in New York City to attorney Joseph Hyde and Catherine McEwen Hyde. Graduated from Princeton Theological Seminary in 1860. Was ordained in 1862, and the degree of Doctor of Divinity was conferred upon him by Williams College in 1872. Married Mary T. Knight in 1865, and they had two children. In 1877, the American Board sent him and his family to Hawai'i. In Honolulu, he helped establish the North Pacific Missionary Institute to train Hawaiian men for ministry. Later, became trustee of five educational trusts. When Bernice Pauahi Bishop wrote her will on October 31, 1883, she named Hyde as one of the original five trustees of her estate. When his health began to fail in 1897, he went on a three months' tour of Japan and China with his wife. Wrote many articles that were published on his travels.

Iokia, Lewa Kalai (1874–1913). Born to a Chinese father and Hawaiian mother. Holds the distinction of being the first Kamehameha School for Girls' graduate to earn a teaching certificate in 1898. Following graduation, she attended the Milwaukee State Normal School in 1900–1901. *The Echo*, the Normal School's yearbook, published that Lewa was from Honolulu, studied English, and was a member of the Young Women's Christian Association. Her yearbook motto was "A dear little mayde from ye sunnie lands." Is mentioned in *True Stories of the Island of Lāna'i* as a teacher of a one-room schoolhouse around 1904. Left to assume leadership of the historic Kaupō school on Maui. In 1907, transferred to Honolulu to become a teacher at Ka'ahumanu School while boarding with Ida Pope at the Kamehameha School for Girls.

Jones, Peter Cushman (1837–1922). Born December 10, 1837, in Boston, Massachusetts, to Peter Cushman and Joan MacIntosh Baldwin. Arrived in Honolulu in 1857. Married Cornelia Hall Jones in 1862, and they had three children. Clerk, Wilcox & Richards (1860); partner, C. L. Richards & Company; partner, then president, C. Brewer & Company (1870–1899); founder and first president, Bank of Hawai'i (1897); minister of finance, Wilcox cabinet (1890–1892) and provisional government (1893). Supporter of the overthrow of Queen Lili'uokalani. Member, Fort Street Church and Central Union Church; trustee and treasurer, Punahou School (1875–1915).

Kahea (Beckley), Grace (ca. 1878–1899). Born to David Kahea (1846–1921) and Maria Kahaawelani Beckley-Kahea, a high chiefess of Hawai'i (1847–1909) custodians of the Royal Mausoleum in Nu'uanu Valley. King Kalākaua appointed Maria as custodian, and she carried this position through the reign of Lili'uokalani and for a number of years thereafter. Upon his wife's death, David K. Kahea took over the responsibility for the resting place of the *ali'i,* and transferred the honor to his son several years before his death in 1921. Grace's mother was a high chiefess, daughter of Kahinu and William Beckley, and granddaughter of Ho'oulu. Her English ancestor Captain George Beckley in the days of Kamehameha I was commander of the fort from which Fort Street takes its name. Grace committed suicide by jumping from a third-story window at the Kamehameha School for Girls, presumably over stress.

Kailipanio, Myra (1879–1934). Born 1879 in Honolulu to Wakeke Ululani; stepdaughter of Joseph Hewakawa Heleluhe, who resided at Washington Place. Her mother was a retainer to Queen Lili'uokalani; her stepfather was the queen's secretary, and her brother was the famous musician Jack Paoakalani Heleluhe. Listed as a student at Kawaiaha'o Seminary beginning 1892. Entered the Kamehameha School for Girls (1895). Queen Lili'uokalani paid her tuition until she dropped out to accompany Queen Lili'uokalani on a trip to the United States. Myra Heleluhe Iona is listed in the 1910 census as the wife of George Iona and mother of Ululani Iona, residents of Honolulu. Married (ca. 1899) George Lumaheihei Iona; they had two children. Obituary in the *Honolulu Advertiser* (May 26, 1934, p. 10) notes that Mrs. Myra Heleluhe Iona accompanied Prince Kūhiō when he was Hawai'i's delegate to Congress, and served in the household of Prince Kūhiō and later Princess Kalaniana'ole. Died in Honolulu.

Ka'iulani, Victoria Kawekiu Lunalilo Kalaninuiahilapalapa Ka'iulani Cleghorn (1875–1899). Born to Scotchman Archibald Scott Cleghorn and Hawaiian princess Miriam Likelike. When her mother died in 1886, Ka'iulani was sent to England to prepare for her future royal duties. Robert Louis Stevenson had been fascinated with the young girl and wrote a departure poem in her honor. In 1891, Queen Lili'uokalani named her heir to the throne. After the coup d'état, Ka'iulani traveled to Washington, D.C., to plead with President Grover Cleveland to restore the monarchy. Died unexpectedly in 1898. Official causes of death were listed as cardiac rheumatism and exophthalmic goiter. Was deeply mourned as evidenced by the 20,000 people who lined the streets as her body was moved to the Royal Mausoleum at Nu'uanu. Today, the many stories, songs, poems, and movies about her keep her memory alive around the world.

Kofoid, Charles Atwood (1865–1947). Born to Nelson Kofoid and Janette Blake in Illinois. Educated Oberlin College, AB (1890); AM (1892); PhD, zoology, Harvard University (1894). Married Carrie Prudence Winter in 1894; they were unable to have children. Instructor in invertebrate morphology, University of Michigan (1894–1895); superintendent, Illinois River Biological Survey; instructor, University of Illinois (1897–1903); professor, University of California (1903–1936); chair, University of California department of biology (1910–1936). Chief scientist and planktologist, Eastern Tropical Pacific Expedition on the USFS *Albatross* with Alexander Agassiz (1904–1905). Assistant director, Scripps Institution for Biological Research (1903–1923). Major, U.S. Sanitary Corps, laboratory car Metchnikoff, Fort Sam Houston, Texas (1918). Died in Berkeley, California.

Lazaro, Julia (ca. 1887–1909). Born in Ho'okena, Kona, to Solomon and Mao Lazaro. Her father was the deputy sheriff of North Kona. She graduated from the Kamehameha School for Girls in 1908 and went to San Francisco to train at the Children's Hospital. Died from a stroke, at age twenty-two, on board the *Alameda* two hours after departing San Francisco for Hawai'i.

Lemmon, Frances A. (1862–1947). Born to Anthony Wayne Lemmon and Delia Ann Bartholomew in Attica, Ohio. Her father died in 1862 and her mother remarried Dr. Hebben Cheyney and had two children, Ida May Cheyney and Anson Cheyney. She graduated from Lake Erie Female Seminary (1888) and became principal of Lagrange High School from 1886 to 1888. Moved to teach at Oberlin High School. In 1896 went to Hawai'i to teach at the Kamehameha School for Girls and assist Ida May Pope with administrative duties. Taught at the school until her retirement, when she went to live at the Kings Daughters Retirement Home. At her death, was buried in the Kings Daughters Plot at Nu'uanu Cemetery, Honolulu.

Lewis, Alice Kalahikiola (1870–1962). Born in Hawai'i to John George Lewis and Amelie Kamahie Lewis. Her father, a successful merchant, constructed The

Queen Emma Summer Palace in 1848. Was a pupil at Kawaiahaʻo Seminary who moved into the role of teacher's assistant in 1891. Married (1896) William F. Ordway, and they had five children, Agnes, Edith, Alice, Anita, and Denise. Raised her daughters alone, with a strong sense of pride in their Hawaiian heritage. Died in Santa Cruz, California.

Liliʻuokalani (1838–1917). The third of ten children born in Honolulu to High Chief Kapaʻakea and High Chiefess Keohokālole. Was given in *hānai* at birth to High Chief Abner Pākī and High Chiefess Kōnia. Her full name was Lydia Liliʻu Loloku Walania Wewehi Kamakaʻeha Pākī-Dominis. Entered into the Chiefs' Children's School at age four. As an adult, was a member of the royal circle and very involved in court life. Married (1862) John Owen Dominis, son of a Boston sea captain of Italian heritage. They had no children together. In 1887, she attended Queen Victoria's jubilee in England. Served as princess regent for her brother King David Kalākaua during his travels in 1881 and 1890. Reigned as Queen Liliʻiuokalani (January 29, 1891–January 17, 1893). Traveled widely in Hawaiʻi interacting with her people of all classes. Gifted singer and composer of songs including "Aloha ʻOe." Established the Liliʻuokalani Educational Society for young Hawaiian girls. Overthrown (1893) and imprisoned in the ʻIolani Palace (1895). Following the coup d'état, resided for two decades in her home known as Washington Place. Became a cherished link with Hawaiʻi's past, and many notables paid their homage to her throughout her life. Was an accomplished pianist and also played many other instruments. Was a masterful composer of many songs. Had a stroke at seventy-nine and is buried in the Royal Mausoleum. Her memoirs were published as *Hawaii's Story by Hawaii's Queen.* Her biography appears in *Notable Women of Hawaii.*

Lovell-Bowers, Julia Kahaunani (1877–1938). Born in Līhuʻe, Kauaʻi, to Daniel Imaikalani Lovell and Loika Halili. Was a graduate of the first class of the Kamehameha School for Girls in 1897. Married (1898) Winfield Lane Bowers (1852–1915) of the Merchants Patrol, and they had one child, Francis Andrew Imaikalani Bowers. Married her second husband, Robert Burns Pauole (1919), a member of the Hawaiian Evangelical Association of Kauaʻi. She was a traveler's aid secretary for the YWCA. Died in Kamiloloa, Molokaʻi, Hawaiʻi.

Lowrey, Cherilla Lillian Storrs (1854–1918). Born in Trenton, New York, to Ephraim Hollister Storrs and Chloe Bill. Was recruited to teach at Kawaiahaʻo Seminary in 1882. In 1883, became assistant principal of Punahou Preparatory School. Married Frederick Jewett Lowrey (1884), and they had three sons and one daughter. In 1909, inspired by the beautiful cities in Europe, became a civic leader and devoted her energy to the beautification of Honolulu. Organized a group of women from the Kilohana Art League to clean up and beautify Honolulu neighborhoods. By 1912, the Outdoor Circle was established with Cherilla as its first president.

McGregor, Louise Aoe Wong Kong (1881–1969). Born in Maui to Lee Wong Kong and Kaakau Kamahalo. Used her middle name, Aoe, throughout her life. Graduated in the first class of the Kamehameha School for Girls in 1897 and in 1899 earned a teaching certificate from Kamehameha. Taught in several different schools. Married Daniel Pamawaho McGregor. When younger sister Lani Hutchinson died in childbirth (1921), added six of her sister's seven to her own six. On August 30, 1920, the *Honolulu Star* indicated that Aoe would go on record as the first woman to be registered in Maui to vote. Was also the first woman in Hawai'i who was awarded a "Hack License" in 1914 to drive an automobile for hire. The Louise Aoe McGregor Award is given each year at Kamehameha Schools. The award is given to the student director who is recognized as having made significant contributions to the entire class and has shown organizational ability, leadership, assistance to others, and persistence. Aoe was the second-longest-living survivor of the first graduating class of the Kamehameha Schools for Girls; her friend Lydia Aholo lived to be 101.

Morley, Fannie Gertrude (1859–1888). Born in Baraboo, Wisconsin, to Nelson Morley and Adaline Serviah Fuller. In her youth, perfected the art of making butter. At twenty, won the grand sweepstakes prize at the Great International Dairy Show in New York in 1879 for the "best butter of any kind, made at any time or place." Was educated at the Oberlin Conservatory of Music (ca. 1882) and arrived in Honolulu to teach music at Kawaiaha'o Seminary in 1886. Was much in demand in the Honolulu community for playing the organ and singing. Died in Honolulu and was sent home to be buried in the Baraboo Cemetery.

Norton, Helen Sarah (1938–1923). Born to Henry Hazard Norton and Lucinda Wakemen in Dexter, Michigan. Graduated from Mount Holyoke (1863) and then taught for a number of years in private schools throughout Michigan, Illinois, and Wisconsin. Was hired by the ABCFM to go to Hawai'i and became principal of Kawaiaha'o Seminary from 1880 to 1884. Returned in bad health to Boston, Massachusetts, to act as a representative for the American Board in the south. Obtained an MA from Wheaton College. Taught for a few years in Florida. Died in Howell, Michigan. Her diary is housed at the HMCS in Honolulu.

Oleson, William Brewster (1851–1915). Born in Portland, Maine, to John Oleson and Matilda Prince. Graduated Theological Seminary, Oberlin (1877); BD, University of Maine (1897); MS (1906). Married twice, to Sophia Mervin Hill and Abigail J. Adams. Had a total of eight children. Was a minister in Gambier, Ohio (1877); principal, Hilo Boarding School (1878–1886); founding principal for the Kamehameha School for Boys (1886–1893); pastor of Congregational churches in Massachusetts for fourteen years. Returned to Hawai'i as secretary of the Hawaiian Evangelical Association (1908–1915). Returning home for health reasons, died in Flagstaff, Arizona.

Parker, Mary Frances "Frank" Stuart (1848–1899). Born in Charlestown, Massachusetts, to Calvin Stuart and Dorothy Furbush. Went by "Frankie" and then "Frank." Graduated from the Boston School of Oratory and was hired to teach there after graduation. Had received a national reputation by the time she married (1882) her second husband, Colonel Francis Wayland Parker, noted pioneer of the progressive school movement in the United States. Was a renowned expert of the Delsarte system of elocution. Was president of the Political Equality League of Women and crusaded for women's rights through "correct dress." Sought to free women from corsets and told women to dress according to their personality. Had two daughters from a failed first marriage when she married Colonel Parker. Even though she was dying from cancer, gave lectures in Hawai'i for the teacher summer institutes and took the time to give private lessons in elocution to Ida Pope's pupils. Is buried with her husband in Manchester, New Hampshire.

Pepoon, Helen Abby (1856–1944). Born in Painesville, Ohio, to Benjamin Pepoon, a farmer who ran a station on the Underground Railroad, and Eliza Ann Hollister. Graduated from Oberlin College (1878) and became a teacher and then principal of the Wisconsin Female College (1880–1888). In 1889, went to Kawaiaha'o Seminary (1889–1891) as principal. On her return to the United States, was hired as a teacher at the Grand River Institute in Ohio (1892–1893) and also earned a PhB in 1892 from Oberlin. Moved to Washington to become a professor of Latin, Whitman College (1893–1921). Toured Europe and Asia on leave (1910–1912), and taught Latin to Chinese students at the ABCFM Mission at Foochow, China, where she survived the Boxer Rebellion. Resided in Walla Walla near Whitman College for many years with her elder sister, Julia, then retired to Seattle, where she died. Whitman College Archives holds some of her letters and a biographical file.

Pope, Anne Elizabeth (1871–1932). The youngest daughter of seven children born in Ohio to William Pope and Cornelia Rochester Waring. Weighed only three pounds at birth and was never expected to survive. Was frail throughout her life. A fall from a hayloft when she was seven injured her hip, requiring her to wear shoe lifts and endure full body castings and traction throughout the years. Graduated from the Chicago Kindergarten Training School in 1896 and joined her sister in Hawai'i in 1897. Was the first kindergarten director for the Pālama Settlement in Honolulu. Ill health required her to return to Chicago in 1899. Her success among the disadvantaged in Honolulu was legendary, and her entire passage was paid home.

Pope, Cornelia Rochester Waring (1831–1910). Born in Franklinville, Otsego County, New York. Was the youngest child of William Waring and Catherine Waring (same name, no relation). Was orphaned at a very early age and brought up by an older unmarried sister, Julia. At fifteen, taught in a one-room school. Married Dr. William Pope (1856) and moved to Crestline, Ohio. All seven of their children were born in Crestline: William, Lois, Ida, Katherine, Henry, Anne, and Frank. When the family moved to Bucyrus, she became the bookkeeper for the Franz-Pope Knitting Machine Company until its bankruptcy in 1890. Worked with her husband until his death in 1890. Is buried at Oakwood Cemetery in Bucyrus, Ohio, beside her husband, son William, and daughter Ida.

Pope, Henry (1868–1947). One of seven children born in Ohio to William Pope and Cornelia Rochester Waring. Graduated from Bucyrus High School at age fifteen. Immediately following his father's death in 1890, assumed the full financial responsibility of the family and moved the family to Chicago in 1891. One of the assets his father left was the first seamless hosiery-knitting machine with semiautomatic features. In 1893 Pope founded the Paramount Knitting Company in Chicago. In 1922 the firm was reorganized as the Bear Brand Hosiery Company. He continued to serve as its president until 1936, at which time he became chairman of the board. Married Adele Prufrock (1898), and they had four children: Margaret, Henry Jr., William, and John. Pope became known as one of the most prominent and successful hosiery executives in the United States. During World War I, served on the Council of National Defense as chairman of the Committee on Knit Goods. Was one of the original members who mapped out the Chicago Beautiful Plan, organized following Chicago's first world's fair. During the Depression years of 1933 and 1934, set aside funds in order that the family of any of his employees who was in need might immediately receive assistance. Was known for steady employment through all the depressions of a half-century. With President Franklin D. Roosevelt, organized and founded the Warm Springs Georgia Foundation in 1927. On this occasion donated the land on which the foundation stands. In 1934, created the Pope Foundation, a non-profit organization for the purpose of eradicating human suffering and disease through scientific research. His daughter Margaret contracted polio, inspiring him to manufacture the Klenzak leg brace as an affordable type of orthopedic appliance. Is considered by many as the lay originator of the hot water treatment for infantile paralysis. The original wooden tank of 1923 was developed and redeveloped with Mr. Pope's guidance and financial aid and is known today as the Hubbard Tank. President Roosevelt, in his publicized address from Warm Springs, Georgia, on Thanksgiving Day, November 30, 1933, stated that he "found a very wonderful man from out in Chicago who dreamt the same dream that I did, and he came along. Through his generosity—more than generosity—through his faith and his belief in what we might accomplish, we held in the spring of 1926 what was called the Medical Experiment, and through that we sold the idea of Warm Springs to the medical profession. The man who made possible that period of proving what we believed in was Henry Pope." Although he never smoked, he chewed on a cigar for years and died of cancer of the tongue.

Pope, Katherine (1865–1958). One of seven children born in Ohio to William Pope and Cornelia Rochester Waring. In 1891, moved from Ohio to Chicago with her family and worked as a contributing journalist for the Western Newspaper Union. Taught English at the Kamehameha School for Boys (1893) and later at the Kamehameha School for Girls. Left Hawai'i after her sister Ida's 1914 death. Homesteaded 160 acres in northern Wisconsin. Lived many years in a "little log cabin in the forest." Author of *Hawaii, the Rainbow Land* (1924), a book that described Hawai'i's folktales and early history, dedicated to her sister Ida May Pope. Continued to freelance as a journalist and published a wide variety of articles about Hawai'i. Spent her last years living in a Chicago apartment as "Aunt Kay" to her numerous nieces and nephews. Took care of her invalid sister Anne until her death. At 92, was the longest-living child of William and Cornelia Pope. Died in St. Luke's hospital in Chicago.

Pope, William (1825–1890). One of twelve children born to Perry Pope and Hanna Webster in Otsego, New York. In 1852, became a self-taught medical doctor. Married Cornelia Rochester Waring (1856) and moved to Crestline, Ohio. While practicing medicine, engaged in several business ventures, the first of which was organizing the Crestline petroleum company in 1866. Unsuccessful, he partnered with William Franz, and through their combined efforts, a patent was obtained for a knitting machine in 1869. Within two years, the business was thriving in Bucyrus, Ohio, and he became president of the Franz & Pope

Knitting Machine Company. His obituaries highlight his gentleness and love of family. Buried at Oakwood Cemetery in Bucyrus, Crawford, Ohio, beside his wife, son William, and daughter Ida.

Pope-Prosser, Lois (1860–1932). Eldest daughter of seven children born in Ohio to William Pope and Cornelia Rochester Waring. Graduated from Crestline High School in 1877. Married Joseph George Prosser (1891), and they had three children, Thomas, Ruth, and Ida Katherine. Moved from Bucyrus in 1903 and joined the family in Kankakee, Illinois. Her husband, Joseph, went into business with her brother Henry at the Paramount Knitting Company. Buried in Pasadena, California.

Powers, Margaret (Maggie) (1873–1939). Born in Honolulu to Captain A. R. Powers and Mary Francis Powers. William O. Smith was her guardian after her father was lost at sea in 1877. Her mother contracted Hansen's disease and was sent to Kalaupapa in May 1888. In December of the same year, her afflicted sister Emma joined her mother. Her composition "Changes at the Kawaiahao Seminary" notes that she arrived at Kawaiahaʻo Seminary at the age of five around the time her father died. In 1892, appointed teacher at a government school on the island of Hawaiʻi with Helen Hoppin. Teacher at Makapala in Kōhala District 1892, teacher at Pohukaina School (1913–1938). Married Frederick Waldron in Kōhala (1897), Hawaiʻi; they had three children. In later life her students, who knew her as Mother Waldron, revered her. She was "tough and respected." On her fiftieth birthday, the boys and girls of Kakaʻako presented her with a pin inscribed "Mother," which she wore the rest of her life. According to Bob Dye, the stories left behind about 300-pound Mother Waldron are the "stuff of legends." A playground in Honolulu was named in her honor.

Prosser-McLain, Ruth Waring (1895–1978). One of three children (along with Thomas and Ida Katherine) born to Lois Pope and Joe Prosser in Bucyrus, Ohio. Married Ralf C. McLain (1922) in Chicago. Was the family historian and compiled *A Bridge to the Past of Prosser and Pope Families*.

Rath, James Arthur (1870–1929). Born in Hyderabad, India, to James and Elizabeth Baker Rath. Educated at military and private schools in India; graduated from the YMCA College, Springfield, Massachusetts. Married Ragna Helsher (1904) in Concord, Massachusetts. Recruited by the Hawaiian Board of Missions to relocate to Honolulu, Hawaiʻi, to reorganize tiny Pālama Chapel into a relevant social service agency. Incorporated Pālama Settlement in 1910. Visionary social worker whose tenacity and strong work ethic transformed a tiny chapel into the thriving Pālama Settlement, now in its 120th year. Established public health nursing in Honolulu and offered innovative recreation, social, educational, arts, and athletic programs to Oʻahu's poorest community.

Rath, Paula Ragna (1947–Present). Born in Oakland, California, to Robert Helsher and Jacqueline Jacobs Rath while the Honolulu residents were on a business trip. One son, Duncan Scott Graham. Married to Gerald W. Mayfield, MD. Educated at Punahou School in Honolulu, Hawaiʻi, and Goucher College in Baltimore, Maryland. Began her forty-five-year journalism career as office manager at CBS News Hong Kong during the Vietnam War. Went on to write for *Puisano Newspaper* in Botswana, *Today's Woman* magazine in Nigeria, KHVH All-News Radio in Honolulu, and the *Honolulu Advertiser.* Currently serves as an emeritus board member at Pālama Settlement and is writing a book about her family's legacy and Pālama Settlement's history.

Rath, Ragna Helsher (1879–1981). Born in Concord, Massachusetts, to Martinus O. Helsher and Eline Evensen, who left Norway in 1872. Educated in Concord schools and at Fitchburg Normal School. Raised five children: James Jr., Elizabeth, Henry, Margaret, and Robert. Worked closely with her husband, James Arthur Rath, to establish Pālama Settlement in Honolulu, Hawaiʻi. Taught English as a second language, hygiene, home economics, nutrition, and cooking to the residents of Pālama, the island's poorest neighborhood. A powerhouse at ninety-eight pounds, was the epitome of "the woman behind the man." Lived until she was 102 years old.

Richards, Theodore (1867–1948). Born in Montclair, New Jersey, to Joseph H. Richards and Frances Baker. Attended Adelphia Academy, Brooklyn; AB (1888), MA (1892), Wesleyan University; attended Columbia Law School. Married (1892) Mary ("May") Atherton and had five children. Music teacher at Kamehameha Schools (1889–1891); principal (1891–1893); field secretary, Hawaiian Board of Missions (1899–1900); treasurer, Mid-Pacific Institute; first president, Anti-Saloon League, Honolulu. Died May 27, 1948; buried at Kawaiahaʻo Church. Listed in *Men of Hawaii.* The Theodore Richards Collection is housed in the archives of Kamehameha Schools. Gwenfread Allen published a 1970 book, *Bridge Builders: The Story of Theodore and Mary Atherton Richards.*

Sturgeon-Cooke, Margaret Elnora "Nora" (1883–1980). Born in Bucyrus, Ohio, to Ida Whan and John H. Sturgeon. Came to Hawaiʻi when she was ten to live at the Kawaiahaʻo Seminary with her mother, who was hired by Ida Pope to be a matron. Moved with her mother to the Kamehameha Schools for Girls in 1894 when her mother left to be the matron of the domestic department. Attended Punahou while she boarded at the girl's school. Became the second wife of widower Clarence Hyde Cooke in 1935. After Clarence's death in 1944, she aided Ida Pope in many civic causes. Her final resting place is in Kawaiahaʻo Church's cemetery alongside her mother, Ida Whan Waterhouse.

Thompson, Uldrick (1849–1942). Born to Ambrose Thompson and Phoebe Reynolds in New York. Orphaned at age four when his parents died of tuberculosis, he was raised by his uncle, Uldrick Reynolds, until he was sixteen. Advanced diploma, Oswego Normal School (1879). Teacher, public schools in Peconic Bay (1881); teacher, Hoboken German Academy. Arrived (1889) in Honolulu at the invitation of General Armstrong. Teacher, Kamehameha Schools (1889–1892; 1901–1922); principal (1898–1901). Married (1882) Alice Haviland; four children, Alice Ranny, Rebecca Hull, Uldrick, and Robert Haviland. His memoir, *Reminiscences of Old Hawaii with Account of Early Life,* was published in Honolulu by Kamehameha Schools (1941). Died in Dobbs Ferry, New York.

Waterhouse, Eleanor (Nellie) (1870–1938). Born in Honolulu to Henry Waterhouse and Julia Hawkins Dimond. Attended Oberlin College as a conservatory student (1887–1891). Teacher, Chinese Mission, Honolulu. Married (1893) Arthur Bacon Wood; one child. Active in YMCA and other philanthropic organizations in Hawaiʻi and California. Author of *Memoirs of the Family* (1930). Died in Honolulu.

Waterhouse-Sturgeon, Ida Whan (1861–1944). Born in Beaver, Pennsylvania, to William Whan and Margaret Marshall. Her first marriage, to attorney John H. Sturgeon, ended in divorce after he embezzled money in Bucyrus, Ohio. Disgraced in the community, she and her ten-year-old daughter, Margaret Elnora "Nora" Sturgeon (Cooke), left for Hawaiʻi with Ida Pope in 1893 to be a matron at Kawaiahaʻo Seminary and later the Kamehameha School for Girls. Her second marriage was to widower Henry Waterhouse in 1899. Was Ida Pope's closest friend and aided her in all her civic causes. Her final resting place is in Kawaiahaʻo Church's cemetery alongside her daughter, Nora Sturgeon-Cooke.

Winter-Kofoid, Carrie Prudence (1866–1942). Born in South Coventry, Connecticut, to Reverend Alpheus Winter and Flora Damaris Thompson. Graduated from Oberlin College in 1890 and earned her MA from the University of Illinois

(1903). Teacher, Kawaiahaʻo Seminary (1890–1893). Married (1894) Charles Atwood Kofoid. Author of a series of articles on Hawaiʻi for the *Hartford Courant* (1893). Member, Congregational Church of Berkeley, California; president of the Women's Association of the Church; member, missionary committee of the church; teacher at church school. Resident, Michigan (1895), Illinois (1896–1903), Berkeley (1903–1942). Traveled extensively abroad with her husband. In Berkeley, member of the Women's Faculty Club, Town and Gown Club, Mobilized Women of Berkeley, and League of Women Voters. Died in Berkeley, California.

NOTES

Abbreviations

CAK   Charles Atwood Kofoid
CPW   Carrie Prudence Winter
CRB   Charles Reed Bishop
HMCS   Hawaiian Mission Children's Society
IMP   Ida May Pope
KS   Kamehameha Schools Archives
LEA   Lilla Estelle Appleton
UCSD   University of California Libraries, San Diego

Introduction

1. Uldrick Thompson Sr., *Reminiscences of Old Hawaii with Account of Early Life* (unpublished manuscript, 1941), 164, KS.

2. Sandra Bonura and Deborah Day, *An American Girl in the Hawaiian Islands: Letters of Carrie Prudence Winter, 1890–1893* (Honolulu: University of Hawai'i Press, 2012).

3. IMP to LEA, April 1, 1896, Lilla Estelle Appleton Papers, Oberlin College Archives.

4. Cynthia L. Morris, "The Prison Songs of Liliuokalani" (master's thesis, University of California, Santa Cruz, 2013), 52.

5. Michelle Keown, *Pacific Islands Writing: The Postcolonial Literatures of Aotearoa/New Zealand and Oceania* (Oxford: Oxford University Press, 2007), 129.

6. "A Service in Memory of Miss Ida M. Pope," *Bishop Memorial Church Service Bulletin,* September 20, 1915, KS.

Chapter 1. Ida's Heritage, 1862–1914

1. Janet Wethy Foley, *Early Settlers of New York State: Their Ancestors and Descendants,* vols. 1–4, pt. 2 (Akron, NY: Heritage Books: 1993), iv–vi, 448.

2. Ibid.

3. LEA to Cousin Hila, May 18, 1930, Charlotte Mitchell, personal collection.

4. Ida Pope and Katherine Pope, *Family Tales & Other Data Handed Down,* comp. John W. Pope (1960), family memoirs held by William Pope.

5. Dora Pope Worden, William Franklin Langworthy, Blanche Emogene Page Burch, and Franklin Leonard Pope, *Genealogy of Thomas Pope (1608–1883) and His Descendants* (Hamilton, NY: Republican Press, 1917), 5.

6. Franklin Leonard Pope, *Genealogy of Thomas Pope of Plymouth* (Boston: Press of David Class & Son, 1888), 6.

7. Ibid.

8. Ibid.

9. Albert Christopher Addison, *The Romantic Story of the Mayflower Pilgrims* (Boston: Page Co., 1911), 140.

10. Worden et al., *Genealogy of Thomas Pope.*

11. James E. McJunkin, ed., *History of Crawford County Ohio* (Hamilton, NY: Crawford Historical Foundation, 1976), 246.

12. *Ohio State Gazette and Business Directory for 1860–61* (Indianapolis: George W. Hawes, 1860), 292.

13. William Waring Pope, born December 5, 1857; Lois Pope, born April 21, 1860; Ida, born July 30, 1862; Katherine Pope, born December 24, 1865; Henry Pope, born October 23, 1868; Anne Pope, born December 23, 1871; Frank Pope, born December 19, 1874.

14. Ruth Prosser McLain, comp., *A Bridge to the Past of the Prosser and Pope Families,* Lois Taylor, private collection.

15. Ibid.

16. Ibid.

17. Ibid.

18. Ibid.

19. Daniel G. Arnold, *About Bucyrus* (Indianapolis: McM, 1971), 59.

20. Newton Bateman and Paul Selby, *Historical Encyclopedia of Illinois,* vol. 2 (Chicago: Munsell Publishing Co., 1913).

21. *History of Crawford County and Ohio* (Chicago: Baskin & Battey, Historical Publishers, 1881), 383.

22. Bateman and Selby, *Historical Encyclopedia of Illinois.*

23. *History of Crawford County and Ohio,* 59.

24. McLain, *Bridge to the Past of the Prosser and Pope Families.*

25. Julia McNair Wright, *Practical Life: Ways and Means for Developing Character and Resources* (Philadelphia: Bradley, Garretson, & Co., 1882), 530.

26. Ibid.

27. "Dr. William Pope," *Bucyrus Journal,* September 5, 1890.

28. *Scientific American* 32 (1875): 173.

29. *Decisions of the Commissioner of Patents and of the United States Courts in Patent and Trademark and Copyright Cases United States* (Washington, DC: U.S. Government Printing Office, Patent Office, 1882), 201.

30. William Dwight Porter Bliss and Rudolph Michael Binder, eds., *The New Encyclopedia of Social Reform: Including All Social Reform Movements and Activities, and the Economic, Industrial, and Sociological Facts and Statistics of All Countries and All Social Objects* (New York: Funk & Wagnalls, 1908), 273.

31. Linda Eisenmann, ed., *Historical Dictionary of Women's Education in the United States* (Westport, CT: Greenwood Publishing Group, 1998), 313.

32. *Catalogue of Oberlin College for the Year 1907,* General Catalogue of Oberlin College 1833–1908, Oberlin College Archives, 221.

33. *The Ohio Educational Monthly and the National Teacher: A Journal of Education,* vol. 38 (W. D. Henkle, 1889).

34. *Thirty-Second Annual Report of the Trustees and Superintendent of the Ohio Institution for Feeble-Minded Youth to the Governor of the State of Ohio for the Year 1888* (Columbus, OH: The Westbote Co., 1889), 89.

35. C. H. Krishef, *An Introduction to Mental Retardation* (Springfield, IL: Charles C. Thomas, 1983).

36. *Thirty-Second Annual Report,* 11.

37. Ibid., 9.

38. W. S. Eagleson, "Care and Education of The Deaf," *Proceedings of the Fifth Annual Ohio State Conference of Charities and Correction: Held at Delaware, Ohio, October 15th–18th 1895* (Columbus, OH: The Westbote Co., 1896).

39. Ibid.

40. Anne Pope to Trustees of Kamehameha Schools, 1914, KS.

41. *Proceedings of the Meeting[s] of the American Association of Instructors of the Blind, Perkins Institution for the Blind, Boston, August 20–22, 1872* (Boston: Rand, Avery & Co., 1873), 119.

Chapter 2. The Extraordinary Nineteenth Century

1. Alice Stone Blackwell, *Lucy Stone: Pioneer of Woman's Rights* (Charlottesville: University of Virginia Press, 1930), xx.

2. Dorothy A. Mays, *Women in Early America: Struggle, Survival, and Freedom in a New World* (Santa Barbara, CA: ABC-CLIO, 2004), 166.

3. William A. Mowry and Blanche Mowry, *American Pioneers,* vol. 1 (New York: Silver, Burdett, 1905), 281.

4. Beth Bradford Gilchrist, *The Life of Mary Lyon* (Boston: Houghton Mifflin, 1910), 198.

5. Mowry and Mowry, *American Pioneers,* 288.

6. Claude Eggertson, ed., *Studies in the History of American Education* (Ann Arbor: University of Michigan, School of Education, 1947), 3.

7. Amos Starr Cooke's May 14, 1839 journal entry, quoted in Mary Atherton Richards, ed., *Amos Starr Cooke and Juliette Montague Cooke: Their Autobiographies Gleaned from Their Journals and Letters 1838–1840* (1941; repr. Honolulu: Daughters of Hawai'i, 1987), 172.

8. Hiram Bingham, *A Residence of Twenty-One Years in the Sandwich Islands* (New York: Praeger Publishers, 1969), 580.

9. Laura Fish Judd and D. L. Morgan, *Honolulu: Sketches of Life in the Hawaiian Islands from 1828 to 1861* (Chicago: Lakeside Classics, Lakeside Press, 1966), 114.

10. Ibid.

11. A. L. Shumway and C. De W. Brower, eds., *Oberliniana: A Jubilee Volume of Semi-Historical Anecdotes Connected with the Past and Present of Oberlin College* (Cleveland: Printed by Home Pub. Co., 1883).

12. "Proportion of Men to Women in the United States," supplement, *Scientific American* 58, no. 1512 (1904): 24231.

13. Drew Gilpin Faust, *This Republic of Suffering: Death and the American Civil War* (New York: Knopf Doubleday, 2008), x1.

14. Gail Collins, *America's Women: Four Hundred Years of Dolls, Drudges, Helpmates, and Heroines* (New York: Perennial Books, 2004), 255–256.

15. "The Inception of the Woman's Board of Missions of Pacific Isles: A Reminiscence," *Twenty-Fifth Annual Report of the Woman's Board of Missions for the Pacific Islands*

(excerpt from Mount Holyoke College Archives and Special Collections, South Hadley, MA, 1896), 64.

16. Ibid.

17. Ibid.

18. Julia McNair Wright, *Practical Life; or Ways and Means for Developing Character and Resources* (Philadelphia: J. C. McCurdy, 1882), 349.

19. Ibid.

20. R. F. Dearborn, *Saratoga, and How to See It: Containing a Description of the Watering Place* (Albany, NY: Weed, Parsons, 1873), 5.

21. Roger William Vaughan, Archbishop of Sydney, South Wales, *The Position of Christian Womanhood in the World*, vol. 6 (Boston: T. B. Noonan and Co., 1882), 488.

22. Dana Goldstein, *The Teacher Wars: A History of America's Most Embattled Profession* (New York: Doubleday, 2014).

23. Gabriella Ahmansson, *A Life and Its Mirrors: A Feminist Reading of L. M. Montgomery's Fiction* (Stockholm: Almqvist & Wiksell, 1991), 120.

24. Cousin Hila from Lilla Appleton, May 18, 1930, Charlotte Mitchell, personal collection.

25. McNair Wright, *Practical Life*, 357.

26. Ibid., 358.

27. Ibid., 360.

28. Ibid.

29. Joseph King Goodrich, *The Coming Hawaii*, The World Today Series (Chicago: A. C. McClurg, 1914), 50.

30. Juliette Cooke, quoted in "Jubilee Celebration of the Arrival of the Missionary Reinforcement of 1837," *Hawaiian Mission Children's Society* (Honolulu: Daily Bulletin Stream Print, 1887), 151.

31. H. G. Pratt, *The Story of Mid-Pacific Institute* (Honolulu: Tongg, 1957), 2.

32. Carl Kalani Beyer, "Manual and Industrial Education for Hawaiians during the 19th Century," *Hawaiian Journal of History* 28 (1994).

33. *Oberlin Review* 18, no. 4 (1890): 59.

Chapter 3. Kawaiaha'o Seminary

1. "Rev. Luther Halsey Gulick, M.D.," *Chinese Recorder* 22 (1891): 327.

2. Lydia Bingham Coan, "Early Days at Kawaiahao," *Friend* 64, no. 7 (July 1906): 9.

3. *Midpac*, self-published booklet to introduce the history of its institution, undated, unnumbered.

4. "Kawaiahao Seminary Celebrates Fiftieth Anniversary," *Friend* 72, no. 12 (December 1914): 275.

5. Martha Chamberlain, "Memories of the Past, Linked to Scenes of the Present, in the History of Kawaiahao Seminary," 1889, HMCS, 13.

6. Coan, "Early Days at Kawaiahao," 9.

7. Lydia Bingham to Trustees of Oahu College, June 12, 1867, HMCS.

8. Ibid.

9. Oscar E. Maurer, *How the Gospel Came to Hawaii*, 2nd ed. (Honolulu: Board of the Hawaiian Evangelical Association, 1952), 13.

10. Coan, "Early Days at Kawaiahao," 9.

11. Julieanna Frost, *Images of America* (Charleston, SC: Arcadia Publishing, 2011), 58.

12. *Friend* 72, no. 12 (December 1, 1914): 275.

13. Coan, "Early Days at Kawaiahao."

14. Ibid.

15. Martha Chamberlain, "Memories of the Past, Linked to Scenes of the Present, in the History of Kawaiahao Seminary" (unpublished paper, HMCS, January 24, 1898), 15.

16. Margaret Powers, "Changes at the Kawaiahao Seminary," *Hawaiian Gazette*, June 16, 1891.

17. John A. Erdman, "Brief Historical Sketch of the Hawaiian Board of Missions," *The Centennial Book: One Hundred Years of Christian Civilization in Hawaii, 1820–1920* (Honolulu: Central Committee of the Hawaiian Mission Centennial, 1920), 77.

18. John Erdman, "The Hawaiian Board of Missions," *Friend* 107, no. 4 (April 1937): 63.

19. *Life and Light for Woman*, vol. 30 (Boston: Women's Board of Missions, 1900), 346.

20. *Sixty-third Annual Report of the Mission Children's Society* (Honolulu: T. H. Paradise of the Pacific Print, 1915), 45.

21. Report to the Hawaiian Board, June 26, 1876, HMCS.

22. Harold Winfield Kent, *Dr. Hyde and Mr. Stevenson: The Life of the Rev Dr. Charles McEwen Hyde, Including a Discussion of the Open Letter of Robert Louis Stevenson* (Rutland, VT: Tuttle Publishing, 1973), 97.

23. C. Kalani Beyer, introduction to *An American Girl in the Hawaiian Islands: Letters of Carrie Prudence Winter, 1890–1893,* ed. Sandra Bonura and Deborah Day (Honolulu: University of Hawai'i Press, 2012), 12.

24. Chamberlain, "Memories of the Past," 3.

25. Lizzie Bingham to Rev. S. E. Bishop, Hilo, October 14, 1879, Sereno E. Bishop Papers, The Huntington Library, San Marino, CA.

26. Ibid.

27. Henry K. Hyde, *Charles McEwen Hyde: A Memorial* (Ware, MA: Eddy Press, 1901), 46.

28. Kent, *Dr. Hyde and Mr. Stevenson,* 100.

29. Ibid., 99.

30. LEA to her mother, Fanny Reed Wooster, February 12, 1887, quoted in "Lilla Estelle Appleton Papers, 1848–1937," Oberlin College Archives.

31. Kent, *Dr. Hyde and Mr. Stevenson,* 99.

32. Ibid., 100.

33. LEA to her mother, Fanny Reed Wooster, February 12, 1887.

34. Kent, *Dr. Hyde and Mr. Stevenson,* 99.

35. Charles Reed Bishop, Letter File, comp. and ed. Harold Winfield Kent, prepared for the sesquicentennial of Charles Reed Bishop, January 25, 1972, Bishop Museum, Honolulu, 1972, 56.

36. Rev. C. M. Hyde, DD, "Letter of Resignation. As a Trustee of Kawaiahao Female Seminary," January 11, 1887, Mission, Mission Houses Museum Library; Kent, *Dr. Hyde and Mr. Stevenson,* 100–101.

37. Liliuokalani, *Hawaii's Story by Hawaii's Queen, Liliuokalani* (Boston: Lee and Shepard, 1898), 383.

38. Ibid.

39. Ibid., 113–114.

40. Sandra Bonura, Lydia Aholo Oral History Transcription (2013; transcription of recorded interview of Lydia Kaonohiponiponiokalani Aholo by Helena Allen in 1969; hereafter cited as Lydia Aholo Transcription), 5.

41. John F. McDermott Jr., Wen-Shing Tseng, and Thomas W. Maretzski, eds., *People and Cultures of Hawai'i: A Psychocultural Profile* (Honolulu: University of Hawai'i Press, 1980), 13; Katharine K. Luomala, "Reality and Fantasy: The Foster Child in Hawaiian Myths and Customs," *Pacific Studies* 10, no. 2 (March 1987): 17.

42. Ruth Prosser McLain, comp., *A Bridge to the Past of the Prosser and Pope Families*, Lois Taylor, private collection.

43. Sandra Bonura, and Sally Witmer, "Lydia K. Aholo, Her Story," *Hawaiian Journal of History* 47 (2013): 107.

44. Lydia Aholo Transcription, 3.

45. Liliuokalani, *Hawaii's Story by Hawaii's Queen*, 6.

46. Lydia Aholo, "My Life as a Schoolgirl in Honolulu," 1892, quoted in Sandra Bonura and Deborah Day, *An American Girl in the Hawaiian Islands: Letters of Carrie Prudence Winter, 1890–1893* (Honolulu: University of Hawai'i Press, 2012), 41–43.

47. Ibid., 10.

48. Ibid., 370.

49. Ibid.

50. LEA, Nancy Malone to LEA, Honolulu, June 1, 1886, Oberlin College Archives.

51. Ibid.

52. LEA, "Kawaiahao Seminary," written and read for the Cousins Society, 1886 or 1887, Oberlin College Archives.

53. Ibid.

54. Ibid.

55. Ibid.

56. H. G. Pratt, *The Story of Mid-Pacific Institute* (Honolulu: Tongg Publishing, 1957), 27.

57. *Annual Report of the Hawaiian Evangelical Association*, vol. 25 (Honolulu: Hawaiian Evangelical Association Board, 1888), 11

58. "Martha Ellwood McLennan's Death," *Oberlin Review*, January 20, 1897.

Chapter 4. Ida to the Kingdom, 1890–1892

1. Carrie Prudence Winter, "An American Girl in the Hawaiian Islands," *Southern Magazine* 1 (November 1892).

2. Ruth Prosser McLain, comp., *A Bridge to the Past of the Prosser and Pope Families* (undated, unnumbered), Lois Taylor, private collection.

3. CPW to CAK, August 16, 1890, UCSD.

4. CPW to CAK, August 21, 1890, UCSD.

5. CPW to CAK, September 9, 1890, UCSD.

6. Winter, "American Girl in the Hawaiian Islands."

7. Ibid.

8. Ibid.

9. Ibid.

10. CPW to CAK, August 27, 1890, UCSD.

11. Winter, "American Girl in the Hawaiian Islands."

12. CPW to CAK, August 27, 1890.

13. CPW to CAK, August 29, 1890, UCSD.

14. Winter, "American Girl in the Hawaiian Islands."

15. Ibid.

16. Ibid.

17. CPW to CAK, September 26, 1891, UCSD.

18. CPW to CAK, August 29, 1890.

19. Ibid.

20. CPW to CAK, October 20, 1890, UCSD.

21. CPW to CAK, June 12, 1892, UCSD.

22. CPW to CAK, October 1, 1892, UCSD.

23. CPW to CAK, December 14, 1890, UCSD.

24. "The King Slept Here," *Honolulu Star-Bulletin,* January 11, 2009.

25. *San Diego Union,* undated newspaper clipping, Coronado Historical Society Archives, Coronado, CA.

26. Ibid.

27. IMP to "My Dear Popes," February 2, 1891, Ida May Pope Papers, The Huntington Library, San Marino, CA.

28. Ibid.

29. Ibid.

30. Ibid.

31. Ibid.

32. Ibid.

33. Harold Winfield Kent, *Dr. Hyde and Mr. Stevenson* (Rutland, VT: Charles E. Tuttle, 1973), 225–226.

34. IMP to "My Dear Popes."

35. LEA, Lilla Appleton Papers, Oberlin College Archives.

36. Ibid.

37. CPW to CAK, September 9, 1890, UCSD.

38. McLain, *Bridge to the Past of the Prosser and Pope Families.*

39. CPW to CAK, September 21, 1890, UCSD.

Chapter 5. Miss Pope in Charge

1. IMP to Lois Prosser, February 2, 1891, Ida May Pope Papers, The Huntington Library, San Marino, CA.

2. W. B. Powell; Emma Todd, *The Normal Course in Reading: Fifth Reader* (New York: Silver Burdett, 1892), 6.

3. *Proceedings of the Washington Academy of Sciences* 10, no. 1 (1908): 230.

4. Ibid., 229.

5. CPW to CAK, September 13, 1891, UCSD.

6. Ibid.

7. Ibid.

8. LEA to Fanny Reed Wooster Appleton, March 1, 1891, Oberlin College Archives, 30.

9. Ibid.

10. Ibid.

11. CPW to CAK, September 6, 1891, UCSD.

12. Ibid.

13. Ibid.

14. Ibid.

15. Ibid.

16. Ibid.

17. Ibid.

18. CPW to CAK, September 21, 1891, UCSD.

19. CPW to CAK, September 6, 1891.

20. CPW to CAK, October 5, 1891, UCSD.

21. CPW to CAK, February 6, 1892, UCSD.

22. CPW to CAK, April 4, 1893, UCSD.

23. CPW to CAK, April 14, 1893, UCSD.

24. CPW to CAK, January 26, 1892, UCSD

25. CPW to CAK, July 17, 1892, UCSD.

26. CPW to CAK, August1, 1892, UCSD.

27. CPW to CAK, December 25, 1892, UCSD.

28. CPW to CAK, January 20, 1893, UCSD.

29. CPW to CAK, January 3, 1893, UCSD.

30. IMP to Lois Prosser.

31. CRB, Letter File, comp. and ed. Harold Winfield Kent, prepared for the sesquicentennial of Charles Reed Bishop, January 25, 1972, Bishop Museum, Honolulu, 1972, 65.

32. "Local and General," *Hawaiian Gazette,* November 10, 1891.

33. CPW to CAK, October 5, 1891.

34. Sandra Bonura, Lydia Aholo Oral History Transcription (2013; transcription of recorded interview of Lydia Kaonohiponiponiokalani Aholo by Helena Allen in 1969; hereafter cited as Lydia Aholo Transcription), 60.

35. CPW to CAK, March 15, 1891, UCSD.

36. CPW to CAK, April 15, 1891, UCSD.

37. Ibid.

38. Ibid.

39. Ibid.

40. Ibid.

41. Lydia Aholo Transcription, 48.

42. CPW to CAK, April 15, 1891.

43. CPW to CAK, January 6, 1892, UCSD.

44. CPW to CAK, March 13, 1892, UCSD.

45. "Kawaiahao Seminary: The Annual Public Examination of the School," *Daily Bulletin* (Honolulu, HI), June 8, 1892.

46. CPW to CAK, June 12, 1892, UCSD.

47. Sandra Bonura and Deborah Day, *An American Girl in the Hawaiian Islands: Letters of Carrie Prudence Winter, 1890–1893* (Honolulu: University of Hawai'i Press, 2012), xxx.

48. "Educational Annual Examination of Kawaiahao Seminary," undated and unnamed newspaper clipping, UCSD.

49. Ida Pope, "The Education of Hawaiians at the Kamehameha School for Girls," *Southern Workman* 29, no. 1 (January 1900): 470.

50. Mary Atherton Richards, ed., *Amos Starr Cooke and Juliette Montague Cooke: Their Autobiographies Gleaned from Their Journals and Letters 1838–1840* (1941; repr. Honolulu: Daughters of Hawai'i, 1987), 566.

51. CPW to CAK, December 20, 1891, UCSD.

52. CPW to CAK, March 13, 1892.

53. CRB, Letter File, 49.

Chapter 6. Pilikia

1. Grace Hortense Tower, "Child's Life in Hawaii," *Pacific Monthly* 6 (January 1909): 71.

2. Mary Kawena Pukui, E. W. Haertig, and Catherine A. Lee, *Nānā i ke kumu* (Look to the source), vol. 2 (Honolulu: Hui Hānai, 1972), 65.

3. CPW to CAK, September 9, 1891, UCSD.

4. CPW to CAK, December 14, 1890, UCSD.

5. CPW to CAK, September 13, 1891, UCSD.

6. Sandra Bonura, Lydia Aholo Oral History Transcription (2013; transcription of re-corded interview of Lydia Kaonohiponiponiokalani Aholo by Helena Allen in 1969), 15.

7. Ibid., 3.

8. Liliuokalani, *Hawaii's Story by Hawaii's Queen, Liliuokalani* (Boston: Lee and Shepard, 1898), 117.

9. CPW to CAK, November 27, 1890, UCSD.

10. CPW to CAK September 21, 1891, UCSD.

11. "Women in Hawaii," *Chicago Sunday Tribune,* March 26, 1893.

12. CPW to CAK, October 26, 1890, UCSD.

13. CPW to CAK, November 27, 1890.

14. CPW to CAK, March 30, 1892, UCSD.

15. Ibid.

16. *Hawaiian Gazette,* January 26, 1889, 3, UCSD.

17. Ibid.

18. Lydia Aholo, "My Life as a School-Girl in Honolulu" (1892), in *An American Girl in the Hawaiian Islands: Letters of Carrie Prudence Winter, 1890–1893,* ed. Sandra Bonura and Deb-orah Day (Honolulu: University of Hawai'i Press, 2012), 41–44.

19. "Brilliant State Ball," *Daily Bulletin,* March 18, 1892.

20. CPW to CAK, March 13, 1892, UCSD.

21. Correspondence between author and Sheila Johnson (December 2014).

22. CPW to CAK, September 21, 1891.

23. IMP to Lois Prosser, February 2, 1891, Ida May Pope Papers, The Huntington Library, San Marino, CA.

24. LEA, journal entry 11, 1893, Oberlin College Archives.

25. IMP to CPW, January 31, 1894, UCSD.

26. CPW to CAK, March 12, 1891, UCSD.

27. LEA to mother, February 6, 1893, Oberlin College Archives.

28. CPW to CAK, April 10, 1892, UCSD.

29. IMP to CPW, January 31, 1894, UCSD.

30. CPW to CAK, May 9, 1891, UCSD.

31. LEA letter to trustees, 1888, KS.

32. CPW to CAK, November 27, 1890, UCSD.

33. CPW to CAK, September 13, 1891.

34. CPW to CAK, January 15, 1891, UCSD.

35. LEA, journal entry, January 19, 1893, Oberlin College Archives.

36. CPW to CAK, June 25, 1891, UCSD.

37. Ibid.

38. CPW to CAK, January 6, 1892, UCSD.

39. Mary Kawena Pukui and Samuel H. Elbert, *Hawaiian Dictionary* (Honolulu: University of Hawai'i Press, 1986).

40. LEA to mother, February 17, 1893, Oberlin College Archives.

41. CPW to CAK, November 29, 1891, UCSD.

42. "Murderous Affair in Kawaiahao Lane," *Hawaiian Gazette*, October 11, 1904.

43. *Lomi lomi* "rub rub" massages have traditionally been part of Hawaiian healing rituals.

44. LEA to mother, February 4, 1893, Oberlin College Archives.

45. First Catalogue, Kamehameha School for Girls, 1897–1898, Hawaiian Gazette Print, 46.

Chapter 7. Off to Moloka'i with the Queen, 1892

1. IMP to Lois Prosser, May 31, 1891, Ida May Papers, The Huntington Library, San Marino, CA.

2. Although leprosy is now officially known as Hansen's disease, the correct medical term is ignored in favor of the historical "leprosy" and "lepers" used in the nineteenth century.

3. Report of the President of the Board of Health to the Legislative Assembly of 1884 (Office of the Board of Health Honolulu, April 24, 1884), 4.

4. Ron Amundson and Akira O. Ruddle-Miyato, "A Wholesome Horror: The Stigmas of Leprosy in 19th Century Hawaii," *Disability Studies Quarterly* 30, no. 3/4 (2010).

5. Pennie Moblo, "Ethnic Intercession: Leadership at Kalaupapa Leprosy Colony," *Journal of the Polynesian Society* 111, no. 4 (1999): 311–338.

6. Harry Frank, *Roaming in Hawaii with Harry A. Franck* (New York: Grosset & Dunlap, 1937).

7. Mary H. Krout, *Hawaii and a Revolution* (New York: Dodd, Mead, 1898), 197.

8. Ibid.

9. "Leprosy in Hawaii—An Official Report," letter book of news clippings, *Pacific Commercial Advertiser,* June 28, 1913, 22.

10. Report of the President of the Board of Health to the Legislative Assembly of 1884, xxxvii.

11. Ibid.

12. Ibid.

13. Kara Rogers, *Infectious Diseases* (New York: Britannica Educational Pub. in association with Rosen Educational Services, 2011), 31.

14. CPW to CAK, April 27, 1891, UCSD.

15. CPW to CAK, May 5, 1892, UCSD.

16. Perley Horne, President Kamehameha Schools to the Trustees, February 16, 1912, KS.

17. Ibid.

18. Ibid.

19. Ibid.

20. CPW to CAK, May 9, 1891, UCSD.

21. CPW to CAK, November 13, 1897, UCSD.

22. Esther Kwon Arinaga and Caroline Axtell Garrett, "Murder, a Trial, a Hanging: The Kapea Case of 1897–1898," *Hawaiian Journal of History* 42 (2008): 42.

23. CPW to CAK, November 27, 1890, UCSD.

24. *Chinese Recorder and Missionary Journal* 22 (1891): 117.

25. Michel Tibayrenc, ed., *The Encyclopedia of Infectious Diseases: Modern Methodologies* (Hoboken, NJ: Wiley, 2007), 179.

26. Anne Pope to Miss Cross, May 19, 1898, The Huntington Library, San Marino, CA.

27. IMP to Lois Prosser, May 3, 1891, The Huntington Library, San Marino, CA.

28. Adreinne Stone, *Hawaii's Queen Liliuokalani* (New York: Julian Messner, 1950), 151.

29. Ibid., 152.

30. IMP to Lois Prosser, May 3, 1891.

31. Ibid.

32. CPW to CAK, April 26, 1891, UCSD.

33. IMP to Lois Prosser, May 3, 1891.

34. Ibid.

35. Ibid.

36. Ibid.

37. Clifford Gessler, *Hawaii: Isles of Enchantment* (New York: D. Appleton-Century, 1938), 267.

38. IMP to Lois Prosser, May 3, 1891.

39. Helen Sarah Norton Diary, October 24, 1881, James Benjamin, private collection.

40. Ibid.

41. "Board of Health Answers Queries," *Evening Bulletin,* March 21, 1907.

42. Ibid.

43. Ibid.

44. Ibid.

45. IMP to Lois Prosser, May 3, 1891, UCSD.

46. Ibid.

47. Ibid.

48. Robert Louis Stevenson, *The Works of Robert Louis Stevenson,* vol. 15 (New York: Charles Scribner's Sons, 1922), 481.

49. Harry Franck, *Roaming in Hawaii with Harry A. Franck* (New York: Grosset & Dunlap, 1937), 201.

50. CPW to CAK, May 12, 1893, UCSD.

51. IMP to Lois Prosser, May 3, 1891. Jacob Adler and Gwynn Barrett, *Diaries of Walter Murray Gibson 1886, 1887* (Honolulu: University of Hawai'i Press, 1973), 185.

52. IMP to Lois Prosser, May 3, 1891.

Chapter 8. Prayer and Politics

1. "Death of H.R.H. The Prince Consort," *Hawaiian Gazette,* September 1, 1891.

2. Liliuokalani, *Hawaii's Story by Hawaii's Queen, Liliuokalani* (Boston: Lee and Shepard, 1898), 382–383.

3. Ibid., 382.

4. Alexander S. Twombly, *Hawaii and Its People: The Land of Rainbow and Palm* (New York, Boston: Silver Burdett, 1899), 327.

5. William F. Blackman, *The Making of Hawaii: A Study in Social Evolution* (New York: Macmillan, 1906), 131.

6. "Transcript of Journal of Lilla Appleton's Revolutionary," Oberlin College Archives, 17.

7. Ibid., 4.

8. Ibid., 2.

9. Ibid.

10. Ibid.

11. W. D. Alexander, *History of the Later Years of the Hawaiian Monarchy and the Revolution of 1893* (Honolulu: Hawaiian Gazette Company, 1896), 34.

12. Ibid.

13. *Appletons' Annual Cyclopedia and Register of Important Events*, vol. 17 (New York: D. Appleton, 1893), 334.

14. Alexander, *Later Years of the Hawaiian Monarchy*, 35.

15. "Transcript of Journal of Lilla Appleton's Revolutionary," 3.

16. Ibid.

17. Ibid., 2.

18. Ibid., 3.

19. CPW to CAK, January 15, 1893, UCSD.

20. Carrie Winter, "Blount Is Very Busy," *Hartford Courant*, May 29, 1893.

21. Alexander, *Later Years of the Hawaiian Monarchy*, 39.

22. Ibid., 41.

23. CPW to CAK, January 15, 1893.

24. Alexander, *Later Years of the Hawaiian Monarchy*, 43.

25. Ibid., 44.

26. Ibid., 50–51.

27. Ibid., 50.

28. "Transcript of Journal of Lilla Appleton's Revolutionary," 1.

29. Ibid., 4.

30. Ibid., 44.

31. Alexander, *Later Years of the Hawaiian Monarchy*, 39.

32. CPW to CAK, January 15, 1893, UCSD.

33. "Transcript of Journal of Lilla Appleton's Revolutionary," 6.

34. CPW to CAK, January 15, 1893.

35. "Transcript of Journal of Lilla Appleton's Revolutionary," 4.

36. Ibid.

37. Ibid.

38. Ibid., 5.

39. Ibid.

40. Ibid.

41. Ibid., 4.

42. George, W. Browne, *The Paradise of the Pacific: The Hawaiian Islands* (Boston: D. Estes, 1900), 128–129.

43. Ibid., 130.

44. CPW to CAK, January 20, 1893, UCSD.

45. Caroline Babb to her brother, February 9, 1893, Caroline M. and George Babb letters, 1891–1894, Bancroft Library, UC Berkeley.

46. "President's Message Relating to the Hawaiian Islands, December 18, 1893," *Report of Commissioner to the Hawaiian Islands, January 23, 1893* (Washington, DC: U.S. Government Printing Office, 1893), 324.

47. LEA to mother, March 22, 1893, Oberlin College Archives.

48. *Impressions of Kamehameha: Letters of Eleanor Little to Her Family 1910–1911* (Honolulu: Kamehameha Schools), 42.

49. Caroline Babb to mother, March 6, 1893, Bancroft Library, UC Berkeley.

50. Uldrick Thompson, *Reminiscences of the Kamehameha Schools* (unpublished, typescript manuscript, 1922), KS.

51. "Transcript of Journal of Lilla Appleton's Revolutionary," 6.

52. Ibid., 6–7.

53. LEA to mother, January 15, 1893, Oberlin College Archives.

54. "Transcript of Journal of Lilla Appleton's Revolutionary," 8.

55. "The Ex-Queen's Investments," *Boston Evening Transcript,* August 1, 1894,

56. "Transcript of Journal of Lilla Appleton's Revolutionary," 9.

57. Ibid.

58. Ibid.

59. Ibid.

60. Ibid.

61. "Burglars Again. Attempted Robbery at Kawaiahao Seminary," *Daily Pacific Commercial Advertiser,* February 7, 1893.

62. "Transcript of Journal of Lilla Appleton's Revolutionary," 7.

63. Caroline Babb to mother, March 6, 1893.

64. A. E. McKinley, *The History of North America,* vol. 20, *Island Possessions of the United States* (Philadelphia: George Barrie & Sons, 1907), 178.

65. "Transcript of Journal of Lilla Appleton's Revolutionary," 17.

66. Ibid.

67. Ibid.

68. Ibid., 10.

69. LEA to mother, February 4, 1893, Oberlin College Archives.

70. "Transcript of Journal of Lilla Appleton's Revolutionary," 16.

71. *Journal of the House of Representatives of the United States, Second Session of the Fifty-Third Congress, Begun and Held at the city of Washington December 4, 1893* 53, no. 2 (1894): 51.

72. "Transcript of Journal of Lilla Appleton's Revolutionary," 16.

73. CPW to CAK, February 12, 1893, UCSD.

Chapter 9. Endings

1. "New Teachers from Ohio for the Kawaiahao Seminary," from *Bucyrus Journal,* reprinted in *Hawaiian Gazette,* August 29, 1893.

2. Ibid.

3. "Kawaiahao Seminary," *Friend* 51, no. 9 (September 1893): 72

4. Ibid.

5. IMP to CPW, January 31, 1894, UCSD.

6. "Local and General News," *Daily Bulletin,* September 6, 1893.

7. "The Situation," *Hawaiian Gazette,* September 19, 1893.

8. "The Ex-Queen Certain of Restoration, She Tells a Lady That Orders Will Be Received on Wednesday to Put Her on the Throne," *Hawaiian Star,* September 4, 1893.

9. "The Queen and the Seminary," *Daily Bulletin,* September 6, 1893.

10. Ibid.

11. "Kawaiahao Seminary and the Queen," *Hawaii Holomua,* September 7, 1893.

12. IMP to CPW, January 31, 1894.

13. Liliuokalani, *Hawaii's Story by Hawaii's Queen, Liliuokalani* (Boston: Lee and Shepard, 1898), 111.

14. IMP to CPW, January 31, 1894.

15. Harold W. Kent, *Charles Reed Bishop, Man of Hawaii* (Palo Alto, CA: Pacific Books, 1965), 182.

16. Ibid.

17. *Hawaii, Education in the States, Historical Development and Outlook* (Washington, DC: National Education Association of the United States, 1969), 297.

18. "The Kawaiahao Seminary," *Hawaii Holomua,* June 15, 1894.

19. Kawaiahao Seminary, Report of Board of Managers, Mission Houses Children's Society, October 1894.

20. Ibid.

21. Ibid.

22. Ibid.

23. Ibid.

24. Helen G. Pratt, *The Story of Mid-Pacific Institute* (Honolulu: Tongg Publishing, 1957), 27.

25. Kent, *Charles Reed Bishop,* 182.

26. Helen Gay Pratt, *The Story of Mid-Pacific Institute* (Honolulu: Tongg Publishing Company, 1957), 108.

Chapter 10. Beginnings

1. C. Black and K. Mellen, *Princess Pauahi Bishop and Her Legacy* (Honolulu: Kamehameha Schools Press, 1965), 111.

2. Ibid.

3. Ibid., 113.

4. "Historical Number for Kamehameha Schools 1887–1928," *Friend* 98, no. 12 (1928): 286.

5. "Hoomanao Hookamaemae" [Hypocritical Remembrance], *Ka Makaainana,* December 23, 1895, translated in *HoʻolaupaʻI Hawaiian Nūpepa Collection,* April 12, 2012, https://nupepa-hawaii.com/2012/04/12.

6. Loring Gardner Hudson, "The History of the Kamehameha Schools" (master's thesis, University of Hawaii, 1935).

7. United States Congressional Serial Set, issue 3180 (Washington, DC: United States Government Printing Office, 1895), 502.

8. Harold W. Kent, *Charles Reed Bishop, Man of Hawaii* (Palo Alto, CA: Pacific Books, 1965), 308.

9. Ibid., 182.

10. CRB, Letter File, comp. and ed. Harold Winfield Kent, prepared for the sesquicentennial of CRB, January 25, 1972, Bishop Museum, Honolulu, 1972, 47.

11. Ibid., 25.

12. "The New School for Girls," *Hawaiian Gazette,* August 3, 1894.

13. Uldrick Thompson, *Reminiscences of the Kamehameha Schools* (unpublished, typescript manuscript, 1922), KS.

14. Ibid.

15. Eleanor Little Baker, "Impressions of Kamehameha, Letters of Eleanor Little Baker to Her Family 1910–1911," 17, KS.

16. "New School for Girls."

17. Ibid.

18. Ibid.

19. Donald Kiolani Mitchell, *Kū Kilakila ʻo Kamehameha: A Historical Account of the Campuses of the Kamehameha Schools* (Honolulu: Kamehameha Schools/Bernice Pauahi Bishop Estate, 1993).

20. Ibid.

21. IMP, "The Education of Hawaiians at the Kamehameha School for Girls," *Southern Workman* 29, no. 1 (January 1900): 477.

22. Charles Reed Bishop, Letter File, 27.

23. Ibid., 26.

24. "New School for Girls."

25. Bishop, Letter File, 21–22.

26. Trustee Report, December 1895, 1, KS.

27. Sandra Bonura, Lydia Aholo Oral History Transcription (2013; transcription of recorded interview of Lydia Kaonohiponiponiokalani Aholo by Helena Allen in 1969; hereafter cited as Lydia Aholo Transcription), 4.

28. First Catalogue, Kamehameha School for Girls, 1897–1898, Hawaiian Gazette Print.

29. "New School for Girls."

30. "Historical Number for Kamehameha Schools," 284.

31. First Catalogue, 46.

32. John R. Musick, *Hawaii: Our New Possessions* (New York: Funk & Wagnalls, 1898), 49.

33. Committee of the Hawaiian Mission, *The Centennial Book: One Hundred Years of Christian Civilization in Hawaii 1820–1920* (Honolulu: Hawaiian Mission, 1920), 58.

34. Sadie Brown, Flora Albright, Nettie Hammond, Cornelia Clymer, Clara Peters, Ida Sturgeon, Mary Kinney.

35. Lydia Aholo Transcription, 35.

36. Pierre Bowman, "From an Almost Forgotten Past," *Honolulu Advertiser,* February 25, 1980.

37. Ibid.

38. Ida May Pope Memory Book, KS.

39. Bishop, Letter File, 51.

40. Ibid.

41. Frank J. Cavaioli, *Farmingdale State College: A History* (Albany: Excelsior Editions/State University of New York Press, 2012), 140.

42. Kent, *Charles Reed Bishop,* 171.

43. Helen G. Pratt, *In Hawaii: A Hundred Years* (New York: Charles Scribner's Sons, 1939), 295.

44. First Catalogue, 16.

45. Ibid.

46. *Makers of Destiny—Hawaiian Style: the Lives of Pioneer Women Educators in Hawaii* (Honolulu: Delta Kappa Gamma Society, International, Beta Beta State, 1981), 184.

47. Ibid., 185.

48. "Historical Number for Kamehameha Schools," 286.

49. Thompson, *Remembrances of Kamehameha Schools*, 164, 170.

50. Ibid.

51. Ibid.

52. Ibid., 161.

53. First Catalogue, 46.

54. Ibid.

55. IMP, Annual Report to the Trustees, 1896.

56. Ibid., 217.

57. IMP, Annual Report to Trustees, June 30, 1904.

58. Ruth Prosser McLain, comp., *A Bridge to the Past of the Prosser and Pope Families*, Lois Taylor, private collection.

Chapter 11. The Foundational Years

1. Sandra Bonura, Lydia Aholo Oral History Transcription (2013; transcription of recorded interview of Lydia Kaonohiponiponiokalani Aholo by Helena Allen in 1969; hereafter, cited as Lydia Aholo Transcription), 12–13.

2. Ibid., 60–61.

3. "Best Musicians from Kamehameha Schools to Be Heard Tomorrow," *Maui News*, August 5, 1921.

4. IMP to LEA, July 29, 1895, Lilla Estelle Appleton Papers, Oberlin College Archives.

5. Andrew Hollis, *The Contribution of the Oswego Normal School to Educational Progress in the United States* (Boston: D. C. Heath, 1898), 15.

6. Ibid., 18.

7. Ibid.

8. Ibid., 17.

9. IMP to LEA, July 29, 1895.

10. James C. Mohr, *Plague and Fire: Battling Black Death and the 1900 Burning of Honolulu's Chinatown* (New York: Oxford University Press, 2004), 32.

11. Hawaii Department of Health, Annual Report, 1896, 9.

12. Lydia Aholo, "Reminiscences," *Friend* 73, no. 1 (January 1, 1915): 11–12.

13. Kamehameha School for Girls Trustees Report, January 25, 1896, 2.

14. Lydia Aholo Transcription, 28.

15. "Historical Number for Kamehameha Schools, 1887–1928," *Friend* 98, no. 12 (1928): 286.

16. Liliuokalani, *Hawaii's Story by Hawaii's Queen by Liliuokalani, Queen of Hawaii: 1838–1917* (Boston: Lee and Shepard, 1898), 33.

17. Aholo, "Reminiscences," 11–12.

18. IMP to LEA, April 1, 1896, Oberlin College Archives.

19. LEA to Dr. Hyde, April 21, 1897, KS.

20. IMP to LEA, June 23, 1896, Oberlin College Archives.

21. Helen Harding, "What Would Froebel Say?," in *The Inland Educator* (Terre Haute, IN: The Inland Educator Company, 1895), 253.

22. IMP to LEA, October 15, 1896, Oberlin College Archives.

23. Annual Report to Trustees, July 1897, KS, 2.

24. IMP to LEA, October 15, 1896.

25. IMP to Ruth and Tom, October 10, 1896, The Huntington Library, San Marino, CA.

26. Ruth Prosser McLain, comp., *A Bridge to the Past of the Prosser and Pope Families,* Lois Taylor, private collection.

27. Ibid.

28. "First Commencement," *Evening Bulletin,* June 30, 1897.

29. Ibid.

30. Liliuokalani to J. O. Carter from Washington, DC, June 19, 1897, Hawaiian State Archives, David Forbes Collection, compliments of Elinor Langer.

31. Lydia Aholo Transcription, 19.

32. Transcript of interview conducted by Katherine B. Allen with Johanna Niau Wilcox, August 6, 1971, as a part of the Watumull Foundation Oral History Project, Honolulu, 21–22, http://hdl.handle.net/10524/48655.

33. Ibid.

34. Queen Liliuokalani to J. O. Carter, 1899, image of partial autograph letter signed "Lili-uokalani," Bonhams, https://www.bonhams.com/auctions/19421/lot/1027/.

35. Lydia Aholo Transcription, 15.

36. Ibid., 5.

37. IMP report to Trustees, July 26, 1897, KS.

38. Ibid.

39. CRB to Henry Holmes, Esq., September 2, 1897, 213, KS.

40. Ibid.

41. CRB, Letter File, comp. and ed. Harold Winfield Kent, prepared for the sesquicentennial of CRB, January 25, 1972, Bishop Museum, Honolulu, 1972, 77.

42. Ibid., 30.

43. CRB to Henry Holmes.

44. Mary Yu Danico, ed., *Asian American Society: An Encyclopedia* (Los Angeles: Sage Publications, 2014), 444.

Chapter 12. Outside the School Gates

1. Ida Pope, "Within and without the Gates at Kamehameha," *Handicraft* 10, no. 7 (March 1898): 3.

2. Ibid.

3. Ibid.

4. CRB, Letter File, comp. and ed. Harold Winfield Kent, prepared for the sesquicentennial of CRB, January 25, 1972, Bishop Museum, Honolulu, 1972, 23.

5. Pope, "Within and without the Gates at Kamehameha," 3.

6. Ibid., 4.

7. Ibid.

8. Ibid., 3.

9. Ibid.

10. Report of the Rev. J. M. Lewis, in charge of Palama Chapel, Annual Report of the Hawaiian Evangelical Association, 1895, 59.

11. Pope, "Within and without the Gates at Kamehameha," 4.

12. Ibid.

13. Ida Pope, "Palama Hull House," Forty-fourth Annual Report of the Hawaiian Mission Children's Society, Minutes of the Annual Meeting Held May 31, 1896 (Honolulu: Press Publishing Company Print, 1896).

14. Ibid.

15. Guy S. Millberry, *A Study of the Dental Problem in Hawaii: A Survey of the Dental Health Educational Program in the Public Schools and Dental Service in Palama Settlement and in Other Public and Private Institutions* (Press of J. J. Gillick, 1930), 11.

16. Trustee Report, January 25, 1896, 5, KS.

17. Report of the Rev. J. M. Lewis, 58.

18. Ibid., 60.

19. Annual Report to Trustees, July 1897, 1, KS.

20. "Palama Settlement, Founded June 1, 1896" (unnamed, unnumbered report, Palama Settlement).

21. Pope, "Within and without the Gates at Kamehameha," 4.

22. Ibid.

23. Annual Report to Trustees, July 1898, 2, KS.

24. Ruth Prosser McLain, comp., *A Bridge to the Past of the Prosser and Pope Families,* Lois Taylor, private collection.

25. Barbara Beatty, *Historical Dictionary of American Education,* ed. Richard J. Altenbaugh (Westport, CT: Greenwood Press, 1999), 144.

26. Ibid.

27. Alfred L. Castle, "Harriet Castle and the Beginnings of Progressive Kindergarten Education in Hawaii, 1894–1900," *Hawaiian Journal of History* 23 (1989): 26–27.

28. Trustee Report, June 30, 1896, 3, KS.

29. McLain, *Bridge to the Past of the Prosser and Pope Families.*

30. Ibid.

31. Sandra Bonura, Lydia Oral History Transcription (2013; transcription of recorded interview of Lydia Kaonohiponiponiokalani Aholo by Helena Allen in 1969, hereafter Lydia Oral History Transcription), 26.

32. Anne Pope to Miss Cross, May 19, 1898, Ida May Pope Papers, The Huntington Library, San Marino, CA.

33. "A Pioneer at Palama," *Friend* 151, no. 7 (July 1932): 451.

34. Ibid.

35. Anne Pope to Miss Cross.

36. "Mixed Children: Various Nationalities in the Palama Kindergarten," *Pacific Commercial Advertiser,* March 24, 1898.

37. Anne Pope to Miss Cross.

38. "Pioneer at Palama," 451.

39. "Are Encouraged," *Hawaiian Gazette,* January 11, 1898.

40. Anne Pope to Miss Cross.

41. "Mixed Children."

42. Lydia Aholo Transcription, 57.

43. Ibid.

44. "Pioneer at Palama," 451.

45. Ibid.

46. Geertje Boschma, *The Rise of Mental Health Nursing: A History of Psychiatric Care in Dutch Asylums, 1890–1920* (Amsterdam: Amsterdam University Press, 2003), 77.

47. McLain, *Bridge to the Past of the Prosser and Pope Families.*

48. Ibid., 456.

49. "Pioneer at Palama," 451.

50. John E. Bishop, *Kajukenbo—The Original Mixed Martial Art* (Collierville, TN: Instant-Publisher.com, 2006), 19.

51. A. L. Castle, *A Century of Philanthropy: A History of the Samuel N. and Mary Castle Foundation* (Honolulu: University of Hawaiʻi Press, 2004), 238.

52. Robert Archey Woods and Albert Joseph Kennedy, eds., *Handbook of Settlements* (New York: Charities Publication Committee, 1911), 303.

Chapter 13. The Turbulent Ending of the Nineteenth Century

1. Modern research suggests that a combustion fire in the ship's coalbunker might have actually caused the explosion.

2. Edward B. Scott, *The Saga of the Sandwich Islands* (Crystal Bay, NV: Sierra-Tahoe, 1968), 301–305.

3. Ibid.

4. Uldrick Thompson, *Reminiscences of Kamehameha Schools* (unpublished, typescript manuscript, 1922), KS.

5. Cora Albright, *The Normal Advance* (Oshkosh, WI) 5, no. 3 (November 1898): 41–43.

6. C. L. Rickets, *Frances Stuart Parker, Reminiscences and Letters* (Chicago, privately printed, 1907).

7. IMP to Lois Prosser, July 31, 1898, The Huntington Library, San Marino, CA.

8. Bernice Pilani Irwin, *I Knew Queen Liliuokalani* (Honolulu: South Sea Sales, 1960), 71.

9. Ibid.

10. Rickets, *Frances Stuart Parker,* 73.

11. Terry L. Marzell, *Chalkboard Heroes, Twelve Courageous Teachers and Their Deeds of Valor* (Tucson, AZ: Wheatmark, 2015).

12. Ibid.

13. Ibid., 96.

14. Ibid.

15. Albright, *Normal Advance.*

16. Sandra Bonura, Lydia Aholo Oral History Transcription (2013; transcription of recorded interview of Lydia Kaonohiponiponiokalani Aholo by Helena Allen in 1969), 13.

17. IMP, Annual Report to Trustees, 1897–1898, 24–25, KS.

18. "The Tragic Death of Miss Kahea," *Hawaiian Star,* January 23, 1899.

19. "A Sad Tragedy," *Friend* 57, no. 2 (February 1899): 11.

20. "Suicide or Accident?," *Hawaiian Star,* January 23, 1899.

21. "Princess Kaiulani Dead," *Little Falls Weekly Transcript,* March 21, 1899.

22. "Funeral of Princess Kaiulani Takes Place at Honolulu," *Record-Union* (Sacramento, CA), March 25, 1899.

23. The colors normally used in royal feather work were red, yellow, and black.

24. Ibid.

25. Annual Report, Kamehameha School for Girls, 1901–1902, KS.

26. Ibid.

27. CRB, Letter File, comp. and ed. Harold Winfield Kent, prepared for the sesquicentennial of CRB, January 25, 1972, Bishop Museum, Honolulu, 1972, 33.

28. CRB to J. O. Carter, August 22, 1899, KS.

29. Bishop, Letter File, 28.

30. George Mause to Trustees of the Bishop Estate, September 6, 1899, KS.

31. "Hull House," in *Encyclopedia of Social Reforms; Including Political Economy, Political Science, Sociology and Statistics,* ed. William Dwight Porter Bliss (New York: Funk & Wagnalls, 1897), 701.

32. Ibid.

33. Marybeth Gasman and Katherine V. Sedgwick, eds., *Uplifting a People, African American Philanthropy and Education* (New York: Lang, 2005), 19.

34. Trustee Report, 1899, KS.

35. IMP to Lois Prosser, October 7, 1898, Ida May Pope Papers, The Huntington Library, San Marino, CA.

Chapter 14. Up and Away in the New Century

1. IMP to Lois Prosser, January 15, 1900, The Huntington Library, San Marino, CA.

2. Ibid.

3. IMP to Lois Prosser, January 18, 1900, The Huntington Library, San Marino, CA.

4. James K. Ikeda, "A Brief History of Bubonic Plague in Hawaii," *Proceedings, Hawaiian Entomological Society* 25 (March 1, 1985): 77.

5. James C. Mohr, *Battling Black Death and the 1900 Bunning of Honolulu's Chinatown* (New York: Oxford University Press, 2005), 59.

6. *Handicraft,* February 1900, KS.

7. George Kanahele, "Kamehameha Schools' First Hundred Years" (unedited draft materials for reference and research only), KS.

8. Uldrick Thompson, *Reminiscences of Kamehameha Schools* (unpublished, typescript manuscript, 1922), KS.

9. Charles Bartlett Dyke, "Essential Features in the Education of the Child Races," *Journal of the Proceedings and Addresses of the Annual Meeting of the National Educational Association* (1909): 930.

10. Ibid., 928–932.

11. Trustee Report, February 1900, KS.

12. "Kamehameha Girls Lay Aside Studies, a Marked Departure at Commencement Exercises. Much Hawaiian Legendary Lore," *Honolulu Republican,* June 26, 1901.

13. Nathaniel B. Emerson, "Unwritten Literature of Hawaii: The Sacred Songs of the Hula," Smithsonian Institution, *Bureau of American Ethnology Bulletin,* no. 38 (Washington, DC: U.S. Government Printing Office, 1909), 161.

14. Ibid.

15. "Kamehameha Girls Lay Aside Studies."

16. Ibid.

17. Ibid.

18. Edward B. Scott, *The Saga of the Sandwich Islands* (Lake Tahoe, NV: Sierra-Tahoe Publishing, Co., 1968), 337–338.

19. Trustee Report, "My Dear Mr. Horne," November 29, 1913.

20. "Kamehameha School for Girls," *Friend* 58, no. 11 (November 1900): 94.

21. Annual Report, KSG, 1901–1902, KSA.

22. "The Reunion of the Kamehameha Alumnae," *Friend* 60, no. 7 (July 1902): 13.

23. Annual Report, KSG.

24. Ida Pope, "The Education of Hawaiians at the Kamehameha School for Girls," *Southern Workman* 29, no. 1 (January 1900): 470–478.

25. Ibid.

26. Ibid.

27. Ibid.

28. Ibid.

29. Ibid.

30. Ibid.

31. Ruth Prosser McLain, comp., *A Bridge to the Past of the Prosser and Pope Families,* Lois Taylor, private collection.

32. "Oberlin Business College," July 1907 newspaper clipping, Ida May Pope Memory Book, KS.

33. Ellen Browning Scripps Diary, 1902, Scripps College, compliments of Molly McClain.

34. "Rest and Air Cures at Sea," *Norddeutscher Lloyd Bremen* (Bremen: Hauschild, 1910), 32.

35. IMP European Travel Diary, 1906, Ida May Pope Papers, The Huntington Library, San Marino, CA.

36. Ibid.

37. Ellen Anderson Gholson Glasgow (1873–1945) was an American Pulitzer-Prize winner who rejected the Victorian definitions of femininity dominating the social attitudes of her day.

38. IMP European Travel Diary.

39. CPW to CAK, March 13, 1892, UCSD.

40. IMP European Travel Diary.

41. Ibid.

42. Ibid.

Chapter 15. A Dream Realized

1. Bishop to J. O. Carter, November 8, 1900, KS.

2. Dyke to Bishop, March 12, 1902, KS.

3. Bishop to Dyke, March 21, 1902, KS.

4. Bishop to Carter, May 9, 1902, KS.

5. CRB to IMP, April 24, 1903, KS.

6. Ibid.

7. Annual Report, Kamehameha School for Girls, June 1903, KS.

8. "New Home for Girls," *Pacific Commercial Advertiser,* July 11, 1903.

9. Ibid.

10. Ibid.

11. "Paradise of the Pacific Print," *Fifty-Second Annual Report of the Hawaiian Mission Children's Society* (Honolulu, 1904).

12. "Thanks from the Kaiulani Home," *Pacific Commercial Advertiser*, December 31, 1903.

13. "Paradise of the Pacific Print."

14. "Money for the Kaiulani Home from C. R. Bishop," *Sunday Advertiser*, August 27, 1905.

15. CRB to J. O. Carter, May 25, 1905, KS.

16. Ibid.

17. "Kaiulani Home Will Build," *Hawaiian Star*, February 8, 1906.

18. Ibid.

19. *Pacific Commercial Advertiser*, January 6, 1907.

20. "Will Build Annex to Kaiulani Home," *Honolulu Star-Bulletin*, July 26, 1912.

21. "Cabinet Members Guest of Princess at a Real Luau," *Honolulu Star-Bulletin,* October 3, 1912.

22. Ibid.

23. Ibid.

24. "Communications," *Honolulu Star-Bulletin*, March 12, 1913.

25. "Distinctive Hawaiian Feast Is Provided: Army and Navy Well Represented," *Honolulu Star-Bulletin,* October 3, 1912.

26. "Local and General," *Honolulu Star-Bulletin*, June 24, 1913.

27. "Working Girls Home Opened Saturday," *Honolulu Star-Bulletin*, March 17, 1913.

Chapter 16. Taking Honolulu by Storm

1. Jon M. Shephard, *Sociology* (Boston: Cengage Learning, 2012), 17.

2. Craig Kridel, Robert V. Bullough Jr., and Paul Shaker, *Teachers and Mentors: Profiles of Distinguished Twentieth-Century* (New York: Garland Publishing, 1996), 22.

3. Marvin Olasky and John Perry, *Monkey Business: The True Story of the Scopes Trial* (Nashville, TN: B&H Publishing Group, 2005), 76.

4. Ernest W. Burgess, "William I. Thomas as a Teacher," *Sociology and Social Research* 32 (1947): 760–764.

5. Herbert M. Kliebard, "Three Currents of American Curriculum Thought," in *Current Thought on Curriculum,* ed. Molnar (Alexandria, VA: Association for Supervision and Curriculum Development, 1985), 81.

6. Burgess, "William I. Thomas as a Teacher," 760–764.

7. Axel R. Schafer, "Social Ethics Social Control and the Organic Society: The Sociology of Charles Richmond Henderson," in *American Progressives and German Social Reform, 1875–1920: Social Ethics, Moral Control, and the Regulatory State in a Transatlantic Context* (Stuttgart: Franz Steiner Verlag, 2000), 163.

8. Kliebard, "Three Currents of American Curriculum Thought," 82.

9. Shephard, *Sociology,* 17.

10. Office of Education, *Statistics of Land Grant Colleges and Universities,* vol. 2, issues 16–30 (Washington, DC: U.S. Government Printing Office, 1913), 69.

11. Meyer Bloomfield, ed., *Readings in Vocational Guidance* (Boston, New York: Ginn and Company, 1915), 8.

12. "The National Vocational Guidance Association," *Vocational Guidance Magazine* 3, no. 5 (1925): 154.

13. Carol Aronovici, *The Social Survey* (Philadelphia: Harper Press, 1916).

14. Robin Rogers-Dillon, *Welfare Experiments: Politics and Policy Evaluation* (Stanford, CA: Stanford University Press, 2004), 28.

15. "Miss Blascoer Explains Work," *Honolulu Star-Bulletin,* July 2, 1912.

16. "Report of Committee on the Social Evil: Honolulu Social Survey," *Honolulu Star-Bulletin,* May 1914.

17. Frances Blascoer, *The Industrial Condition of Women and Girls in Honolulu; A Social Study* (Honolulu: Paradise of the Pacific Printers, 1912), 6.

18. William Burgess and Harry Olson, *The World's Social Evil: A Historical Review and Study of the Problems Relating to the Subject* (Chicago: Saul Brothers, 1914), 5–6.

19. "Report of Committee on the Social Evil."

20. "The Hawaii Survey," *Friend,* 70, no. 7 ((July 1912): 1.

21. "Miss Blascoer Explains Work."

22. "Expert Talks of Charity Problem," *Hawaiian Gazette,* June 14, 1912.

23. "Hawaii Survey."

24. Ibid.

25. "Report of Committee on the Social Evil."

26. Ruth Prosser McLain, comp., *A Bridge to the Past of Prosser and Pope Families,* Lois Taylor, private collection.

27. Frances Blascoer, *The Industrial Condition of Women and Girls in Honolulu: A Social Study* (Honolulu: Paradise of the Pacific Printers, 1912).

28. IMP, foreword to *The Industrial Condition of Women and Girls in Honolulu: A Social Study,* by Frances Blascoer (Honolulu: Paradise of the Pacific Printers, 1912).

29. "City's Shame, Their Topic," *Hawaiian Gazette,* August 16, 1912.

30. Ibid.

31. Ibid.

32. *Ohio Bulletin of Charities and Correction,* vols. 20–21 (Columbus: Ohio Board of State Charities, 1914), 67.

33. "City's Shame."

34. Ibid.

35. Ibid.

36. Ibid.

37. *Bulletin of the Bureau of Labor,* Congressional Series of United States Public Documents, vol. 6272 (Washington, DC: U.S. Government Printing Office, 1912), 403.

38. Blascoer, *Industrial Condition of Women and Girls in Honolulu,* 90.

39. *Ohio Bulletin of Charities and Correction,* 67.

40. Margit M. Watts, *High Tea at Halekulani: Feminist Theory and American Clubwomen* (Brooklyn, NY: Carlson, 1993), 96.

41. Barbara Bennett Person, ed., *Notable Women of Hawaii* (Honolulu: University of Hawai'i Press, 1984), 245–246.

42. Watts, *High Tea at Halekulani,* 99.

43. *Bulletin of the Russell Sage Foundation Library,* issues 1–20 (New York: Russell Sage Foundation Library, 1913), 245.

44. "Our Women," *Friend* 70, no. 10 (October 1912): 284.

45. "New Social Program," *Hawaiian Gazette,* November 12, 1912.

46. Ibid.

47. Richard Hawkins, *A Pacific Industry: The History of Pineapple Canning in Hawaii* (London: I. B. Tauris, 2011), 148.

48. *The American Labor Year Book 1919–1920,* vol. 3 (New York: The Rand School of Social Science, 1920), 221.

49. "Some Weird Facts Unearthed Here," *Hawaiian Gazette,* April 13, 1917.

50. Ibid.

Chapter 17. The Changing Hawaiian Islands

1. Katherine Pope, *Hawaii, the Rainbow Land* (New York: Thomas Y. Crowell, 1924), 245, 257.

2. Ibid., 258–259.

3. CRB to J. O. Carter, February 22, 1902, KS.

4. Trustee Report, June 30, 1904, 18–28, KS.

5. Ibid.

6. Ibid., 28.

7. Ibid.

8. Ibid., 23.

9. "Chicago School Children Write Honolulu Pupils," *Pacific Commercial Advertiser,* May 9, 1903.

10. Ida May Pope Memory Book, October 16, 1904, KS.

11. "Girls Who Do Things," newspaper clipping, Miss Pope's Memory Book, 1905, KS.

12. Ibid.

13. President's Report: 20th Annual, June 30, 1907, KS.

14. Anna M. Reid, "The Second Decade," *Friend* 73, no. 1 (January 1915): 1.

15. "Miss Julia Lazaro Died at Sea," *Evening Bulletin,* November 26, 1909.

16. "Ancient Hawaii," *Evening Bulletin,* July 16, 1908.

17. Reprinted in "Tribute to Charles R. Bishop," January 25, 1912, 19–20, KS.

18. Anna M. Reid, "The Second Decade," *Friend* 53, no. 1 (January 1915): 1.

19. CRB to A. F. Judd, October 19, 1914, KS.

20. CRB to trustees, June 7, 1899, KS.

21. Philippians 4:8 (King James version).

22. "Woman's World: Sorosis Celebrates Her 25th Anniversary," *The Day* (New London, CT), March 31, 1893.

23. Kathleen L. Endres and Therese L. Lueck, eds., *Women's Periodicals in the United States: Social and Political Issues* (Westport, CT: Greenwood Publishing Group, 1996), 133.

24. "The Women's Clubs. The State Federation Meeting—Good Club News from Honolulu—Local Notes and Happenings," *Boston Evening Transcript,* February 16, 1901.

25. Trustee Report, May 31, 1913, KS.

26. Newspaper clipping, Miss Pope's Memory Book, KS.

27. Trustee Report, 1909, Alumnae, 6, KS.

28. Ibid.

29. *Handicraft* 15, no. 8 (May 1910).

30. Ibid.

31. "Travelers' Aid Work Done by Efficient Secretary," *Honolulu Star-Bulletin,* January 27, 1917.

32. Ibid.

33. Ibid.

34. Ibid.

35. "Vive la Hawaii?," manuscript, letters, and photos held in KS.

36. "Reunion of the Kamehameha Alumnae," *Friend* 60, no. 7 (July 1902): 13

37. Ida May Pope Memory Book, December 17, 1904.

38. David Kanuha later changed his last name to Ainoa.

39. "Gladys Brandt, Champion of Hawaiian Culture," *Honolulu Advertiser,* January 17, 2003.

40. Terry L. Marzell, *Chalkboard Champions: Twelve Remarkable Teachers Who Educated America's Disenfranchised Students* (Tucson, AZ: Wheatmark, 2012), 176.

41. David Yount, *Who Runs the University?: The Politics of Higher Education in Hawaii, 1985–1992* (Honolulu: University of Hawaii Press, 1996), 130.

42. Marzell, *Chalkboard Champions,* 169.

43. "Honor and Trust Fund," *Hawaiian Star,* August 20, 1908.

44. Trustee Report, 1909, Alumnae, 6–7, KS.

45. Ibid.

46. Report of Kamehameha Alumnae Association for 1912–1913, 37, KS.

47. "Wooing of Umi and Piikea Witnessed by Thousands," *Pacific Commercial Advertiser,* February 20, 1914.

48. "Old Hawaiian Story Being Told on Waikiki Beach This Afternoon," *Star Bulletin,* February 19, 1914.

49. "Wooing of Umi and Piikea."

50. Trustee Report, February 28, 1914, KS.

51. Trustee Report, September 30, 1913, KS.

52. Trustee Report, May 31, 1913, KS.

53. Ida Pope Memory Book.

54. Frances Lemmon to Lois Prosser, July 18, 1914, Ida May Pope Papers, The Huntington Library, San Marino, CA.

Chapter 18. Last Aloha to Mother Pope, 1914

1. "Body of Teacher Rests in Oakwood," unnamed newspaper clipping, Ida May Pope Memory Book, KS.

2. "Letter from Miss Anne Pope to the Children of Miss Ida M. Pope," *Friend* 72, no. 8 (September 1915): 202–204.

3. IMP to Lois Prosser, July 13, 1914, The Huntington Library, San Marino, CA.

4. Anne Pope, "To the Trustees of the Kamehameha Schools of the Hawaiian Islands," July 27, 1914, KS.

5. A. C. McClurg was a Chicago publishing house and bookstore that had just made notoriety by publishing the Tarzan of the Apes novels.

6. IMP to Lois Prosser, July 9, 1914, The Huntington Library, San Marino, CA.

7. Ibid.

8. "Letter from Miss Anne Pope to the Children of Miss Ida M. Pope."

9. Ibid.

10. Ibid.

11. "Miss Pope Died Very Suddenly," unnamed newspaper clipping, Ida May Pope Memory Book, KS.

12. "Letter from Miss Anne Pope to the Children of Miss Ida M. Pope."

13. Ibid.

14. "The Death of Miss Pope Is an Irretrievable Loss to the Kamehameha Schools and to the Hawaiian Race," *Pacific Commercial Advertiser,* July 16, 1914.

15. "Mother—Ida Pope," *Advertiser,* July 19, 1914.

16. "Ida M. Pope," *Friend* 72, no. 8 (August 1914): 1.

17. The trustees approved the construction of the Rest House while Ida was in Chicago.

18. Pope, "To the Trustees of the Kamehameha Schools."

19. Ibid.

20. "A Sketch of the Life of Miss Ida M. Pope," *Maui News,* February 6, 1920.

21. "Funeral of Princess Kaiulani Takes Place at Honolulu," *Record-Union* (Sacramento, CA), March 25, 1899.

22. *Thrum's Hawaiian Annual,* vols. 44–47 (Honolulu: Star-Bulletin Press, 1917), 107.

23. Uldrick Thompson, *Reminiscences of the Kamehameha Schools* (unpublished, typescript manuscript, 1922), 164–165, KS.

24. Michelle Keown, *Pacific Islands Writing: The Postcolonial Literatures of Aotearoa/New Zealand and Oceania* (Oxford: Oxford University Press, 2007), 129.

25. "The Pope Fund—A Scholarship Loan," *Ke Aliʻi Pauahi,* March 1956.

26. "Ida Pope Fund Will Supply Scholarships for Hawaiian Girls," unnamed newspaper clipping, June 29, 1923, 1–2, KS.

27. Ibid.

28. Ruth Prosser McLain, comp., *A Bridge to the Past of the Prosser & Pope Families,* Lois Taylor, private collection.

29. Ibid.

30. Marie A. McDonald, *Ka lei: The Leis of Hawaii* (Honolulu: Topgallant, 1985), 24.

31. Sandra Bonura, Lydia Aholo Oral History Transcription (2013; transcription of recorded interview of Lydia Kaonohiponiponiokalani Aholo by Helena Allen in 1969; hereafter cited as Lydia Aholo Transcription), 22.

32. Alice Stone Blackwell, *The Woman Citizen,* vol. 3 (New York: Leslie Woman Suffrage Commission, 1917–1927), 67.

33. "Mrs. Wm. Hyde Rice First to Register," *Garden Island,* September 7, 1920.

34. "Ida Pope," in *Makers of Destiny, Hawaiian Style: The Lives of Pioneer Women Educators in Hawaii* (Honolulu: Delta Kappa Gamma Society International Beta Beta State, 1981), 183.

35. Ibid.

36. Ibid., 183.

37. Ibid., 185.

38. Ibid.

39. Ibid.

40. Ibid., 185–186.

Index

ABOUT THE AUTHOR

SANDRA E. BONURA lives in Southern California and teaches in higher education. She is deeply interested in education, history, and Hawai'i, and when they merge, there is instant engagement. Her previously published works emanating from primary sources are "Queen Lili'uokalani's Beloved Kawaiaha'o Seminary" in the *Hawaiian Journal of History* (volume 51, 2017), *An American Girl in the Hawaiian Islands: The Letters of Carrie Prudence Winter (1890–1893)* (University of Hawai'i Press, 2012), and "Lydia K. Aholo—Her Story Recovering the Lost Voice" in the *Hawaiian Journal of History* (volume 47, 2013). She is a frequent storyteller and lecturer on the importance of using a multitude of primary sources to gain perspectives on significant events in history.